WITHOUT FEAR OR FAVOR

D1447220

Stanford Studies in Law and Politics

A series edited by Keith J. Bybee

A full list of titles in the series can be found online at www.sup.org/lawandpolitics

WITHOUT FEAR OR FAVOR

*Judicial Independence and Judicial
Accountability in the States*

G. Alan Tarr

Stanford University Press
Stanford, California

Stanford University Press
Stanford, California

Printed in the United States of America on acid-free, archival-quality paper.

Library of Congress Cataloging-in-Publication Data

Tarr, G. Alan (George Alan)
   Without fear or favor : judicial independence and judicial accountability in the states / G. Alan Tarr.
     p. cm. — (Stanford studies in law and politics)
   Includes bibliographical references and index.
   ISBN 978-0-8047-6039-3 (cloth : alk. paper)
   ISBN 978-0-8047-6040-9 (pbk. : alk. paper)
   1. Judicial process—United States—States.   2. Judicial independence—United States—States. I. Title.
KF8736.T373   2012
347.73'5—dc23
                                                  2012020088

For Susan, as always

At present it will be sufficient to remark that no citizen of Virginia can be prejudiced either in his person or his property, by any of the government of this commonwealth (or of the United States) so long as the judiciary departments of those governments, respectively, remain uncorrupt, and independent of legislative or executive control. But whenever the reverse of this happens, by whatever means it may be effected (whether fear or favour), liberty will be no more, and property but a shadow.

St. George Tucker, 1803

Those who effect to scout the phrase 'sovereign people' ask much in a jargon, understood by none but themselves, about '*the independence of the Judges.*' Are they to be independent of THE PEOPLE? If they are to be independent of the people, and the people are not also to be independent of the judges; we may as well call them *superior to the people*, at once, and [be] done with it.

New-Hampshire Gazette, February 19, 1805

Contents

Introduction

THE CHARGES ARE FAMILIAR. CONSERVATIVE CRITICS INSIST THAT judicial activism is rampant, with liberal judges "legislating from the bench" on social policy issues, such as abortion and same-sex marriage, ignoring long-standing community sentiment on issues such as the pledge of allegiance and school prayer, and "making law rather than enforcing it" in overturning the convictions in criminal cases.[1] For these critics, the solution is obvious. Out-of-control judges must be held accountable for their overreaching, so that self-government and the rule of law can be restored and "judicial dictatorship" ended.[2] Indeed, some wish to go further. As the chief of staff for Oklahoma Senator Tom Coburn declared, "I don't want to impeach judges. I want to impale them."[3]

Equally familiar are the counterclaims. Harsh criticism of judges and their rulings allegedly galvanizes public frustration over hot-button issues, so this "pernicious rhetoric" must stop, lest it erode the public's confidence in judicial impartiality and threaten the rule of law.[4] Legislative steps to curtail judicial power are portrayed as attempts to intimidate judges and threaten their independence.[5] Efforts to hold state judges electorally accountable for their rulings are condemned for the same reasons.[6] So too are judicial election campaigns, which purportedly promote a politics of "slogans and thirty-second television spots singularly inappropriate to the evaluation of judicial candidates."[7] Even inquiries into the political views and legal perspectives of judges before they ascend the bench are criticized as an American version of the "telephone justice" common in authoritarian regimes.[8] Only when these threats are eliminated, it is argued, can the rule of law flourish and judges fulfill their responsibility of dispensing equal justice under law.[9]

Both sides in the contemporary debate over judicial independence and judicial accountability—we shall refer to them as the Bashers and the Defenders—claim to support the rule of law, but they disagree about what threatens it. Defenders see the danger as coming from external pressures on judges by those who seek to influence or intimidate them or induce them to abandon their commitment to the law in favor of what is popular or politically acceptable. But Bashers view the danger as rooted in the absence of checks on judges, which frees them to pursue their political or ideological or professional or class agendas at the expense of fidelity to the law. Impartial decision making, according to Bashers, is best promoted by the prospect of retribution for judicial activism, which keeps in line judges who might otherwise be tempted to read their own preferences into the law.

The current debate reflects as well differing conceptions of the role courts and judges should play in governing. Defenders typically celebrate the role courts have played in protecting rights, especially those of unpopular minorities, and tend to applaud vigorous judicial intervention.[10] Bashers, by contrast, characteristically emphasize the importance of self-government and decry judicial involvement in policy-making as undemocratic. In part, inevitably, the conflict over judicial independence and accountability is tied to satisfaction—or dissatisfaction—with salient judicial decisions. If one is pleased with the general tenor of judicial rulings, one is more likely to champion judicial independence. If one is distressed by those rulings, one is more likely to demand that judges be held accountable. The current assumption on both the Right and the Left seems to be that the more independent judges are, the more liberal their rulings are likely to be, so promoting greater accountability will move decisions in a conservative direction. One may well question whether this assumption is accurate, especially in the Roberts Court era, or merely represents liberal nostalgia for and conservative antipathy toward the Warren Court. Whatever the accuracy of the assumption, it contrasts sharply with the perspective of earlier eras, when accountability was sought to counter judicial conservatism.[11]

Connected with these differing conceptions of the role of courts are divergent portrayals of the judicial process. Defenders emphasize conflict resolution, with their prototypical example being a trial judge applying the law to resolve a dispute between two litigants. Framing the issue in this fashion underscores the importance of impartiality and obscures the courts' policy role. Bashers, by contrast, highlight judicial policy-making, with their prototypical example an appellate court announcing a ruling with broad societal implications on an issue that had already been addressed—and resolved differently—by the other branches of government.

The contemporary debate has generated far more heat than light. For critics of judicial activism, the very term "judicial independence" has become anathema. For the critics of these critics, so has "judicial accountability."[12] Yet in an era of overheated rhetoric, in which "judicial independence exists primarily as a rhetorical notion rather than as a subject of sustained, organized study," a dispassionate discussion of judicial independence and accountability is sorely needed.[13] This volume provides such an assessment, focusing on the American states, where the current debate is most heated and where historically the relation between independence and accountability has been the subject of wide-ranging and enlightening discussion.

Chapters 1–3 trace the debate over judicial independence and accountability in the states from the American founding to the present day, seeking to place this debate in a broader historical context. Chapter 1 examines the development of the idea of judicial independence during the antebellum era. Recalling the abuses of the colonial era, the founding generation sought to protect judges from the influence of the executive but debated whether judges should be insulated from popular influence as well. Moreover, the definition of the judicial function was itself contested. From the perspective of the present, questions about the character and legitimacy of judicial review stand out. However, also at issue were the division of responsibility between judge and jury, the legitimacy of legislative intervention to overturn judicial rulings or order new trials, the range of disputes to be settled by courts rather than by private laws, and the participation of nonjudges in appellate review. The history we examine reveals that two key issues—from whom judges should be independent, and what the scope of their responsibilities should be—dominate the debate in the states during the antebellum era. Put differently, the contemporary debate over judicial independence and judicial accountability is not simply a continuation of a debate that began in the American founding. Only after a consensus was achieved about the function that judges should serve could discussion begin about what influences inappropriately impinged on the performance of that function.

Chapter 2 traces the debate in the states over judicial selection and tenure through the early twentieth century. The federal Constitution grants federal judges tenure during good behavior, thereby coming down emphatically on the side of judicial independence. However, the states have approached judicial tenure quite differently. Several states established tenure during good behavior in their initial constitutions but then actively enforced the good-behavior requirement through impeachment, other forms of removal, and the abolition of courts and judgeships, thus ensuring accountability to the people's representatives. Only when limited terms of office provided an opportunity for regularized assessments of judicial performance did these weapons fade into obsolescence. Also, beginning in the mid-nineteenth century, most states moved from appointment or legislative election of judges to popular election. This shift did not ignite an early version of the contemporary debate; the impetus for this change and the debate that it engendered were distinctive. The shift to judicial elections was part of a set of constitutional reforms designed to impose restraints on state legislatures in the wake of their reckless promotional efforts, which brought several states to the brink of financial ruin. Moreover, those who favored judicial elections sought to empower judges, not rein them in. They argued that electing judges would free them from partisan control, and this greater independence, together with their electoral connection to the people, would embolden them to actively police the state legislature to ensure it stayed within constitutional bounds. Interestingly, judicial elections at the outset found significant support even within the legal profession.

Only during the Progressive era, when the issue of judicial selection again became controversial, did the debate shift to the arguments made familiar by Bashers and Defenders today. Defenders during the Progressive era sought to replace partisan election of judges with nonpartisan elections and later with merit selection, in order to insulate judges from external pressures. But Bashers championed judicial elections and sought additional weapons, such as the recall of judges and judicial decisions, to enforce judicial conformity with the popular will. Even so, the Progressive-era debate differed in some respects from the current debate. The Bashers of the Progressive era were on the political Left, while Defenders were on the political Right, although most of the legal profession supported elimination of contested judicial elections. Also, both Bashers and Defenders shared an expectation that, absent effective mechanisms of judicial accountability, judges would render conservative rather than liberal decisions. So if the arguments are familiar, the identity of those making them is not.

Chapter 3 describes the current controversy over judicial independence and accountability in the states, which focuses on judicial selection and identifies the political and legal developments that have contributed to it. It describes the politicization of judicial elections in the states, as shown in the dramatic rise in the cost of campaigns for judicial office, the proliferation of televised attack ads, and the increasing efforts of interest groups to influence their outcomes. It explains how the development of more contested and contentious judicial elections is rooted in trends that are unlikely to change in the near future. These include the rise of two-party competition in the states, the increasing activism of state courts, and the activation of interest groups committed to influencing court rulings by reshaping the composition of state supreme courts.

Chapter 4 shifts the focus from the historical to the analytical. Defenders' arguments for judicial independence have tended to be long on pieties and short on precision. The Bashers' calls for judicial accountability too have often substituted outrage for analysis. This chapter clarifies the terms of the debate, identifies the elements of judicial independence (decisional and institutional), the forms of judicial accountability (decisional, institutional, and behavioral), the mechanisms by which accountability is enforced, and the identity of those who might be held accountable (the individual judge, the court, or the judiciary as a whole). In assessing the current debate, this chapter finds serious weaknesses in both the Defender and Basher perspectives. The Defenders' case for judicial independence typically rests on a simplistic understanding of law and judging that ignores what political scientists and legal scholars have demonstrated about indeterminacies in law and the necessity of judicial choice. Bashers tend to endorse the same simplistic understanding of law and judging, which enables them to condemn as intentional departures from proper interpretation rulings that may simply reflect good-faith efforts to deal with legal complexity and indeterminacy. The critique of these positions should point the way to an understanding of judicial independence and accountability that is compatible with a more sophisticated account of law and judging.

Much of the contemporary debate about judicial independence and judicial accountability in the states revolves around judicial elections. Over the last few decades, the importance of the issue has increased in the wake of greater electoral competition, escalating campaign spending by both candidates and independent groups, and "nastier, noisier, and costlier" campaigns for judicial office.[14] Defenders have long opposed judicial elections as a threat to judicial independence, their perspective best captured in the pithy title of an article by Charles Geyh: "Why Judicial Elections Stink." Chapter 5 challenges the Defender consensus. It analyzes the Defenders' attacks on judicial elections in light of social science research into voting behavior, both in judicial elections and in low-salience elections more generally, and into the effects of campaigns and political advertising on voter choice and on voter attitudes toward the courts. The chapter also examines the available evidence on how the mode of selection affects the quality of the bench and the decisions judges render. The chapter concludes that the case against judicial elections is weak when elections do not involve incumbents, who might be tempted to modify their rulings in order to attract the support of voters or interest groups. It further argues that partisan judicial elections have virtues in terms of judicial accountability not present in nonpartisan elections or retention elections. However, this does not prove the case for judicial elections; it merely establishes that they remain a legitimate mode of judicial selection.

Chapter 6 addresses what is to be done, examining recent proposals designed to safeguard judicial independence or promote accountability, namely, the greater use of recusal and disqualification for judges who receive campaigns contributions, the public financing of judicial elections, and the establishment of a single nonrenewable term for state supreme court justices. It concludes by acknowledging that the need to respect judicial independence imposes severe limits on judicial accountability, and it therefore encourages a shift in popular focus from those interpreting the law to the substance of the law itself. It surveys the ease with which voters and legislators in the states can respond to judicial rulings with which they disagree. In particular, it suggests that the ease of constitutional amendment in the states creates an opportunity for a popular constitutionalism that respects the independence of judges while giving the people the final say.

My research on judicial independence and accountability has spanned more than a decade, and I have accumulated more intellectual debts over that period than I can easily list. My work on the topic was jump-started by the opportunity to contribute an essay to *Justice in Jeopardy*, a report of the American Bar Association's Task Force on the 21st Century Judiciary. Involvement with that project led to a long and fruitful collaboration with Edward

("Ned") Madeira, who chaired the task force and later the ABA's Standing Committee on Judicial Independence. In 2006 the National Endowment for the Humanities awarded me a fellowship that provided an opportunity for concentrated research on the history of judicial independence and accountability in the states. As dean and then acting chancellor at Rutgers University-Camden, Margaret Marsh created an exemplary intellectual environment and provided encouragement and support throughout my research. I have benefited immensely from discussions with my Rutgers colleagues, most notably Robert F. Williams, Richard Harris, and Aman McLeod. I have also benefited from the advice and suggestions of numerous other scholars, among them Luke Bierman, Keith Bybee, Michael Dimino, John Dinan, Christian Fritz, Charles Geyh, Leslie Goldstein, Norman Green, Robert Peck, and Mary Cornelia Porter. Some of them will likely conclude that this would have been a better book had I followed more of their suggestions.

I am likewise grateful for opportunities to present my research at the University of Missouri Law School, at Willamette Law School, at the University of Ottawa, and at Harvard Law School. Portions of this volume appeared initially as articles: "Contesting the Judicial Power," *Harvard Journal of Law and Public Policy* (2012); "Do Retention Elections Work?" *Missouri Law Review* 74 (2009); and "Rethinking the Selection of State Supreme Court Justices," *Willamette Law Review* 39 (2003). I also want to thank those journals for permission to use material from those articles.

Sylvia Somers and Karen McGrath did a wonderful job in transforming disjointed and sometimes illegible material into a coherent manuscript, and Kyle Weber provided excellent research assistance. My wife, Susan, and my sons, Bob and Andy, have made all the work worthwhile.

1 Creating and Debating Judicial Independence and Accountability

CURRENTLY THE CONFLICT IN THE STATES OVER JUDICIAL INDEPEN-
dence and accountability focuses on judicial selection and tenure.
Historically, however, the debate in the states has been far broader, a continuing
constitutional conversation about the role of courts and judges in a republican polity. This conversation has involved the character of the judicial function and the place of legal professionals and laypeople in the administration of
justice. It has also addressed from whom judges must be independent and for
what purposes, to whom they should be accountable, and how that might be
accomplished without jeopardizing independence. The states have tried various answers to these questions, and even states that resolved these issues at one
point in time later revisited them. Simply put, the history of judicial independence and accountability in the states has been not a steady progression toward
a single ideal but rather a record of competing and diverse conceptions of independence and accountability, with the prevailing understandings changing over
time and among the states. This chapter traces the conflict over the contested
concepts of judicial independence and judicial accountability from the founding era to the mid-nineteenth century. Chapter 2 extends the analysis into the
twentieth century with particular emphasis on judicial selection and judicial
tenure, and Chapter 3 analyzes the current debate. Political practice and political debate in the states highlight the complexities of judicial independence and
judicial accountability and, in so doing, provide the basis for understanding
and assessing current claims and arguments.[1]

Independent of Whom?

Constitutional Arrangements

Before the American Revolution, colonial governors, selected by the Crown, appointed judges, raising concerns that those selected might be biased in favor of royal interests.[2] Those receiving these patronage appointments served at the pleasure of the Crown rather than, like their counterparts in Britain, during good behavior, increasing fears that they might "pronounce that for law, which was most agreeable to the prince or his officers."[3] Thus, the issue of judicial independence first arose in America in reaction to excessive executive control over—and possible manipulation of—the administration of justice.[4] Thus the Declaration of Independence charges the king with "refusing his assent to laws for establishing judiciary powers," with making "judges dependent on his will alone for the tenure of their offices, and the amount and payment of their salaries," with "depriving us in many cases of the benefits of trial by jury," and with "transporting us beyond seas to be tried for pretended offenses."

The Declaration's indictment of the Crown, it should be noted, is framed not in terms of judicial independence but in terms of popular access to justice, understood as encompassing both the availability of judicial forums ("refusing his assent to laws establishing judiciary powers") and proper administration of justice within those forums. Proper administration of justice in turn required that trials be presided over by impartial magistrates (not "judges dependent on his will alone"), in venues subject to public scrutiny (not "beyond seas"), and with independent decision-makers who could be trusted to render impartial verdicts (not "depriving us in many cases of the benefits of trial by jury"). Insofar as the Declaration addresses judicial independence, it emphasizes freeing judges from subservience to an unaccountable executive whose interests differed from those of the general public. The Declaration thus left open whether making the judiciary answerable to the people, either directly or through their elected representatives, posed the same problems for the rule of law or for the impartial administration of justice. Or, put differently, it left open the relationship between republicanism and judicial independence.

Some early state constitutions contain stirring rhetoric on judicial independence. The Massachusetts Declaration of Rights of 1780, for instance, proclaimed it "the right of every citizen to be tried by judges as free, impartial, and independent as the lot of humanity will admit," and the Maryland Declaration of Rights of 1776 noted that "the independency and uprightness of Judges are essential to the impartial administration of justice, and a great security to the rights and liberties of the people."[5] Although proponents of judicial independence never tire of quoting such provisions, the institutional arrangements under eighteenth-century state constitutions emphasized judicial accountability to state legislatures, as "short terms with election and reelection voted by the same lawmakers who set rates of compensation and paid their salaries made judges more dependent than independent."[6] Indeed, those Massachusetts "judges as free, impartial, and independent as the lot of humanity will admit" could be removed upon a vote of two-thirds of the state legislature. In emphasizing judicial accountability to state legislatures, early state constitutions "represented the culmination of what the colonial assemblies had been struggling for in their eighteenth-century contests with the Crown."[7]

State judges in the decades after Independence might be appointed by the executive, by the legislature, or by some combination of the two, but state legislatures generally dominated judicial selection (see Table 1.1).[8] This legislative dominance is explicable on republican grounds. In most states, only legislators were directly elected by the people, and this—combined with their short term of office—encouraged the belief that the legislature embodied the people, whereas other branches did not. Given this understanding, legislatures seemed the safest repository of the appointment power. In addition, legislative dominance was a response to Americans' suspicion of executive power in general and of the executive appointment power in particular. As Gordon Wood has noted, "The power of [executive] appointment to offices" was perceived as "the most insidious and powerful weapon of eighteenth-century despotism."[9] Thus, none of the initial state constitutions gave the governor acting alone the power to appoint judges. By 1800, two states—Delaware (1792) and Pennsylvania (1790)—authorized unilateral gubernatorial appointment, but seven continued to lodge the appointment power exclusively in the state legislature. The remaining states allowed the governor to appoint judges but required that appointments be confirmed by an executive council or the legislature. Even where governors participated in the selection process, their control over the composition of the bench was limited. For in several states the governors themselves were largely creatures of the legislature, chosen by it for short terms and dependent on it for their continuation in office, and this undoubtedly influenced their choices.

TABLE 1.1 State Judiciaries in the Eighteenth Century: Selection and Tenure*

State	Year	Provision	Mode of Selection	Tenure	Address	Removal by Impeachment
CT	No Constitution		4	1 yr.	N	N
DE	1776	Art. 12	3	GB	N	Y
DE	1792	Arts. 3, 8	1	GB	Y	Y
GA	1777		4	Not specified	N	Y
GA	1789		4	3 yrs.	N	Y
GA	1798	Arts. 3, 1	4	3 yrs.	Y	Y
KY	1792	Art. 2	3	GB	Y	Y
KY	1799	Arts. 3, 9	3	GB	Y	Y
MD	1776	Art. 48	2	GB	Y	N
MA	1780	Chs. 2, 1, 9	2	GB	Y	Y
NH	1776	Nothing on Judiciary				
NH	1784	Part II	2	GB	Y	Y
NJ	1776	Art. 12	4	7 yrs.	N	Y
NY	1777	Art. 23	2	GB (60)	N	Y
NC	1776	Art. 13	4	GB	N	Y
PA	1776	Sec. 20	2	7 yrs.	Y	Y
PA	1790	Arts. 2, 8	1	GB	Y	Y
RI	No Constitution		4		N	N
SC	1776	Art. 20	4	GB	Y	Y
SC	1778	Art. 27	4	GB	Y	Y
SC	1790	Arts. 6, 1	4	GB	N	Y
TN	1796		4	GB	N	Y
VT	1777	Art. 18	2	Unclear	N	Y
VT	1786	Chs. 2, 9	4	1 yr.	N	Y
VT	1793	Chs. 2, 9	4	1 yr.	N	Y
VA	1776	None	4	GB	N	Y

* Excluding justices of the peace

1 = Gubernatorial appointment

2 = Gubernatorial appointment and council confirmation

3 = Gubernatorial appointment and legislative confirmation

4 = Legislative appointment

5 = Election

GB = During good behavior

(60) = Retirement age of sixty

Once selected, judges remained under legislative scrutiny. "The Revolutionaries had no intention of curtailing legislative interference in the court structure and in judicial functions, and in fact they meant to increase it."[10] During the colonial era, popular assemblies with some regularity "restored [losing litigants] to the law" by granting them a new trial, which served as a check on abuses by unelected judges. After Independence, those who lost in court might still appeal to the legislature for redress, and legislators could order new trials or pass private bills providing them with the compensation denied them at trial. This practice continued into the nineteenth century, with the Rhode Island Legislature overturning adjudicated verdicts almost to the Civil War.[11]

Judges who issued unpopular rulings might be called before the legislature to explain their decisions. In 1786, for example, after the Rhode Island Supreme Court invalidated a law requiring creditors to accept paper money in payment for debts, its members were summoned before the legislature, and although the legislature took no disciplinary action, it refused to reappoint all but one of the justices when their terms expired.[12] When all else failed, a legislature might get rid of judges by enacting "ripper bills" that abolished the judges' positions or the court on which they sat because the structure of state court systems typically was not entrenched in the state constitution. Thus in 1807, after the Ohio Supreme Court struck down a law extending the jurisdiction of justices of the peace, the legislature passed a resolution depriving the offending justices of their positions when their terms expired.[13] New Hampshire twice legislated out of office all justices of the supreme court by repealing the statute that created the tribunal and establishing another court in its place.[14] In New York in 1821, a new constitution reduced the membership of the supreme court from five to three, and the incumbents' positions were terminated when the constitution went into effect.[15] And in Kentucky in 1823, the legislature, after failing to muster the two-thirds vote necessary to impeach justices who had invalidated a law providing for debt relief, abolished the supreme court and created a new one with new judges.[16]

State constitutions guaranteed the people's representatives control over judges' continuation in office. One-third of eighteenth-century state constitutions established short terms of office for judges, ranging from one year in Vermont to a high of seven years in New Jersey and Pennsylvania (1776). Obviously, in those states the process of periodic reappointment, in which legislators played the central role, determined whether judges would continue in office. The remaining two-thirds of eighteenth-century state constitutions, reacting to the British imposition of service during the pleasure of the Crown, provided for judicial tenure during "good behavior." During the last quarter of the eighteenth century, one can detect a slight movement toward longer judicial terms—for example, Georgia in 1789 increased the term of office to three years, and Pennsylvania in 1790 adopted tenure during "good behavior." But even in the eleven states in which, by 1800, judges served during "good behavior," legislatures scrutinized the judiciary. We understand "good behavior" today as a synonym for life tenure, but during the early decades of the Republic, it was understood as a standard of conduct enforceable by the legislature.[17] Indeed, as a contemporary commentator noted, the nebulous character of that standard virtually invited legislators to apply it "according to disaffection on the one Hand; or Favour on the other."[18]

The legislature might act against "misbehaving" judges through impeachment, and the grounds for impeachment under early state constitutions were considerably broader than those under the federal Constitution.[19] States that defined impeachable offenses in their constitutions did so expansively. Thus New York (1777) and South Carolina (1778) permitted impeachment for "mal and corrupt conduct"; New Hampshire (1784) for "bribery, corruption, malpractice, or maladministration in office"; and New Jersey (1776) for "misbehavior."[20] Other states declined to define—and thereby limit—the grounds for impeachment. For example, in constitutions written after the US Constitution had limited impeachable offenses to "Treason, Bribery, or other high Crimes and Misdemeanors," Georgia (1789), Kentucky (1799), and Tennessee (1796) all provided for impeachment without specifying what offenses justified removal.

Several states supplemented impeachment with provisions authorizing the governor to remove judges upon address by two-thirds of the state legislature, with the gubernatorial role typically more ministerial than discretionary. Rather than merely duplicating impeachment, removal by address offered an additional—and potentially more far-reaching—weapon for legislative control.[21] For one thing, the "address did not have to allege willful or criminal misconduct. It needed only a favorable vote by both houses, not an investigation or trial."[22] Thus, judges were not guaranteed the basic elements of due process before they were removed. They did not have an opportunity to retain counsel, to cross-examine those accusing them, or to call their own witnesses. Early state constitutions did not even require a specification of the grounds for removal, although some later state constitutions mandated that the basis be "stated at length in such address, and on the journal of each house."[23] Thus, the inclusion of removal by address in state constitutions potentially came close to service during the pleasure of the legislature (or at least an extraordinary majority of the legislature), although the guarantee of tenure during "good behavior" implied that some misconduct had to be alleged. Address allowed legislators to hold judges accountable not only in cases of clear wrongdoing, as might be reached by impeachment, but even in instances where their performance could not be characterized as "any misdemeanor in office."[24] The Kentucky Constitution of 1799 made this clear, authorizing removal of judges by address "for any reasonable cause, which shall not be sufficient ground for impeachment."[25] So too did the origins of the practice in England, where address served as a mechanism for inducing the king to remove unpopular ministers, serving as "a vote of censure and no confidence."[26] In rejecting removal of federal judges by address, the delegates to the Constitutional Convention of 1787 indicated their understanding that removal by address potentially had greater reach than did impeachment.[27] Thomas Jefferson agreed with the analysis but not the conclusion. He favored a constitutional amendment to permit removal of federal judges by the president upon address by Congress, insisting that "in a government founded on the public will, [judicial independence] operates in an opposite direction, and against that will."[28]

The Removal of Judges

Although state legislatures maintained close oversight over the judicial branch, their removal powers threatened judges' decisional independence only if those powers were used to influence the substance of decisions or to penalize judges for their rulings. Often this was not the case. For example, New Jersey in 1782 impeached and removed two judges for corruption, and Massachusetts did the same for a justice of the peace in 1799. In 1791 Georgia impeached and removed a judge who misused his office to manipulate an election, and New Hampshire impeached a judge for "maladministration" based on unjustified absences from the court, though the judge resigned before he could be tried. Legislators in Massachusetts removed by address a judge after he was stricken with paralysis, and in 1805 legislators in North Carolina removed a justice of the peace by address for taking bribes and brawling with litigants. In that case legislators expressly recognized removal by address as a compromise between censure and impeachment.[29]

However, state legislatures sometimes did employ their removal powers to advance political objectives or punish courts for their rulings. The use of impeachment for political purposes peaked at the state and federal levels during the first decade of the nineteenth century. This "most sweeping impeachment movement in American history" arose with the electoral triumph of the Republican Party, which prompted a campaign to drive Federalist partisans from the bench.[30] This goal was pursued both wholesale, as in the repeal of the Judiciary Act of 1801, which removed judges appointed by President John Adams from the bench, and on a case-by-case basis against staunch Federalist judges via impeachment. For example, in Pennsylvania in 1803, the same year that Republicans in the federal House of Representatives launched impeachment proceedings against Supreme Court Justice John Pickering, the Pennsylvania Senate by a straight party-line vote removed Alexander Addison, an outspoken Federalist, from the bench.[31] In 1805, the same year that the US Senate acquitted Justice Samuel Chase, the Pennsylvania Senate fell just short of the two-thirds majority needed to convict and evict several members of the state's supreme court.[32]

In a narrow sense, the Republican aim was to remove those who had abused judicial office for partisan purposes and to chasten Federalists still on the bench. But in a broader sense, the Republican complaint was more fundamental. Tenure during good behavior, some Republicans complained, allowed a party in power to pack the bench with partisans who could frustrate efforts to introduce political change. Or, more positively put, tenure during good behavior prevented the appointment to the bench of judges who would reflect in a timely fashion changes in popular sentiment. As James Monroe noted in a letter to Thomas Jefferson, "The [Federalist] party had retired into the judiciary. . . . While in possession of that ground it can check the popular current which runs against them."[33] From the Republican perspective, then, courts in a republican regime should reflect, rather than check, the current of popular opinion.[34] As Thomas Jefferson wrote, "A judge independent of a king or executive alone is a good thing; but independence of the will of the nation is a solecism, at least in a republican government."[35] Indeed, impeachment of judges had a distinctively popular cast, with constituents memorializing legislators demanding the removal of particular judges.

Concerns about a gap between popular sentiment and judicial rulings also underlay the use of impeachment to punish judges for decisions striking down legislation. These conflicts between court and legislature turned less on the overall legitimacy of judicial review, though a few state legislators early on denounced it as an usurpation, than on the response to be made to rulings with which legislators disagreed. Could legislators conclude that a wrong-headed judicial ruling evidenced an underlying evil motive, a bad-faith dereliction of duty, and thus constituted grounds for impeachment? Or even if a judge's legal error might be an honest mistake, did mistaken rulings justify removal from the bench? The issue was debated at both the federal and state levels.[36] At the federal level, the unsuccessful Chase impeachment established that judges would not be removed for honest mistakes.[37] But in the states, resolution of the issue came neither so quickly nor so definitively.

Implications

Our analysis reveals that judicial independence as understood today was not a founding principle in the states—and perhaps not at the federal level either.[38] No one doubted that judges in a republic should be free from influence or manipulation by the executive. But whether they should likewise be immune from influence by the people—or by their agents in the state legislature—was less clear. One commentator has suggested that during the founding "little ink was spilled in attempts to explore the contradictory elements inherent in an independent judiciary as a part of a form of government based on popular sovereignty," but this is not altogether accurate, as revealed in the writings of Brutus, a leading Anti-Federalist.[39] Brutus insisted that the antimonarchial arguments for judicial independence did "not apply to this country, we have no hereditary monarch; those who appoint the judges do not hold their offices for life, nor do they descend to their children. The same arguments, therefore, lose a considerable part of their weight when applied to the state and condition of America." If judges were completely "independent of the people, of the legislature, and of every power under heaven," they would "soon feel themselves independent of heaven itself" and act tyrannically.[40] Thus, unchecked judicial power was in principle as dangerous as any other unchecked power. The system of tenure during good behavior exacerbated concerns about a power not answerable to the people. If there was no periodic assessment of judicial performance, then checks were needed to ensure that judges did not pursue a partisan or ideological or professional agenda, and the people or their representatives would have to supply those checks. Judges might take an oath to decide in accordance with the law, and they might recognize their duty to decide cases without fear or favor, but that did not guarantee the impartial administration of justice.[41]

Our analysis also reveals that the doctrine of the separation of powers, although expressly enshrined in some state constitutions and implicit in the rest, was not understood to preclude active legislative oversight over the judiciary. Rather, according to some scholars, this doctrine was primarily concerned with dual office-holding.[42] Today proponents of judicial independence insist that judges should not be threatened with removal based on disagreement with their rulings. But during the early decades of the Republic, state judges were deemed answerable for those rulings. State legislatures punished judges whose rulings were perceived as exhibiting partisan bias. They also held judges accountable if they acted beyond the scope of their authority, and the very process of holding them accountable served to define the scope of that authority in instances where it was contested. Finally, at least some state legislators believed that judges could be removed for mistaken rulings, even if rendered in good faith, and that question was debated throughout the period.

State legislatures felt justified in exercising such oversight because they believed they were acting—and were widely perceived to be acting—as the agents of the people. State legislators were directly elected by the people—often they were the only state officials who were. In addition, because they served short terms of office—annual election was the rule for lower houses and for some upper houses as well—legislators could be trusted to be responsive to and reflective of popular sentiments. Moreover, given the large size of early American assemblies, legislators were likely to resemble their constituents demographically, were likely to be in close contact with them, and thus were likely to share their perspectives. Finally, the transmission of popular views to legislators via memorials and instructions encouraged a coincidence between popular and legislative views.[43] Thus, if one accepted the notion of republican checks on the judiciary, that judges and the law they enunciated should be subject to popular influence and reflect the sense of the community, the only question was how that popular voice would be transmitted. For eighteenth-century state constitution-makers, the answer was obvious: state legislatures would provide that voice.

Whatever the persuasiveness of this in theory, reality proved recalcitrant. Legislators, despite their democratic pedigree, proved less than faithful agents of the public, and by the 1830s, the popular loss of confidence in their judgment and probity led constitutional reformers to seek controls on state legislatures, rather than relying on them to control courts.[44] New or revised state constitutions mandated that all bills be referred to committee, that they be read three times prior to enactment, that their titles accurately describe their contents, that they embrace a single subject, and so on. Other prohibitions addressed the substance, as well as the process, of legislation. This distrust of state legislatures extended to distrust of their oversight over courts. In fact, the objective shifted to judicial oversight over legislatures, so states began the transition to judicial election. Election of judges not only put control of the judiciary in the hands of the people but also reduced the power of legislatures, which had previously dominated selection. Judicial elections also produced a shift in the understanding of popular government, as popular authority was vested not only in the legislature but, with the direct election of governors as well, in all branches of state government. So elected judges could claim just as strong a connection to the people, the source of all political authority, as legislators could, and this gave them greater legitimacy in challenging legislative enactments.[45] Thus, over time, a more complex understanding developed as to the place of the judiciary in a republican government, a topic we explore in Chapter 2.

Independent as to What?

Even if judges should be safeguarded against undue external pressures so they could exercise their powers independently, what were those powers? The answer to this question was not self-evident, and in fact the definition of the judicial realm changed over time. From a twenty-first-century perspective, it might seem easy to distinguish what responsibilities are inherently judicial, obvious that only judges should deal with those responsibilities, and equally obvious that they should deal only with those responsibilities. But from an eighteenth-century perspective, it was not.[46] The issue that has attracted the most scholarly attention has been judicial review of legislation.[47] Did the state and federal founders believe that judicial review was an appropriate exercise of judicial power, and if so, how broad was this power supposed to be? During the first half century of the Republic, however, this was only one of a host of issues that affected understandings of judicial independence.

An initial issue was whether there was a distinctly judicial function at all. This was not obvious on its face. Indeed, one influential exponent of the separation of powers, John Locke, did not consider the judicial power distinct but rather subsumed it under the executive power.[48] Despite Montesquieu's reformulation of the separation of powers, Locke's analysis carried considerable weight, in part because Blackstone followed Locke in his influential *Commentaries*, subsuming judges under the executive.[49] The New Jersey Constitution of 1776, for instance, "called for a division of government into three branches but also did not include the judiciary among them."[50] Only gradually did one see a proliferation of state constitutional provisions mandating a separation of powers that included the judicial power as one of the three powers.[51]

The Shared Power of Judging: Other Branches

Even if one assumes a distinct judicial function—with dispute resolution on the basis of law the most likely candidate—should that function be lodged exclusively in the judicial branch? Historically, the American judiciary shared responsibility for dispute resolution with the other branches of government. During the colonial period, for example, there was an established practice of legislative adjudication that paralleled adjudication by the courts, a practice that reflected in part a distrust of judges who owed their continuation in office to the favor of the Crown.[52] In addition, the flood of petitions to legislatures to resolve specific disputes led to a proliferation of private bills in which the legislature was making essentially judicial determinations.[53]

After Independence, safeguards were established to prevent misuse of the legislature's adjudicative power—for example, state constitutions prohibited bills of attainder and retrospective laws.[54] But this did not preclude legislative adjudication. In some instances litigants were granted new jury trials by the legislature, in others default judgments were vacated, and in still others a special tribunal was established to resolve particular disputes.[55] Indicative of the extent of this legislative restoring to law was Thomas Jefferson's complaint that the Virginia legislature had assumed "judiciary powers" and by "put[ting] their proceedings into the form of an act of assembly," had "in many instances decided rights which should have been left to judicial controversy."[56] Debate continued in the new states as to whether the practice of legislative adjudication was appropriate only to the colonial situation, in which judges might be influenced by an unelected and unaccountable monarch, or whether it should continue under a republican government, in which those who selected judges were themselves subject to popular control. And if legislative adjudication was to continue, what sorts of disputes were appropriate for legislative resolution?

The early history of the Republic reveals the varying views on these matters. Take, for example, the issue of divorce. In some states during the antebellum era, particularly in the South, divorce was viewed as a legislative responsibility, with divorces granted by the people's representatives on a case-by-case basis. In other states, particularly in the North, divorce was understood as a legal rather than a legislative question. Thus, by 1800 all the New England states, New York, and New Jersey had divorce laws, and divorce cases took the form of ordinary lawsuits.[57] In still other states, divorce was a shared legislative and judicial responsibility. The Georgia Constitution of 1798, for example, authorized the legislature to grant divorces by a two-thirds vote after "the parties shall have had a fair trial before the superior court, and a verdict shall have been obtained authorizing a divorce upon legal principles."[58] As this suggests, the boundaries between those disputes appropriate for legislative resolution and those appropriate for judicial resolution remained unclear—and sometimes contested.

This was particularly true when rulings might impose financial obligations on states. State legislatures claimed the power to approve every grant of money from the public treasury, and this extended to money owed by the government to private claimants, so that redress for such debts lay with the legislature rather than the courts. The doctrine of sovereign immunity meant that courts had the authority to hear claims against the government only if they were authorized to do so by the legislature, and state legislatures often kept to themselves the power of resolving such claims.[59]

Also during the colonial era, nonjudicial bodies—typically, the governor and council—had the final say on appeals. This coincided with the practice in England, where the House of Lords sat as the court of ultimate appeal. However, the practice of nonjudicial bodies exercising ultimate appellate authority continued under several state constitutions. For example, under the New Jersey Constitution of 1776, the governor and Legislative Council sat as the "Court of Appeals in the Last Resort"; under the Vermont Constitution of 1786, the governor and council served as a court of impeachment; and under the Delaware Constitution of 1776, appeal was from the Supreme Court to a "court" consisting of the president (governor), three members appointed by the Legislative Council, and three members appointed by the House of Assembly.[60] Thus, even in the legal realm state courts might share power with other institutions of government.

The Shared Power of Judging: The Jury

Even when the judicial branch alone resolved disputes, judges did not exercise sole authority but rather shared decision making with juries, which ensured popular participation in the administration of justice. As Jack Rakove put it, "Juries were the basic agents of decision making in nearly every matter where the general authority of the state intersected with the private concerns and rights of citizens."[61] It is hard to overestimate the importance that early Americans attached to "the inestimable right of trial by jury," the only right protected in all eighteenth-century state constitutions.[62] The jury's importance lay in its popular character. As Alexis de Tocqueville noted, "The jury system as understood in America seems to me as direct and extreme a consequence of the dogma of the sovereignty of the people as universal suffrage. They are . . . equally powerful means of making the majority prevail."[63]

The key phrase here is "the jury system as understood in America." In England a division of responsibility developed early on in the courts, such that juries were responsible for deciding questions of fact and judges for deciding questions of law. But even prior to the Revolution, juries in America came to exercise the power of rendering judgment on matters of both fact and law in civil and in criminal cases. As John Adams summarized it, the juror's duty was to "find the Verdict according to his own best Understanding, Judgment, and Conscience, though in Direct opposition to the direction of the Court."[64] This view of the jury's responsibility continued after Independence, as early state constitutions attest.[65] Thus the Pennsylvania Constitution of 1776 insisted that the existing right of trial by jury "ought to be held sacred," the Massachusetts Constitution echoed that language, and the Georgia Constitution of 1777 expressly stated that "the jury shall be judges of law as well as of fact."[66] In fact, several state legislatures extended trial by jury to types of cases, such as admiralty cases and paternity cases, that had formerly been tried without juries.[67]

This expansive understanding of the jury's role necessarily diminished the role of the judge. In fact, the judicial role in dispute resolution was even more circumscribed than a description of the jury's authority might suggest. Whereas in theory judges could still influence case outcomes by summarizing the evidence in a case and instructing jurors as to the applicable law, in practice they rarely did so. Whether out of a desire to avoid antagonizing the parties to a case or because of a lack of ability, American judges generally avoided summarizing the evidence in cases.[68] The fact that trials were conducted before multijudge courts, as was the practice in many states, also meant that jurors received seriatim charges, with each judge and both counsel giving their opinions of the law. This in turn allowed jurors to choose whichever interpretation they judged most appropriate.[69] Thus, according to one contemporary account, trial judges did little more than "preserve order and see that the parties had a fair chance with the jury."[70]

During the colonial period, the jury's broad authority served to check abuses by judges who might be susceptible to the blandishments or threats of the Crown, and to block unjust laws by refusing to give them effect. After the Revolution, the selection of judges changed, but the rationale for jury power did not. Commentators analogized the jury to the lower house of the legislature, depicting the jury as representing the people in the administration of law and thereby forestalling judicial arbitrariness and lawlessness. Thus, Thomas Jefferson famously described the jury as "curb[ing] judges and represent[ing] the people in the judicial branch."[71] In fact, Jefferson claimed it was more important that the people be represented in the implementation of the law than in its creation. For present purposes, what is striking is the expectation that the people would control judicial behavior not only indirectly through selection and removal of judges but directly through their participation in judicial decisions.

Such broad power could be assigned to the jury because—in John Adams's words—"the general Rules of Law and common Regulations of Society [were] well enough known to the ordinary Juror."[72] The authority of juries to determine the law in civil and criminal cases rested on the widespread understanding that ordinary citizens had as great an ability as judges to discern what the law was.[73] In part, this stemmed from the fact that the gap between those with legal training and those without was not as broad as it is today. In part, too, it acknowledged that not all of those holding judicial office had the advantage of legal training. This was true not only for justices of the peace, who were generally local notables without formal legal training, but even for members of state trial and appellate courts, as service on the bench during the antebellum period was not a lifetime career for most judges.[74] But most importantly, the jury's authority reflected a particular understanding of the character and sources of the law. Most law was common law, rather than statutory law, and the common law was viewed as arising out of and reflecting the community, rather than as a form of law elaborated by legally trained professionals. Indeed, the jury served as a shield for the local community against "outside interference," whether in the form of plaintiffs taking locals to trial or of appellate courts imposing legal obligations.[75] As Shannon Stimson has put it, jury "powers were premised by an epistemology of law utterly and irrevocably dependent upon local government and on the jurors' first-hand sense of the law."[76] Only when this understanding of law changed would one find a shift in the responsibilities of the jury.

Judicial Power Beyond Judging

Although the American judiciary's role in dispute resolution may have been circumscribed during the colonial era, it also exercised powers beyond what might today be understood as judicial powers. As William Nelson has noted, "The courts . . . protected life and property, apportioned and collected taxes, supervised the construction and maintenance of highways, issued licenses, and regulated licensees' businesses." Thus, the lines typically drawn among legislative, executive, and judicial power were "obscured."[77] This judicial involvement in administration did not cease with independence, so that Stephen Skowronek could characterize American government during the nineteenth century as a system of parties and courts, in which courts played a key administrative role.[78] This was largely a matter of necessity. Throughout the antebellum period and even beyond it, the states (and the federal government) lacked a developed administrative apparatus. Thus, as Alexis de Tocqueville observed, "What most strikes the European who travels through the United States is the absence of what is called among us government or administration." Indeed, looking beyond the township, he noted that "one hardly perceives a trace of an administrative hierarchy."[79] Various factors, including distrust of executive power, contributed to this. For present purposes, the point is that the American states tended to rely on the judiciary, especially justices of the peace but other trial and appellate judges as well, for administrative functions.[80] For example, the Georgia Constitution of 1798 instructed judges to appoint census takers, and courts in Massachusetts and Virginia were involved in "assessing taxes, directing expenditures on local projects, issuing licenses, and in general monitoring the counties over which they presided."[81]

Judicial involvement in political matters extended beyond administration to legislation as well. A prime example was New York's Council of Revision, comprised of the governor, chancellor, and supreme court, which reviewed all pending bills and exercised a limited veto over their passage.[82] The council assessed both the constitutionality and the wisdom of proposed legislation.

Although the council attracted considerable attention at the Philadelphia Convention of 1777, where James Madison championed the concept, no other state followed New York's lead, and ultimately dissatisfaction with judges assessing the desirability of legislation led to its elimination, by unanimous vote, at New York's 1821 constitutional convention.[83]

Judicial responsibilities beyond judging also included the obligation to furnish legal advice to other branches of the government, enshrined in constitutional provisions requiring state supreme courts to issue advisory opinions upon request of the legislature or the executive.[84] One might view the opportunity to issue advisory opinions as an enhancement of judicial power, similar to the abstract review exercised by constitutional courts today. But in practice the requirement to provide advisory opinions subordinated the judicial branch to the legislative and executive branches, which had the judiciary at their beck and call but were not obliged to follow the courts' legal advice.[85]

Finally, state judges sometimes took upon themselves a political role, defending the judicial branch against what they perceived as invasions of their prerogatives by issuing resolutions attacking the constitutionality of legislative enactments. These resolutions were issued not in the course of resolving disputes between contending parties but rather entirely on the initiative of the courts. These judicial efforts to defend the institutional interests of the judiciary were hardly an innovation; they had precedents in the actions of English judges since at least the early eighteenth century.

A conflict in Virginia in 1778 illustrates the aggressive stance taken by some courts. The Virginia General Assembly enacted a law requiring judges of the Virginia Court of Appeals to sit on district courts, in addition to carrying out their other responsibilities. The Court of Appeals responding with a resolution claiming that the law in effect reduced their salaries by imposing responsibilities without compensation for the new duties. Whatever the merits of the controversy, in issuing the resolution the judges asserted a judicial authority to expound the law outside of cases and controversies when the integrity of the judicial branch was at stake. For judges to assume the role of political disputant often proved unproductive because they were confronting the people's representatives. Nevertheless, their willingness to enter the political thicket underscores the lack of clarity as to the confines of the judicial office.[86]

In sum, judges had wide-ranging responsibilities beyond dispute resolution. This in turn discouraged the development of discourse on judicial independence and accountability because the definition of judicial independence and the arguments for it are premised on a picture of judges engaged in the resolution of disputes. When judges' responsibilities extend beyond that core function, when they encompass functions that today are understood as administrative rather than judicial, they raise perplexing questions as to the appropriate scope of judicial independence and judicial accountability, as it becomes "inevitable that the line between what [is] political and what [is] judicatory would be blurred."[87] Or, from a different angle, the development of the modern argument for judicial independence required a distinct judicial function that differentiated the tasks of the courts from those of the other branches and confined the courts to those tasks.

Implications

The eighteenth century produced a distinctive—and to twenty-first-century eyes, unfamiliar—conception of the place of the judiciary in a republican government. The line distinguishing the judicial branch from other branches and the judicial function from other functions proved to be unclear and permeable. Other governmental institutions undertook the resolution of disputes between parties, either though legislative remedies or by passing final judgment on appeals. Meanwhile, judges participated in assessing the wisdom of public policy, in administering the policies that were adopted, and in furnishing legal advice to other branches of government. And those without legal training—whether jurors or nonlawyers appointed to the bench— played a crucial role in enunciating the law and resolving disputes. In such a legal context, the contemporary debate about judicial independence and potential threats to the impartial administration of justice would have been incomprehensible.

For this debate to develop, significant changes had to occur in legal and political institutions, in legal and political practice, and in the law. Courts had to wrest from other governmental institutions exclusive control over the resolution of disputes. Judges also had to make effective a claim that their legal expertise gave them a preeminent claim to enunciate and interpret the law and that effective exercise of that responsibility required judicial independence. The nineteenth century witnessed the beginning of these changes, albeit not without a reaction from political forces championing a more "republican" perspective.

The Changing Judicial Function
and Judicial Independence

During the first half of the nineteenth century, the responsibilities of state judicial branches expanded, such that by the 1850s state courts were exercising more or less the same decisional powers that they do today. States moved to safeguard the judicial sphere by eliminating the participation of other institutions in matters that we today recognize as inherently judicial. New Jersey and New York, among others, eliminated the final appeal to nonjudicial entities and lodged ultimate appellate authority in their state supreme courts.[88] State legislatures largely ceased granting new trials to disappointed litigants, and issues such as divorce were transferred to the courts. Beyond that, various threats to the judicial authority to elaborate the common law were repulsed, including efforts to replace it with a common-sense jurisprudence or with a legal code drafted by the legislature. State courts expanded their authority in familiar areas, taking from juries the power to find the law and undertaking in a self-conscious way to shape the common law. Finally, state courts extended and solidified their power to strike down statutes as unconstitutional. This section describes how the answer to "independent as to what" changed during the antebellum era.

Expanding the Judicial Function: Judicial Review

Judicial review emerged almost immediately following independence as a key issue in defining the scope of judicial authority. The practice had no colonial analogue, and review of the constitutionality of legislation ran counter to the Blackstonian doctrine of legislative supremacy, so it demanded some justification.[89] As Sylvia Snowiss has shown, initially judicial review was understood as a political mechanism rather than as an exercise of legal judgment, "an additional political responsibility outside the judiciary's assigned function."[90] Early judicial review extended only to "concededly unconstitutional laws," so that there was no need for the sort of interpretation that judges engaged in with other legal texts. In many of the early judicial review cases, courts were defending themselves against legislative encroachments on their powers in standard checks-and-balances fashion. Finally, in refusing to give effect to unconstitutional laws, courts were reaffirming the constitution as fundamental law and protecting the people against faithless legislators who sought to transgress it.[91]

Yet justification of judicial review as a political mechanism did not serve to confirm judicial authority, much less judicial supremacy.[92] If courts in reviewing legislation were not exercising a core legal function, if they were not interpreting law, then that function might be dispensed with—after all, courts in Great Britain and in the American colonies did without judicial review. Or the power to invalidate laws might be shared with or assigned to other institutions. For example, in Pennsylvania and Vermont, a Council of Censors was created to identify and report constitutional violations, and in New York the Council of Revision, which included both judges and nonjudges, passed on legislation.[93] Also, insofar as judicial review was confined to concededly unconstitutional laws, it did not provide a basis for asserting the superiority of judicial interpretations of the constitution when its meaning was contested. The establishment of something more akin to contemporary judicial review required a reconceptualization of the practice, one that analogized the practice to the standard judicial function of interpreting ordinary law.

State courts began to exercise judicial review over state legislation in the decade following Independence. According to one count, between 1780 and 1801 state courts in eight cases refused to give effect to state laws, and in at least four others they claimed the power of judicial review, although they declined to invalidate the laws that were challenged.[94] The reception accorded these rulings varied. The New York legislature denounced the decision in *Rutgers v. Waddington* (1784), claiming that judicial review was "in its tendency subversive of all law and good order" and that "therewith will end all our dear bought rights and privileges, and Legislatures become useless."[95] However, an attempt to impeach the judges who authored the opinion in the case failed.[96] In Rhode Island, the legislature summoned the judges who decided *Trevett v. Weeden* (1786) to explain their ruling, and it ultimately refused to reappoint several members of the offending court. However, by the 1790s there was broad acceptance of the legitimacy of judicial review, at least with regard to concededly unconstitutional acts, and "legislative resistance such as that following *Rutgers* and *Trevett* disappeared as opposition became a minority position."[97] Most scholars, although differing among themselves as to exactly when judicial review became institutionalized in the states, concur. Thus, William Nelson writes that "by 1820 the doctrine of judicial review had attained general acceptance," noting that by that year ten of the original thirteen states had either invalidated laws or asserted their authority to do so, and all five of the states admitted to Union from 1790–1815 had also accepted it.[98] Similarly, Robert

Clinton has attributed the muted public reaction to *Marbury v. Madison* (1803) to "the general acceptability of the decision itself and the opinion that justified it," and Larry Kramer has argued that by the time *Marbury* was decided, its "main principles were already widely accepted."[99] For example, from 1825–50 the Ohio Supreme Court handed down eight decisions involving the constitutionality of legislation, striking down four laws, and in no instance did the court's actions prompt a challenge to its authority.[100] Indeed, what did not happen is perhaps as important as what did. Only one state, Kentucky, made any serious effort to prohibit by statute or constitutional amendment the practice of judicial review. (We shall discuss the Kentucky case shortly.) Even in those instances where judicial rulings sparked debate, the controversy typically was confined to attacks on the particular rulings and their perpetrators and did not extend to challenges to the practice of judicial review.[101]

Why did the innovation of judicial review gain such ready acceptance in the states? In part, this was because during the antebellum era it was employed primarily in cases that either were not politically charged or that could be resolved in ways that were not politically divisive. Thus, in a survey of invalidations by southern courts in the antebellum era, Donald Fehrenbacher found thirty instances in which statutes were struck down, but "at least a third of those thirty decisions [were] technical corrections, often of minor consequence."[102] Indeed, "many judicial review cases were of immediate concern only to the rather small number of individuals directly involved."[103] This meant that judicial invalidations did not significantly restrict—and thereby challenge—legislative power. Also, the exercise of judicial review in low-visibility cases served to establish a body of precedent supporting the practice. Then when controversial invalidations occurred, the force of precedent limited those opposing the rulings to attacking the particular outcome, as opposed to the legitimacy of the practice itself.

In part too, judges defused controversy over judicial review by the restraint they showed in striking down state enactments. While it is true that by 1860 more than 150 state laws had been invalidated by state courts, in the vast majority of early cases state judges upheld challenged laws.[104] For example, prior to 1860 the Virginia Supreme Court heard thirty-five challenges to state enactments but declared only four laws unconstitutional, and the Indiana Supreme Court struck down only two laws prior to 1850.[105] Also, state courts adhered, at least rhetorically, to the "doubtful case" doctrine, under which only clearly unconstitutional laws would be invalidated. Illustrative is the Ohio Supreme Court's opinion in *McCormick v. Alexander* (1825).[106] The court reaffirmed its power of judicial review but cautioned that a court should not invalidate a law "unless the statute in question is a plain and palpable violation of the constitution. It should be both against the letter and spirit of the instrument. So long as there is a doubt, the decision of the court should be in favor of the statute."[107] This invocation of the doubtful-case doctrine helped give legitimacy to the exercise of judicial review by basing it on a noncontroversial standard. Thus, when there were challenges to particular rulings, they focused on the court's departure from the standard and did not escalate into attacks on the judicial review itself.

Perhaps most importantly, over time the task of constitutional interpretation came to be seen as no different in character than the uncontested judicial responsibility of applying and enforcing ordinary law. This was a crucial shift. Initially, judicial review meant the authority of judges to strike down unquestionably unconstitutional laws. Judges in such circumstances were expected, no less than other officials, to enforce the constitution in the course of exercising their responsibilities. But over time, through analogy to legal interpretation, judicial review became a judicial power to choose among competing interpretations of the state's constitution. The point is not merely the regularizing of the practice of judicial review, though that was important. Rather, it is that judicial review came to be analogized to other instances of dispute resolution, so that the judicial exposition of the constitution became just another instance of legal interpretation. And because saying what the law is was recognized as an inherently judicial task, the effect of the shift was to make judicial review a core judicial responsibility. Going along with this, the justification for judicial review shifted from a political one to a legal one. The constitution was portrayed as essentially a legal document, and the claim was that judges, by virtue of their legal training, were particularly well-suited to interpret it. Sylvia Snowiss attributes this shift at the federal level to innovations pioneered by Chief Justice John Marshall in his post-*Marbury* rulings, in particular his practice of establishing the meaning of the Constitution, for the purpose of judicial review, through a process of textual exposition following the rules for statutory interpretation, and his relaxation of the doubtful-case rule.[108] It is impossible to determine to what extent Marshall's leadership guided state judges and to what extent the change occurred independently. What is clear is that the shift provided the foundation for the institutionalization of judicial review.

Of course, history is seldom so neat, and the story told thus far finds an apparent outlier in Kentucky.[109] In 1823, the Kentucky Court of Appeals, the state's highest court, struck down a popular debtor-relief statute. The ruling sparked an immediate political reaction, and in an election the following year, opponents of the ruling won a resounding victory. However, their attempt to remove the offending judges by address failed to achieve the required two-thirds vote. The frustrated legislators then enacted a Judicial Reorganization Act that abolished the Court of Appeals, thus unseating its members, and created a new Supreme Court. The old court refused to accept removal from office and continued to sit, producing a "jurisprudential schism unique in American history."[110]

Of particular note in the Kentucky conflict is the sustained and vitriolic opposition to the institution of judicial review itself. As one opponent put it, "We appoint judges . . . but it is never understood that they will judge our laws, because to vest them with such a power, would be to put them over our will, over our law, and . . . they would be our legislators, our masters, our dictators, our sovereigns." Judicial review, another argued, was unnecessary "in our Republican government . . . because the people cannot be their own enemies."[111] From his study of this conflict, Theodore Ruger has concluded that what appeared to others to be a consensus in the states in favor of judicial review was in fact a mirage produced less by acceptance of the practice than by the absence of controversial rulings that might have activated opponents of the practice.

This claim is consistent with the low-visibility exercise of judicial review in most states. But Ruger appears to confuse the strong reaction to an unpopular decision with deep-seated resentment of judicial review. It is true that opponents of the "old court" sometimes couched their complaints in the rhetoric of an attack on judicial review. But when the issue of judicial review was squarely presented to the electorate in 1825 and 1826, divorced in time from the court's ruling, Kentucky voters by comfortable majorities backed the "old court" and judicial review. Thus the Kentucky experience, like that in other states, demonstrates the institutionalization of a new understanding of the scope of judicial responsibility, one initially contested but then rather quickly accepted. And with this acceptance, the debate shifted from the issue of judicial review to the character and independence of those exercising the power, that is, to issues of judicial independence and judicial accountability.

Safeguarding the Judicial Function: The Common Law

After the revolution, some Americans opposed continued reliance on the common law, arguing that it was tainted through its association with "the monarchial and aristocratical institutions of England" and could never "be consistent with republican principles."[112] They also distrusted the common law because it was inaccessible to ordinary citizens, empowering legal professionals (judges and lawyers) who understood the common law to manipulate it for self-interested purposes. More radical opponents proposed to replace the common law's "hodge-podge of mystery" with a commonsense jurisprudence. They favored an easy-to-understand body of law drawn up by the legislature and replacement of the common law's system of pleadings with simplified procedures that would allow litigants to present their cases to local juries directly.[113] They also argued that making the law clearer and more accessible would reduce the incidence of legal disputes, which were often rooted in uncertainty about the law. By increasing the accessibility of the law, they hoped to make it unnecessary for ordinary people to consult legal professionals in order to understand their legal rights and duties. Thus, the positive consequences of legal certainty and accessibility would include freeing the great body of the people from having to rely on the arcane expertise of legal professionals, thereby reducing the power of attorneys and frustrating "the chicanery of law and lawyers." The remedy also served important republican objectives. Judges were suspected of "blocking the emergence of a truly free republic by their stubborn adherence to prewar forms and ceremonies."[114] So it was important that law be made not by judges but by the people themselves (the jury) or by officials directly answerable to the people (legislators).[115] Thus, the aim was to "provide democratic legal and political structures and jurisprudence that would replace the independent judiciary and judicial review and expunge the common law from American life."[116]

Yet despite concerns about its compatibility with republicanism, no state abolished the common law. Instead, the states "received" the common law, albeit with reservations. The New York Constitution of 1777, for example, declared that "such parts of the common law of England . . . as did form the law of the said colony [New York] shall be and continue the law of the state," but made exception for provisions that favored "particular denominations of Christians," recognized "the supremacy, sovereignty, government, or prerogatives claimed by the King of Great Britain," or conflicted with the constitution.[117] The reason for this "reception" of the common law was a practical one.

Legal continuity seemed a necessity because it would have been difficult, if not impossible, to craft an entirely new body of law, particularly in the midst of a revolution. Still, popular criticism of the common law had an effect. Even its most committed defenders came to recognize that to preserve the common law, it would have to be reformed to bring it into harmony with American circumstances and social conditions, and the unnecessary complexities in the common law would have to be eliminated in order to make justice more accessible to ordinary people. This latter concern led to the transformation of the rules of pleading in common law during the early nineteenth century in order to make them less technical and thereby to encourage decision of cases on the merits.[118]

Yet more than simple necessity underlay the states' "reception" of the common law. Many Americans viewed the common law as a foundation of American society and the source and safeguard of their rights. Legal professionals in particular stressed that the common law embodied the "collected wisdom of the ages, combining the principles of original justice with the infinite variety of human concerns."[119] Although acknowledging that it had to be purified of monarchial and aristocratic doctrines, they insisted that the common law's rules of procedure and its methodology should remain part of American law. Underlying this position was a political perspective quite different from that advanced by republican critics of the common law. Those championing the common law "wanted law to come not primarily (and certainly not exclusively) from the legislature but from the opinions of judges who were well-trained lawyers." Such law, they believed, formulated in the resolution of real-life conflicts, would be "better, tougher, and more practical" than that enacted via legislation.[120]

In making this argument, proponents of the common law were not arguing, at least explicitly, for judicial policymaking. They agreed that nonelected officials should not initiate policy. But this did not preclude giving a paramount role to the common law because the prevailing legal understanding was that the common law was "a body of essentially fixed doctrine," with judges serving merely as the expositors of an existing law.[121] Supporting this notion of a fixed and determinate common law was an expectation of strict adherence to precedent. Yet tensions underlay this depiction. For example, the acknowledged need for judges to evaluate common law in order to bring it into conformity with republican institutions was in tension with strict adherence to precedent. And the notion of the common law as furnishing "remedies according to growing wants and varying circumstances of man . . . without waiting for the slow progress of legislative interference" seemed to imply that judges would introduce changes in public policy.[122]

Although fully developed alternatives to the common law, such as common-sense jurisprudence, faded into historical insignificance, elements of these positions survived, albeit transformed over time. Thus, the concerns about reception of the English common law voiced by the proponents of common-sense jurisprudence found echoes in the movement for codification of the law during the mid-nineteenth century.[123] The advocates of codification noted that it placed law-making in the hands of the people's representatives rather than in the hands of the judges and so better accorded with republican principle than did judicial policy-making under the guise of legal interpretation. Also underlying "these demands for codification was a new conviction that much of the English common law itself was the product of the whim of judges."[124] Finally, again echoing earlier critics of the common law, proponents of codification insisted that it made the law more accessible and more certain. A well-organized, written body of law would eliminate the confusion engendered by the multiplicity of precedents. Thus the solution may have changed, and the vocabulary in which the concern was voiced, but there is no mistaking the continuity of the concern or the continuing need for defense of the judiciary's role in crafting American law.

Expanding the Judicial Function: The Common Law

Several factors combined to alter state judges' role in the enunciation of the common law during the early nineteenth century. For a system of case law to operate, judges and attorneys must have easy access to appellate rulings, so the first factor was the development of a readily available body of American case law. In the early Republic, uncertainty as to English and American law was widespread even among legal professionals, "exacerbated by the lack of written case law, and the complete lack of any collected indigenous case reports until very late in the [18th] century."[125] The absence of American case reports, together with the suspicion of English law, encouraged a reliance on community sentiment as a source of the common law. This affected the distribution of authority in trial courts, as juries could plausibly claim special expertise as to community values, "articulat[ing] into positive law the ethical standards of those communities and . . . completely dominat[ing] the legal system's decision-making processes."[126]

This situation changed in the early nineteenth century. In 1804 Massachusetts by statute provided for the publication of appellate opinions, and by 1830 nearly all the states were publishing such reports.[127] This transformed court operations because it meant that there was now a source for the common law other than community sentiment, namely judicial precedent, and this new source was one in which judges, not jurors, were expert. Moreover, a common law based on a body of precedent would no longer be understood as a reflection of local values but rather as explicating statewide or even national standards. Thus jurors' expertise as to local standards became less important. Finally, insofar as judges were expert in case law and juries were not, the shift in the locus of expertise encouraged a corresponding shift in responsibilities. The problem of legal uncertainty, an endemic concern in developing commercial societies, would be addressed by elevating expertise over popular judgment, by placing the determination of the law in the hands of legal professionals rather than in those of ordinary citizens. This produced a realignment of the roles of judge and jury, with the judge's role considerably enhanced. During the nineteenth century, judges began to regularly set aside jury verdicts as contrary to law.[128] Even more important, they claimed broad authority to determine what the law was. By the 1820s in Massachusetts—and likely shortly thereafter in other states as well—"the jury had become the adjunct of the court and had been left only with those fact-finding tasks, such as determining the credibility of witnesses and weighing the inherent probability of competing testimony, for which courts lack special expertise."[129]

This of course was not the only possible outcome. Insofar as jurors did not know or understand the law, one might have attributed the problem to the inaccessibility or uncertainty of the law rather than to inadequacies in the jurors. Such a diagnosis, as we have seen, was behind the campaign for codification of the law. What is noteworthy is that the courts were able to fend off legislative intrusions on their authority, such as codification, even as they were expanding their authority vis-à-vis ordinary citizens.

Also contributing to state judges' altered role in the enunciation of the common law was a new conception of that law and of judges' relation to it. Morton Horwitz has traced this changing understanding to the early decades of the nineteenth century. Whereas at the outset of the 1800s, the common law was perceived as a set of unchanging principles, judges came to view those principles from a functional or purposive perspective, subject to revision based on their social consequences. Put simply, judges could adapt common law principles when they no longer served the purposes for which they were created. Although precedent continued to exert considerable influence, judges came to believe it appropriate to depart from precedent if considerations of social policy justified such a shift or to avoid manifestly unjust results. This instrumental conception of the law encouraged—or at least justified—legal innovation by state judges, involving them in choosing among policy directions rather than merely elaborating unchangeable principles. Their rulings, like statutes, self-consciously enunciated legal standards based on a consideration of consequences, with a recognition that these standards would govern beyond the particular dispute being resolved. The judicial embrace of this instrumentalist view of the common law involved judges in directing the course of social change, so that during the antebellum era "the common law performed at least as great a role as legislation in underwriting and channeling economic development."[130] Yet this shift in the judicial role occurred without a frank acknowledgment that judges were and ought to be participants in policymaking. Most likely, such an endorsement of judicial policymaking would have been counterproductive, analogizing judges to legislators instead of insisting upon their distinctiveness. It was far better to continue to portray judicial decisions as rooted in and dictated by law, though the prevailing understanding of the law and of judgment under law may have changed. This portrayal likely accorded with the self-understanding of state judges in the nineteenth century.

The justification for this enhanced judicial role was tied closely to enhanced professionalization within the judiciary and the legal profession more generally. Although the judiciary was not a lifetime career during the early nineteenth century, lacking the distinctive professional training found in civil-law countries, it did develop a sense of professional identity. The number of nonlawyer judges on the state bench declined, and the substantial growth in the legal profession during the late eighteenth and nineteenth centuries provided a pool of experienced, trained professionals from which to select judges. As Chapter 2 will show, when states shifted from appointment to election of judges, among the key concerns was to rescue the selection process from domination by party caucuses within state legislatures, so as to enhance the quality of those selected and to free them to expound the law without fear of political consequences. An obvious corollary of this move to a more learned and less partisan judiciary was that its members should be free to exercise their professional judgment.

Conclusions

The legal profession tends to depict judges as trained professionals, possessed of expert knowledge, dealing dispassionately with complex, technical, and frequently arcane subject matter. This description helps justify judicial independence, for it follows that nonlawyers lack the legal expertise necessary to understand the responsibilities of judges or to critique their rulings in an informed fashion. Often the public lacks the necessary dispassion as well. As proponents of judicial independence never tire of insisting, it makes no more sense to elect a judge than it does to choose a physician or an engineer by popular vote. Thus the claim of expert knowledge trumps the demand for democratic accountability, even in a republican regime.

Yet as our analysis has shown, this understanding of judicial independence was not present—or at least was not dominant—from the outset of the American republic. Rather, this "new conception of judicial independence," as Gordon Wood has called it, had to be constructed and connected to the rule of law and to the idea of judges as expert and authoritative expositors of that law. This did not occur in the states until the nineteenth century.[131] In addition, the emergence and triumph of this new understanding had to await developments in the law, in the courts, in the legal profession, and in the broader society. Among the most important of these were the institutionalization of judicial review, the "legalization" of the Constitution in order to maintain the distinction between law and politics in the exercise of judicial review, and the proliferation of case law.[132] Salient developments in the courts included the taming of the jury and the solidifying of a judicial monopoly over dispute resolution. Often, these developments were interconnected. The expansion and professionalization of the legal profession during the nineteenth century provided a base of support for the independence of legal professionals on the bench. Meanwhile, the creation of a vibrant market economy placed a premium on legal certainty and on the development of a coherent and predictable body of law elaborated by legally learned professionals. As Jack Rakove has suggested, "Judicial review could only become possible after influential segments of the American political community moved away from the belief that juries were competent triers of law and fact alike, and instead accepted the benefits of allowing professionally expert judges to act as independent sources of legal authority."[133]

Yet to speak of the triumph of the new conception of judicial independence overstates the case. Throughout the antebellum period, efforts to advance judicial independence collided with claims that judges, like other officials in a republican regime, should be responsive to popular concerns and should be accountable to the people or to their representatives. During the nineteenth century, critics insisted that important societal issues should be resolved by popular majorities, not by courts, through such reforms as codification. In doing so, these critics harkened back to themes present since the founding of the Republic, underscoring important continuities in the campaign for chastened and confined courts. Other critics questioned whether judicial independence would free more than professional judgment, whether professional expertise might operate to disguise the pursuit of interests of the judiciary, of the legal profession, or of the class of which judges were a part. This concern found common cause with the Jacksonian concern for privilege, which itself has roots in earlier republican thought about interests distinct from the interests of the people.[134]

What is ironic is that the emergence of the modern conception of judicial independence coincided with the adoption of reforms that today are viewed as anathema to judicial independence, namely, the partisan election of judges and reduction of judicial tenure from "good behavior" to limited terms of office. Between 1847 and 1910, twenty of the twenty-nine states in the Union switched to partisan judicial elections, and all states joining the Union during that period adopted that same process of selection.[135] The new mode of selection did not intimidate state judges—indeed, state supreme courts substantially expanded their exercise of judicial review in the latter half of the nineteenth century.[136] Nor did it lead to large numbers of sitting judges being unseated because of unpopular rulings. Kermit Hall's study of appellate court judges in Midwestern states during the latter half of the nineteenth century found that only about one-fifth of those judges who sought reelection were either denied renomination (2.3 percent) or defeated (18.2 percent).[137] In the next chapter, we trace the debate over judicial independence and accountability from the nineteenth to the twentieth centuries.

2 Institutionalizing Judicial Independence and Accountability

DEVELOPMENTS DURING THE ANTEBELLUM ERA ESTABLISHED a distinctive set of judicial responsibilities and ensured that judges alone would carry out those responsibilities. What remained unsettled, however, was to what extent judges would be insulated in carrying them out from the influence of other branches of state government, political parties, and the general public. To its advocates, such independence was necessary so that judges could decide without fear or favor, rendering impartial decisions according to law. It would also help in attracting qualified persons to the bench and, by shielding them from political retribution for their rulings, encourage them to aggressively police constitutional boundaries and check abuses of political power.

Yet because judicial independence enhanced judicial power, it raised questions about how to hold judges accountable when they abused that power. During the first half of the nineteenth century, reliance on incident-specific mechanisms of judicial accountability, such as impeachment, removal by address, and ripper bills, decreased. States instead opted for more regularized assessments of judicial performance, experimenting with the mode of selection and tenure in office as ways to enhance accountability while preserving appropriate judicial independence. Interestingly, these changes to selection and tenure often were designed to serve other purposes beyond simply striking an appropriate balance between independence and accountability.

Typically, reforms of judicial selection and tenure coincided with other important changes in state government, so this chapter situates those reforms in the political movements of which they were a part. It also analyzes the political context in which the reforms were undertaken, the justifications offered for them, and the expectations about their likely effects. This is vitally important because the debates over judicial independence and accountability during the nineteenth and early twentieth centuries, rather than merely anticipating current arguments and divisions, reveal a far more complex— and more interesting—consideration of the appropriate scope of judicial independence and accountability and about how that might be achieved. We begin by reviewing the eighteenth-century baseline.

The Eighteenth Century

From the patriot perspective, colonial judges had been too much under the sway of the British Crown. To prevent a repetition of excessive executive influence, state constitution-makers reined in state executives, limiting their term of office, granting them very limited powers, and in many states making their continuation in office dependent on the legislature that elected them.[1] With regard to judicial selection, six of the initial state constitutions required that gubernatorial appointees be confirmed by an executive council or by the legislature, while seven transferred the power to select judges to the state legislature. Some states also empowered legislators to select the state executive and various local officials, thus centralizing authority in the hands of the people's representatives.

Yet this consensus on judicial selection did not signal a commitment to modern understandings of judicial independence. The perception was that the problem with executive influence over judges was that it was *executive* influence. This can be seen in how the states dealt with judicial tenure. In eight of the original thirteen states, judges initially served during good behavior, and Pennsylvania in its 1790 constitution and Kentucky in its 1792 constitution also adopted tenure during good behavior. But the 1776 constitutions of New Jersey and Pennsylvania established quite limited judicial terms of office, with judges appointed by the legislature, while judges in Connecticut, Georgia, Rhode Island, and Vermont served at the pleasure of the legislature.[2] Even in those states that provided for tenure during good behavior, judges remained subject to impeachment, removal by address, or ripper bills abolishing their courts or their positions.

The Early Nineteenth Century

Judicial Tenure

During the first half of the nineteenth century, most states abandoned tenure during good behavior in favor of limited judicial terms. This shift toward limiting judicial tenure began early in the nineteenth century, preceding by decades the widespread adoption of judicial elections. Beginning with Ohio in 1803, eleven of the seventeen states that joined the Union between 1801 and 1860 established limited terms of office for judges in their constitutions. Of the six entering states that initially adopted tenure during good behavior, all had abandoned it by the Civil War. So too had Tennessee and several of the original states, including Connecticut, Maryland, New Jersey, New York, and Pennsylvania. The constitutional convention in Massachusetts in 1852 proposed limiting judicial terms, but voters rejected the proposed constitution for reasons unrelated to the tenure issue.[3] By 1860 judges in more than two-thirds of the states were serving limited terms of office.[4]

This shift to limited tenure coincided with a broader democratizing trend, with states eliminating property requirements for voting and expanding the range of offices subject to popular election, reflecting a developing consensus that more people should have a voice in selecting and cashiering their governors and that more officials should be elected.[5] Thus, a delegate in the Maryland constitutional convention of 1851 could without exaggeration insist that unlimited judicial tenure was "not consistent with the progressive spirit of the age."[6] However, more was involved than the democratic ethos. Some states limited tenure as a way of combating what Jack Balkin and Sanford Levinson have referred to as partisan entrenchment, that is, "a particular party using its power over judicial selection to extend temporally that party's authority to change the governing legal regime."[7] Some states limited tenure because of dissatisfaction with particular judicial rulings. For example, in the wake of unpopular decisions on the permissible rate of interest in contracts, Alabama in 1830 limited judicial tenure to six years and applied that standard to the sitting judges.[8] In similar circumstances, when the Maine Supreme Court circumscribed the reach of a statute for the relief of debtors, voters responded by amending the state constitution to reduce terms of office to seven years.[9] When the Ohio Supreme Court struck down a statute expanding the power of justices of the peace in 1807, the state legislature sought to impeach the judges for "willfully, wickedly, and maliciously" attempting "to introduce anarchy and confusion in the government of the state of Ohio," and when the impeachment effort failed by a single vote, it shortened the judges' already limited terms in order to force them out of office.[10]

Not all states limiting judicial tenure did so in response to unpopular decisions—once a constitutional reform has taken root in some states, the processes of horizontal federalism encourage emulation in other states, even when the underlying causes for the change may be absent.[11] Thus what was controversial in pioneering states became the conventional wisdom for later adopters. In addition, the late adopters had the opportunity to see how the innovation worked in other states before embracing it; thus they had a basis for dismissing the parade of horribles presented by opponents of limited tenure. Finally, the adoption of judicial elections accelerated the movement to limit tenure, as it made no sense to elect judges for life terms.

Initially, the movement to shorter judicial tenure was connected with the effort in the early decades of the nineteenth century to curtail judicial independence and discipline judges who issued unpopular rulings. Limiting tenure, then, was one of an arsenal of weapons—together with impeachment, removal by address, and ripper bills—employed to rein in courts. Indeed, as the Ohio example shows, limiting judicial tenure was sometimes employed when these other mechanisms failed. Thus, underlying the early movement to limit judicial terms were the assumptions that the judiciary posed a threat to popular government, and that the legislature could—and should—serve as the agents of the people in keeping watch over the exercise of judicial power and in holding judges accountable. As shall be seen, neither assumption would long survive.[12]

Judicial Elections

In 1846 New York adopted a new constitution under which voters would elect all judges.[13] Following New York's lead, within a decade fifteen of the twenty-nine states in the Union in 1846 had shifted to judicial elections.[14] All states entering the Union from 1846 to 1912 likewise embraced the election of judges, so that at one point 70 percent of the states chose their judges via contested partisan elections.[15] Of the twenty-one states holding constitutional conventions from 1846 to 1860, nineteen approved constitutions that provided for judicial elections.[16] In fact, in only five conventions was the issue of popular election sufficiently controversial as to require a roll-call vote.[17] As states adopted new constitutions, they recognized, in the words of a Minnesota delegate, that "it has become the settled rule throughout the states which have revised their constitutions within any recent date, to provide for an elective judiciary."[18]

New York was not the first state to elect judges. In 1810 Georgia provided for the election of its circuit judges, in 1816 Indiana did the same for its lower-court judges, and in 1832 Mississippi opted to elect all its judges, thereby becoming the first state to elect its supreme court. These early initiatives coincided with a more general shift from appointment to election of other state and local officials that began even prior to the inauguration of Andrew Jackson.[19] Yet the fact that only three states embraced judicial elections during the first four decades of the nineteenth century shows that state constitution-makers were not simply "caught up in a wave of democratic sentiment" nor subject to "a burst of democratic enthusiasm," as some commentators have claimed.[20] Quite the contrary: several states held constitutional conventions after Mississippi's adoption of judicial elections without following its lead. In 1844–45, for example, New Jersey, Louisiana, Iowa, Missouri, and Texas all held conventions, but the only new judicial elections were for Iowa's lower-court judges.[21] In Louisiana, debate on the floor of the convention appeared to favor popular election, as opponents were loath to voice distrust of voters, but the proposal for popular election was defeated by a 40–20 vote.[22] An emerging democratic ethos was a necessary condition for the shift to judicial elections, but it was not a sufficient one.

In states that adopted judicial elections before 1840, concerns about the exercise of judicial power, together with local conditions or controversies, triggered the change. For example, Georgia adopted its constitutional amendment in 1810 instituting popular election of circuit judges in part in reaction to the US Supreme Court's rulings in *Chisholm v. Georgia* and *Fletcher v. Peck*, both of which were highly unpopular in the state and highlighted the threat posed by unchecked judicial power.[23] However, the amendment also reflected a distrust of the state legislature, which had previously selected judges, especially in the wake of the Yazoo Land Scandal. Far from being an isolated reform, the amendment was one of several amendments to the Georgia Constitution designed to move away from "legislative dominance toward a better balance of power between the branches of government."[24] In its initial 1816 constitution, Indiana provided for the election of its circuit-court judges for seven–year terms in reaction to the overbearing behavior of federal judges under the territorial government before statehood.[25]

In Mississippi, judicial selection and tenure were key issues in the selection of delegates for the 1831 constitutional convention, as delegates sought to restrict judicial power and impose greater accountability.[26] Under the state's 1817 constitution, judges were chosen by the state legislature and served during good behavior. This centralized power in the hands of the Natchez commercial elite, which enjoyed disproportionate representation in the legislature, and enabled it to place its political allies on the bench even in frontier districts. Perhaps unsurprisingly, this also led to rulings that, in the eyes of frontier Mississippians, favored commercial interests, as exemplified by the state's supreme court's invalidation of a popular debtor law. Judicial decisions beyond the state's borders—particularly the US Supreme Court's ruling in *Worcester v. Georgia* (1832) limiting state power in dealing with Indian tribes—further fueled popular distrust of the judiciary.[27] Thus, in a convention called to redress the balance of power among regions in the state, judicial selection emerged as a major issue. After lengthy debate, the delegates replaced centralized legislative selection with popular election in districts and substituted relatively short terms of office for tenure during good behavior.[28]

Mississippi was hardly alone in recognizing the importance of restraining judicial power, but other states were reluctant to follow Mississippi's lead because it was both a slave state and a frontier state, and neither consideration encouraged emulation by older or Northern states. In part too, efforts to curtail judicial power in the 1830s and early 1840s were focused elsewhere, on mechanisms such as codification, and this reduced the energy available for pursuing selection reform. Also, few constitutional conventions were called during the 1830s, which meant that reformers would have had to persuade the legislature to propose an amendment, always difficult when the desired change would reduce legislative power. For example, the Michigan legislature in 1845 considered but rejected a proposed amendment that would have required the election of all state officials, including supreme court justices.[29] As Jed Shugerman has suggested, "the movement for judicial elections required a constellation of forces to line up" to gain the momentum, plus an opportunity like a constitutional convention, plus a little luck, to start a sweeping change. Not until the mid-1840s did such a confluence occur, but when it "did, the speed at which judicial elections swept the land between 1846 and 1851 is a historical marvel."[30]

A Broader Perspective

First, insofar as states abandoned tenure during good behavior and/or adopted judicial elections during the early nineteenth century, they did so primarily to curtail judicial power and enforce accountability to the people or, more accurately, to their agents in state legislatures. Thus, the concerns and divisions of the early nineteenth century track those of the late twentieth and early twenty-first centuries. They also were of a piece with the conflicts detailed in Chapter 1. Second, the movement to constrain the courts was fueled, as in the late twentieth and early twenty-first centuries, by specific judicial rulings that suggested a disconnect between popular and judicial views. Interestingly, even decisions beyond the borders of a state, such as those of the US Supreme Court, contributed to efforts to increase the accountability of state judges. Those concerned about judicial power, again as in the current era, often did not differentiate among courts in their condemnations. Third, although the mechanisms relied upon during the early nineteenth century to enforce judicial accountability paralleled those employed to promote official accountability more generally, the adoption of limited tenure and popular election for judges were not a mindless extension of popular reforms to the courts. States that made more positions elective did not necessarily endorse judicial elections, or if they did, they did not necessarily adopt election for all judges. Moreover, in several states there was a significant time lag between extension of election to other officials, state and local, and its extension to judges. Finally, states that were entering the Union and had no court system in place, were more likely to adopt limited tenure for judges than were states that already had provided for tenure during good behavior. In part, this pattern confirms that it is more difficult to justify change than to decide what system to inaugurate. In part too, existing states often had to contend with entrenched interests benefiting from the system of tenure during good behavior. This same dichotomy would arise when states in the late 1840s and 1850s considered the election of judges.

The Shift to Popular Election of Judges

The adoption of popular election of judges in New York in 1846 transformed the experiments in Mississippi, Georgia, and Indiana into a nationwide movement.[31] With "the leading State in the Union in advance," in less than a decade eighteen states—Alabama, Arkansas, California, Connecticut, Florida, Illinois, Indiana, Kentucky, Louisiana, Maryland, Michigan, Missouri, Ohio, Tennessee, Texas, Vermont, Virginia, and Wisconsin—had adopted popular election for some or all of their judges.[32] In addition, Iowa, which had instituted popular election of trial judges in 1845, extended popular election to its supreme court in 1857.

Some regional differences emerged. Massachusetts and New Hampshire held constitutional conventions during the early 1850s but rejected popular election of judges. Some Southern states were also less firmly committed to popular election. South Carolina rejected proposals for judicial elections and clung to its system of legislative election of judges.[33] Although Virginia adopted popular election in 1850, it reverted to legislative election in 1864 and repulsed all subsequent efforts to institute popular election.[34] Other Southern states adopted judicial election only gradually or reluctantly. For example, Alabama instituted elections for lower-court judges in 1850 but did not provide for supreme court elections until 1867, and during the convention that proposed the 1867 constitution, it gave serious consideration to returning to gubernatorial appointment of all judges. Moreover, a majority of the delegates at the state's 1875 convention "wanted to give the election of judges to the General Assembly, or to provide that they should be appointed by the governor with the consent of the Senate, but were restrained from doing so by the fear that it would defeat the new constitution when submitted to the people."[35]

Nevertheless, the fifteen years after New York adopted judicial elections witnessed a remarkable shift: between 1846 and 1861, eighteen states held constitutional conventions, and sixteen of those states adopted judicial elections in the course of revising their existing constitutions.[36] This reliance on constitutional revision rather than constitutional amendment was significant. Almost all states that adopted judicial elections did so not as an isolated action but as part of a set of reforms designed to address broader problems in state government, and the aims and character of the shift to popular election of judges must be understood in that broader context.

The Context of Reform

During the 1820s and 1830s, state governments offered corporations and other private entities a wide array of inducements to encourage them to develop canals, railroads, and other infrastructure in the hope of spurring economic growth.[37] Southern states borrowed funds to enlarge banking facilities and support railroad development, issuing state bonds to supply working capital. Northern and Midwestern states constructed canals and other public works, usually in partnership with private concerns, in order to facilitate the transportation of goods to major markets. Often state legislatures granted special privileges to private corporations, ranging from special corporate charters to subsidies to outright grants of monopoly privileges, all in order to induce their participation. Political corruption all too often determined who received these benefits, and even when it did not, several state legislatures were extraordinarily reckless in their promotional efforts. The development bubble burst with the economic depression of 1837. By 1841, states owed $198 million on outstanding bonds issued to finance investments in canals, railroads, and banks. By 1842, eight states were in default on their debts. Ultimately, Mississippi and Florida repudiated their debts outright, and Louisiana, Arkansas, and Michigan repudiated part of their debts, while Alabama, New York, and Ohio barely avoided default.[38]

This economic imbroglio spurred a wave of constitutional revision in the states. Reform efforts were not limited to those states that had been particularly overzealous in underwriting economic development; rather, their experience served a cautionary function, as other states constructed constitutional barriers to prevent such abuses within their own borders.[39] If the agenda for reform went beyond restricting ill-considered or corrupt forays into economic boosterism, the economic crisis nonetheless taught state constitution-makers several lessons. Perhaps the main one was that popular election did not ensure that legislators would forego private advantage or narrow partisan interests and pursue the public good. Whether accurate or not, the perception was that problems arose not from legislators too eagerly following the popular will but from their ignoring it. In the wake of the economic crisis, few states were willing to forego altogether the benefits of state promotion of economic development. However, their loss of faith in the judgment and probity of legislators meant that they believed it necessary to devise mechanisms for channeling and constraining legislative choice. One approach state constitution-makers used was to impose stringent procedural restrictions on state legislatures. These were meant to promote greater transparency in the legislative process, with the assumption that facilitating public scrutiny would deter misbehavior or make its detection easier.[40] Other constitutional restrictions required generality in law making—for example, bans on special laws and the requirement of general incorporation laws—or mandated popular involvement, as in requirements of voter approval before money could be borrowed to finance projects.[41] Taken altogether, these restrictions were designed to combat politics as usual by limiting the influence of powerful interests and to change political outcomes by altering the way in which policy was developed.

Yet constitutional safeguards against legislative misconduct were deemed insufficient. State constitution-makers believed it essential to enlist other institutions to keep the legislature in check. This required a redistribution of power among the branches of state government, exemplified by provisions introducing or strengthening the gubernatorial veto. It also required a redesign of state institutions, reducing the number of offices subject to legislative appointment and control and expanding the number subject to popular election.[42] These reforms not only increased popular control over those officials but, equally important, enabled those officials to claim that they had just as strong a connection to the people as did legislators. This latter consideration figured prominently in the shift to popular election of judges.

Debating Judicial Elections

Like their counterparts in Mississippi a generation earlier, some radicals at midcentury constitutional conventions denounced judicial appointment as "a relic of monarchy" and the "last vestige of aristocracy" and insisted that judicial selection be made "consonant with our theory of government."[43] This rhetoric prompted a familiar response from conservatives, who insisted that judicial elections would promote popular or partisan interference with the exercise of legal expertise and jeopardize judicial independence. But these arguments had little influence.

The delegates who favored judicial elections acknowledged the importance of judicial independence but denied that the existing modes of judicial selection safeguarded it. They saw the system of judicial appointment as thoroughly corrupted by partisanship, with party leaders, "the selfish manipulators of legislative assemblies," dominating the process.[44] If anything, the shift to limited tenure for judges had exacerbated the problem by multiplying opportunities for party leaders to dictate the composition of the bench. Thus, a delegate to the Maryland convention of 1851 characterized gubernatorial appointment as "a great political engine, by which the interests of a large portion of the people have been sacrificed to the elevation of others."[45] Similarly, a delegate to the Ohio convention of 1850 complained that judicial selection by the legislature had become "a mere political arena, embittering the feelings of party spirit, and corrupting the pure fountain of justice."[46] Whatever the nominal mode of selection, in practice the party caucus controlled the process. In the words of one New York delegate, "Which party had the governor . . . made their caucus nominations, and that was virtually an appointment."[47] This contributed to partisan imbalance on the bench—as a Massachusetts delegate complained, "How does it happen that only two judges of the supreme court were members of the Democratic party, for more than half a century?"[48] Even more importantly, it reduced the competence of the state bench because those chosen as judges were typically patronage appointees, who owed their selection to "service to the party" rather than to "legal skills or judicial temperament," with courts becoming "asylums for broken down or defeated politicians."[49] Meanwhile, skilled lawyers who lacked political contacts did not even seek appointment. The low quality of the judges in turn undermined respect for the bench, which was a precondition for popular support of judicial independence.

According to its proponents, popular election of judges would promote judicial independence by freeing judges from partisan control. Some delegates insisted that all that voters would require of judges was the impartial administration of justice: "You have nothing to do but to be an upright judge, to deal out justice fairly, to sell it to none, and the people will stand by you."[50] Less sanguine delegates acknowledged the potential for popular influence on judicial decisions but concluded that the popular threat to independence was less severe—or less detrimental—than that posed by powerful interests or by the other branches of state government. As David Davis concluded in the Illinois convention, he would "rather see judges the weather-cocks of public sentiment" than to see them "the instruments of power . . . registering the mandates of the Legislature, and the edicts of the Governor."[51] Other delegates framed the choice as one between influence by the populace as a whole, which contributed to justice, versus influence by a segment of the society that sought only its own advantage.

Underlying the preference for popular election was a suspicion of the fidelity of governors and legislators to the interests and will of the people. But this suspicion of the people's agents did not extend to the people themselves. As an Illinois delegate observed, "The old system was to place the judiciary independent of the people, and dependent on the Governor and Legislature; the elective plan was to make them independent of the Governor and Legislature, and dependent on the people for support against the other branches of the government."[52] This in part reflected what Kermit Hall has called "the traditional notion that [the] popular, majoritarian will was capable of defeating narrow partisanship."[53] But it also reflected the republican conviction that judicial independence of the people was not necessarily a good thing.

Tied to the notion of ensuring judicial independence from the other branches of state government, especially from the legislature, were changed expectations as to what the judiciary should do, recalling the "independence for what" discussion in Chapter 1. Convention delegates embraced judicial independence of the governor and legislature so that judges could be more aggressive in policing legislative abuses of power. As James Borden, an Indiana delegate, put it, unless the judiciary was placed "beyond the control of the other branches of the government," constitutional provisions "to protect the rights of the people, and to preserve a proper equilibrium between the different departments of the government" would remain "parchment barriers."[54] Judicial elections not only removed the selection process from the self-interested control of governors and legislators, but also gave judges an independent political base, a claim to democratic legitimacy equal to that of legislators. As Abner Keyes summed it up in the Massachusetts convention, "Elect your judges, and you will energize them, and make them independent, and put them on a par with the other branches of government."[55]

This energizing was important because judges under the revised state constitutions were expected to assume a broader role in governing. The constitutional conventions of the 1840s and 1850s had imposed various procedural and substantive restrictions on the legislature, and judges would be responsible for enforcing those restraints. This would require replacing judicial deference with judicial forcefulness. Beyond that, as Michael Hoffman explained in the New York convention, "in reorganizing the legislative department we have made it less powerful for general legislation . . . [so] a larger share of judicial legislation will be inevitable, and we must endeavor to supply it" through popular election of judges.[56]

Securing the Independence of Elected Judges

The states' simultaneous commitment to judicial elections and to judicial independence from political influence is underscored by the various measures states adopted to moderate the political effects of election. One such device was electing justices of the state supreme court in geographic districts. Proponents of districting contended that smaller constituencies would foster greater personal knowledge of candidates, which in turn would decrease voting based on party affiliation. Opponents of districting likewise supported judicial independence but doubted that districting would have that effect. Districting implied—incorrectly, in their view—that judges were representatives and therefore similar to other political officials. As a delegate to the Illinois constitutional convention of 1870 put it, "The judiciary are not created for the purpose of representing interests at all. They are not created to represent persons or to act for a constituency."[57] Opponents of districting also insisted that voters would be more likely to find highly qualified persons to serve on the bench if their choices were not limited to the residents of a single district. They were more likely to choose such persons in a larger area, whereas a judge in a small district might "owe his election to his immediate neighbors."[58] Finally, opponents of districting claimed that it was undesirable for people to have no voice in the selection of six of the seven justices who would decide their fates.[59]

For some delegates the arguments on districting may have masked partisan calculations: decentralizing selection meant that political parties that were in the minority statewide might still be able to elect their adherents in local strongholds. Yet even here broader concerns also may have figured in. As one delegate observed, "A decision of a partisan court . . . has no weight whatever with the American people, [whereas] the decision of a court composed of men of both parties will command the respect of the better class of thinking minds of the country."[60] The arguments for districting may also have reflected intrastate political differences: in antebellum Kentucky, for example, proslavery delegates embraced districts in order to shift control away from urban Whigs, many of whom espoused gradual abolition.[61] But what the debates seem to reveal is a shared commitment to freeing judges from the control of party politicians—the only question was what system of districting would most effectively achieve that objective. Whatever the outcome of the districting debate in a particular state, the movement to judicial election did have a decentralizing effect on selection, in that trial-court judges were elected in the districts in which they served rather than being chosen by the governor or state legislature.

Another device, adopted by more than half the states with judicial elections, was staggered judicial terms. This arrangement moderated the political effects of elections by ensuring that a single election would not transform the composition of the state bench. A further way to insulate judicial elections from political pressures was scheduling those elections separately from the elections for other offices. For example, the Michigan Constitution of 1850 stipulated that elections for circuit-court judges would be held the first Monday in April in each election year, while elections for other offices would take place in November.[62] This reform was designed to ensure that the outcome of judicial races would not be affected by party-line voting or by races at the top of the ticket.[63] However, the commitment to this reform was sometimes short-lived: Tennessee abandoned separate elections in 1870, and California did so in 1879 because of their cost and because of low turnout in the absence of other races on the ballot.[64] Finally, some states established more stringent qualifications for serving as a judge, seeking to make its elected judiciary more professionalized.[65]

The Effects of Popular Election

According to its nineteenth-century proponents, popular election would empower judges by giving them democratic legitimacy, liberate them from the control of political elites and special interests, and thereby embolden them to strike down legislative enactments that violated constitutional norms. To what extent did judicial elections fulfill these hopes?

The available data on the exercise of judicial review are consistent with the notion that popular election freed judges to scrutinize legislative enactments more closely. Several scholars have documented a rise in the exercise of judicial review in the states in the latter half of the nineteenth century. For example, the Virginia Supreme Court heard only thirty-five constitutional cases from 1789 to 1861 and declared only two laws unconstitutional; but from 1861 to 1902, it heard one hundred thirty constitutional cases and invalidated more than forty laws.[66] The Ohio Supreme Court, which had struck down only six statutes from 1800 to 1850, invalidated sixteen statutes during the 1850s and fifty-seven more from 1880 to 1900.[67] The New York Court of Appeals, which had invalidated only sixty-five laws prior to the Civil War, struck down almost two hundred from 1870 to 1900; the Supreme Judicial Court of Massachusetts, which had declared only ten laws unconstitutional prior to the Civil War, struck down thirty-one from 1860 to 1893.[68] In his comprehensive study of state courts' exercise of judicial review, Jed Shugerman found that courts in the twenty-four states that had joined the Union by 1821 struck down only forty-seven statutes from 1830–39 and sixty-six from 1840–49. However, those same courts struck down one hundred sixty-four state laws from 1850–59 and another seventy-four from 1860–65. Of particular note is the fact that one hundred forty of the one hundred sixty-four invalidations from 1850–59 and sixty-seven of the seventy-four invalidations from 1860–65 were by courts whose judges were popularly elected.[69] While to some extent the substance of the statutes that were invalidated in the 1850s coincided with that of statutes in earlier decades—for example, laws impairing the obligation of contracts—Shugerman found that "the largest share shifted to the protection and definition of judicial power and jurisdiction, consistent with the conventions' goal of increasing judicial power. The next largest share was in the realm of takings, eminent domain, and internal improvements unsurprisingly. New cases emerged from the new constitutions' limits on taxation, public debt, legislative procedures, and from the validity of local referenda."[70]

Of course these figures hardly prove that popular election caused judges to strike down state enactments. Other factors may also have contributed to the rise in invalidations, ranging from the more detailed constitutional limitations imposed on state legislatures to the proliferation of state economic regulation after midcentury to the new inclusion of express endorsements of judicial review in some state constitutions.[71] The widespread distrust of state legislatures, which fueled the shift to judicial elections, also likely emboldened state judges. Nonetheless, at a minimum, the exercise of judicial review in the aftermath of the switch to popular election is consistent with the notion that judges felt free to interpret and apply the law without fear of political repercussions. This, of course, is the very definition of judicial independence.

This is particularly striking because popular election of judges clearly did not banish partisan politics from judicial selection. Nominees for judicial office were, until the advent of primary elections in the early twentieth century, chosen by party conventions and ran on party labels. Those nominated were typically party stalwarts—more than 90 percent of state appellate judges in the latter half of the nineteenth century had previously been served in partisan political office.[72] This did not mean that conventions chose unqualified candidates for the bench. As James Bryce observed, the party leaders at the conventions were often lawyers themselves, so they had "a professional dislike to the entrusting of law to incapable hands" and tended to choose "as competent a member of the party as can be got to take the post."[73] Nonetheless, political parties dominated the initial stage of the selection process.

The fragmentary data available on voting patterns in state judicial elections also indicate the continuing influence of political parties. These data reveal that political parties regularly contested judicial elections. In states with strong two-party competition, such as California and Ohio, both parties nominated candidates for appellate judgeships—less than 5 percent of elections were uncontested.[74] Moreover, judicial elections in those states were remarkably competitive. In California, the winning candidates garnered less than 55 percent of the vote in almost three-quarters of the judicial elections, and in Ohio this was true in more than 80 percent of judicial elections.[75] Furthermore, in competitive two-party states, voters tended to choose judges based on their party affiliation. The prevalence of party voting reflected the importance of parties in an era of strong partisan allegiances, as well as the usefulness of a party as a voting cue in the absence of other information that might have informed voter choice. Finally, voting procedures facilitated party-line voting. Until the introduction of the Australian ballot late in the nineteenth century, most states used party-strip ballots, and this open balloting strongly encouraged voters to adhere to the party ticket for all offices.

However, electoral data also reveal that incumbency had a pronounced effect in judicial races. In Mississippi, for example, the court's chief justice was reelected three times, even though he was a Whig in a staunchly Democratic state; a Whig chief justice was elected in staunchly Democratic Missouri as well.[76] Surveying judicial elections in California, Ohio, Tennessee, and Texas from 1850 to 1920, Kermit Hall found that only 16.8 percent of sitting state appellate judges were denied renomination or reelection. These data should be viewed with caution, as they are skewed by the extremely low (4 percent) nonretention rate in Texas, a one-party state. Moreover, more than one-quarter of incumbents did not seek reelection, and at least some may have declined to do so because they expected to be defeated if they sought to remain on the bench.[77] Nonetheless, Hall is likely correct in concluding that it was "limited terms of service rather than popular election [that] created a turnover that was higher on the state bench than on the federal bench."[78]

Reconsidering Judicial Elections and Judicial Tenure

Early critics of judicial elections decried the influence of parties on judicial selection and proposed a return to an appointive system. A delegate to Pennsylvania's 1872 convention asserted that "if it was safe to elect judges in 1850, when our elections were free and pure, it is not safe to elect them now, when, by common consent, popular elections have ceased to be either free or pure."[79] Another Pennsylvania delegate claimed that judges were still chosen by "pot-house politicians" and those "who understood the manipulation of party politics and the control of primary elections."[80] However, voters were reluctant to surrender their newly acquired power of selection to governors or state legislatures. A few Southern states—Georgia in 1861, Virginia in 1864, and Mississippi in 1868—did abandon popular election, but their switch was tied to racial politics within their borders rather than to concerns about judicial independence. In Northern and Western states, the opponents of judicial elections enjoyed no success.

Yet if voters clung to judicial elections, they were amenable to lengthening judicial tenure, and beginning in the 1860s, several states did so. In Maryland, delegates to the state's 1864 constitutional convention extended the judicial term of office to fifteen years, and this remained the standard when the state revised its constitution in 1867. During the 1870s, California, Connecticut, Louisiana, Missouri, New York, Pennsylvania, and Wisconsin all increased judicial terms of office.[81] In some instances the extensions were dramatic: New York shifted the judicial term of office from eight to fourteen years, and Pennsylvania the term of supreme court justices from fifteen years to a single twenty-one–year term. Such long terms resembled tenure during good behavior because during the latter half of the nineteenth century, "the average term in office for a state judge was 8.9 years."[82]

While acknowledging that longer terms of office reduced the frequency of public scrutiny, their proponents insisted they encouraged judicial independence.[83] Yet the proponents of longer tenure differed among themselves as to the threat they were combating. Some advocates of longer terms opposed popular election of judges and so were seeking to reduce popular influence over the administration of justice. However, most saw the threat as coming from party leaders who were able to manipulate the selection process. They advocated longer terms in order to reduce the influence of party leaders and the possibility of corruption in judicial selection, not to insulate judges from popular control. From a broader perspective, what is noteworthy is that the concern about judicial willfulness that led to restrictions on tenure early in the nineteenth century had been replaced with concern about external influences on judges and about the need to safeguard against them.

Summary Observations

During the mid-nineteenth century and thereafter, the mode of state judicial selection and the length of judicial tenure changed dramatically, as states embraced popular election of judges. According to some advocates of judicial elections, they enhanced judicial independence by liberating judges from the influence of partisan appointing authorities. For others, the choice was between partisan influence exercised through the institutions of government that controlled judicial selection and popular influence outside of these institutions through the direct election of judges. Proponents of judicial elections contended that elections were less partisan, even if candidates were nominated in party conventions and bore party labels, than were other modes of selection, in which party leaders directly determined who would sit on the bench. They also believed that state legislators could not satisfactorily substitute for the voting public in judicial selection because legislators were themselves susceptible to influence by special interests and could not be counted on to faithfully represent the public interest or the popular will. They therefore understood political parties not as a tool toward democratic accountability but as an impediment to it.

Underlying the midcentury shift to judicial elections was also a dramatic change in the understanding of the problems that this reform was meant to address. Those who adopted judicial elections early in the nineteenth century distrusted judges, and they wanted judicial elections to curb judicial willfulness, constrain judicial power, and enhance accountability.[84] But later proponents of judicial elections distrusted state legislatures and believed that judicial elections would free judges to review legislation more aggressively. Thus the same reform was expected, at different points in time, to serve diametrically opposed purposes. In addition, many in the legal profession were comfortable endorsing judicial elections because they expected that the reform would free the bench from domination by political parties and that voters would be more likely than party bosses to choose attorneys of stature to serve on the bench.[85] When concerns about the misuse of judicial power reemerged in the late nineteenth and early twentieth centuries, the battle over judicial independence and judicial accountability heated up once again. And when it did, the concepts of democratic accountability and professional development that had seemed mutually reinforcing in the 1850s would appear increasingly at odds.[86]

Judicial Independence and Accountability in the Progressive Era

When the issue of judicial independence and accountability reemerged in the late nineteenth century, the debate changed significantly. For one thing, it was national in character, with similar concerns being voiced, often by the same critics, about the involvement of both federal and state courts in making public policy. This led to identical proposals both nationally and within individual states, such as the recall of judges and of judicial decisions, although such reforms enjoyed greater success at the state level. It also led to the proposal of measures at the national level, such as the election of judges and limits on their term of office, that were already in place in the states, but these proposals never attracted substantial backing.

The mention of recall suggests another change, namely, an expansion in the mechanisms proposed to enforce judicial accountability or—in the eyes of critics—to invade judicial independence.[87] By the mid-nineteenth century, states had abandoned using removal by address to punish judges who announced unpopular decisions. After the 1850s, the states did the same with impeachment, emulating the practice at the national level.[88] It is no coincidence that the obsolescence of impeachment and address coincided with the rise of elections and with limited judicial tenure, both of which seemed to provide alternative avenues for accountability.[89] But with the extension of judicial terms late in the nineteenth century and the reluctance of voters to unseat incumbent judges, advocates of judicial accountability again found it necessary to seek other ways to call judges to account, such as the recall of judges and of judicial decisions.

A third change was in the attitudes of groups concerned about judicial independence and accountability. In the mid-nineteenth century the legal profession had largely endorsed popular election of judges, but by the turn of the century the organized bar strongly condemned partisan judicial elections. Initially the bar supported nonpartisan elections, but it soon abandoned contested judicial elections altogether in favor of merit selection. Popular attitudes likewise shifted. During the mid-nineteenth century popular majorities, distrustful of state legislatures, championed elections so that independent judges could aggressively scrutinize legislation. But by the end of the century, many believed that these aggressive judges were usurping legislative power and protecting vested interests, and this led to proposals to rein them in. Thus judges went from being perceived as a solution to problems to being perceived as the problem themselves.

Finally, the debate during the late nineteenth and early twentieth centuries was complex and multisided. On one level, the conflict was between critics of the courts (including populists, progressives, and the labor movement) and their defenders. Yet there were important areas of agreement among these groups as well. There was a consensus that major changes were necessary in the administration of justice—even William Howard Taft, perhaps the paramount Defender, characterized "the administration of criminal justice in this country [as] a disgrace to civilization."[90] There was also agreement that steps were necessary to prevent—or end—the politicization of the courts. Yet on the issue of judicial independence and judicial accountability, serious differences surfaced.

The Bashers of the Progressive era charged that judicial rulings betrayed a strong class bias, that judges regularly read their own social and economic theories into the law, and that they willfully misconstrued the Fourteenth Amendment to strike down needed reforms and protect business interests.[91] As one commentator put it, "Judges habitually think in the terms of the rich and the powerful. The training, sympathies, experiences, and general view of life of most judges have made this inevitable."[92] The "absolute power of veto" that judges exercised via judicial review meant that they had become "political organs of the government" that "exercise definite political power without a corresponding political responsibility."[93] Indeed, in reaching out to strike down social legislation, judges had virtually displaced the people's representatives. One union organizer sarcastically observed that "under the present condition, I would say that the legislature is an unnecessary expense, on account of the courts setting aside anything the legislature may do."[94]

Legal conservatives agreed that politicization of the judiciary was a concern, but they rejected the critics' diagnosis and the remedies they prescribed. Legal conservatives attributed the problem of politicization not to judicial activism or class bias but to the processes by which judges were selected. In particular, they argued that judicial elections enmeshed the judiciary in politics, undermined respect for the courts, and discouraged the selection of highly qualified jurists. As Nebraska Governor Chester Aldrich put it in 1911, "Probably a whole lot of this trouble comes from the fact that in many instances these inferior courts are composed of lawyers who owe their position, not so much to legal attainment and profound learning, as they do to political services rendered."[95] In his famous address to the American Bar Association in 1906, Roscoe Pound charged that "putting courts into politics, and compelling judges to become politicians in many jurisdictions . . . [had] almost destroyed the traditional respect for the bench."[96] And William Howard Taft, who as president had denounced the recall of judges as "legalized terrorism," claimed that it was "disgraceful" for candidates for the bench to be campaigning and promising that their decisions would serve the interests of a particular social class.[97] He declared that "the People at the polls, no more than kings upon the throne, are unfit to pass upon questions involving the judicial interpretation of the law."[98] Legal conservatives believed that the way to rebuild popular support for judges and for the rule of law was by removing judges from politics and elevating more qualified persons to the bench.

Even within the ranks of the Bashers, there were differences of substance and emphasis.[99] Populists tended to believe that court rulings favored railroads and other corporations that exploited farmers; more generally, they distrusted courts as bastions of elitism and favored measures that made judges more directly accountable to the public. The labor movement was most concerned about injunctions and rulings restricting union activities and favored a reorientation of the bench—the replacement of judges who practiced "government by injunction" or favored business interests—rather than fundamental structural reforms. Progressives were most critical of rulings, such as *Lochner v. New York* and *Standard Oil Co. of New Jersey v. United States*, which nullified social legislation or blunted its effects.[100] So court critics differed as to whether the problems with the judiciary were attributable to the orientation of those on the bench, to the absence of judicial accountability, or to more fundamental factors.

Let us turn to the proposals of the Bashers and Defenders and to the understandings of judicial independence and accountability underlying them.

Popular Recall of Judges

One major shift in the debate was the consideration of ways other than judicial selection and tenure for constraining judicial power and enforcing accountability. Chief among these was the recall, under which voters would be able to remove judges from office prior to the expiration of their terms. The recall was first adopted by progressives in Oregon in 1908 as a check upon officials more generally, and the campaign for its adoption did not highlight judicial misconduct. By 1915, nine additional states had adopted the recall, although four—Idaho, Illinois, Kansas, and Washington—refused to extend the recall to judges.[101] Nevertheless, Bashers immediately saw its potential for enhancing judicial accountability, while Defenders saw it as a fundamental threat to judicial independence.

"The judicial recall movement agitated the newly organized American bar to a greater extent than any other public issue before the 1930's."[102] In 1912 the American Bar Association adopted a resolution that decried the judicial recall as "destructive of our system of government" and established the ABA Committee to Oppose the Judicial Recall. State bar associations followed suit. The issue came to a head when President Taft vetoed a bill admitting Arizona to the Union because the prospective state's constitution authorized the recall of judges. Arizona's constitution-makers duly removed the offending provision. But after the state was admitted to the Union in February 1912, voters amended its constitution in November of the same year to reinstate the recall of judges.[103]

Defenders believed the recall posed an even greater threat than elections because it promised immediate retribution for unpopular decisions. Judges fearful of removal would "consult the popular omens rather than the sources of law," and this would undermine the rule of law. According to its opponents, the recall would "substitute for the fearless and independent judge a spineless, flabby, cowardly judge, a reed shaken by the wind" and encourage "timorous and unprincipled office-seekers and office-holders . . . to change what they call their principles as quickly as they change their clothes, if a few votes are to be gained thereby."[104] In some instances party bosses might manipulate popular sentiment to remove upstanding judges. As one commentator put it, the political boss "will touch the mysterious sources of his unjust powers with deft and secret sign, and swarms of satraps will rise in mockery of the voice of an outraged community to indict the fearless judge."[105] Sometimes public opinion might be unstable or tyrannical, so the recall would enable majorities to threaten the rights of minorities. Judges who issued rulings based on the law might find themselves confronted with what one opponent called "a howling mass of men drunk with power bent upon doing [them] mischief."[106]

Whereas judges subject to impeachment had the opportunity to hear the charges against them and defend themselves, the recall offered no such guarantee of due process. In the words of one critic, "Can anyone outside of Bedlam support a public policy such as this?"[107]

Defenders also insisted that the recall undermined the rule of law. When judges made unpopular decisions, they were merely following what the law required, and thus the recall unjustly targeted judges when their real complaint was with the substance of the law. Because the recall was invoked when the populace disagreed with judicial rulings, it reflected popular willfulness, rather than a desire to uphold the law against judicial usurpations. Implicit in this argument, of course, were several crucial assumptions: first, that because of their legal expertise, judges were the most competent interpreters of the law; second, that their unpopular rulings reflected the requirements of the law rather than their own predilections; and third, that popular disagreement with rulings meant the substitution of a political judgment for a legal one.

If opponents of the recall emphasized the rule of law and the protection of minority rights, its proponents harkened to Thomas Jefferson, who had highlighted the anomaly in a republic of a judge "independent of the will of the nation." Denying the exceptionality of judicial responsibilities, Bashers insisted that "while the judges are bound to act in accordance with the established law and to interpret and apply that law to specific controversies, they ought to be just as responsible to the people as the governor and the legislature are for the performance of their respective functions."[108] They denied that recall posed a threat to conscientious judges, analogizing it to removal by address, which had not undermined judicial independence, the only difference being a transfer of power from the people's agents to the people themselves. Moreover, Bashers noted that the same people who elected judges would vote on recall, so it was hard to dismiss it as mob rule. Indeed, one proponent claimed, "no judge was ever defeated for reelection, and none will ever be recalled because of an erroneous decision involving only the private rights of individual litigants."[109] The real issue was the political role assumed by judges. This might involve judicial invalidation of social legislation. As Gilbert Roe put it, "The litigation of this country is becoming more and more quasi-political in character, involving questions of governmental policy concerning which the people have the same right to be heard that they have when the Congress passes upon the same or similar measures."[110] It might also involve judicial intrusion in labor disputes—in Arizona, for example, what prompted extension of the recall to judges was judges' use of the injunction against strikers during the territorial period.[111] This did not mean that judges would constantly be recalled. Rather, the threat of recall would suffice: judges "will not set aside state or federal laws nor legislate under the color of judicial decisions, and they will so conduct themselves that the use of the recall will be unnecessary."[112]

The Recall of Judicial Decisions

As an alternative to the recall of judges, Theodore Roosevelt in 1912 proposed that voters have the power to recall judicial decisions in which judges ruled that a law violated either the federal Constitution or a state constitution. Under Roosevelt's proposal, when "any considerable number of the people" believed that a judicial decision striking down a law was "in defiance of justice," they could petition to place on the ballot the question of whether the ruling should be overturned.[113] If voters agreed that it should, then the judgment between plaintiff and defendant would remain in effect, but the court's construction of the constitution would be overturned, the precedential value of its decision would be nullified, and judges could not invalidate the statute in subsequent cases. Recall of decisions thus would enable the populace to overturn judicial interpretations of the constitution without a constitutional amendment.[114] This was crucial because Bashers did not want to repeal the due process clause or amend its language, lest important constitutional protections against arbitrary government action be lost. Rather, they wanted it interpreted in a way that reflected "current realities." More specifically, they wanted "a method of obtaining legislation which does correspond to the prevailing ideas of social justice, while at the same time retaining in our constitutions the principle that no act which is arbitrary or unfair should be recognized as law."[115] If judges failed to supply such an interpretation, perverting the Fourteenth Amendment and its state analogues to protect "property privileges [and] vested rights to exploit others," then the recall of decisions allowed the people to correct the error.[116]

Theodore Roosevelt contended that his proposal safeguarded judicial independence better than the judicial recall did because it permitted the correction of judicial "mistakes" without intimidating judges by threatening their positions. He also argued that the recall of decisions would not encourage hasty or thoughtless popular action because of the inevitable delay between a judicial ruling and the voters' verdict on it at the polls.[117] His allies pointed out that the recall of decisions was "more precise and effective" because "the question is shifted from men to principles and the issue is made impersonal and concrete."[118]

Despite this, Roosevelt's proposal was broadly attacked, with the strongest criticism emanating from the legal profession.[119] President Taft dismissed his predecessor's proposal as "utterly without merit" and insisted that the American people "will never give up the Constitution, and they are not going to be honey-fugled out of it by being told that they are fit to interpret nice questions of constitutional law just as well or better than judges."[120] He darkly predicted that if recall of judicial decisions were adopted, it would result in "application of constitutional guarantees according to popular whim."[121] Other critics maintained that such a popular intrusion into the legal realm would politicize legal issues and threaten basic constitutional freedoms. These arguments persuaded even some progressives. For example, Gilbert Roe, a law partner of Senator Robert LaFollette, defended the recall of judges, but he rejected the recall of judicial decisions because it involved "the wholly untrained layman" in "the highly specialized and technical work of a judge" and because it "would be used as a means of amending the Constitution by a majority vote."[122]

Only Colorado adopted Roosevelt's proposal, ratifying a constitutional initiative in 1912 under which the state supreme court was the only court that could invalidate a state or municipal law and voters could revoke any such ruling. In 1920 the Colorado Supreme Court effectively gutted the measure, ruling that the state constitution could not prevent lower state courts from adjudicating issues under the federal Constitution nor allow voters to review state supreme court rulings based on that constitution.[123] A year later it also struck down the amendment's application to state constitutional rulings, holding that this denied due process rights to criminal defendants.[124] By the time these rulings were announced, they excited little controversy, and thus the recall of judicial decisions—like the recall of judges—had no practical effect on judicial independence.

Extraordinary Majorities for the Invalidation of Legislation

During the early twentieth century, Nebraska, North Dakota, and Ohio amended their constitutions to require a super-majority of justices to invalidate statutes.[125] In Ohio the amendment, adopted in 1912 as an alternative to the recall of judicial decisions, was part of a set of seven amendments, including recall of judges, that either directly overruled decisions of the Ohio Supreme Court or removed potential judicial barriers to legislative action.[126] Ohio required the concurrence of all but one justice to declare a statute unconstitutional, and Nebraska and North Dakota followed Ohio's lead.[127]

Underlying such super-majority requirements was a belief that judges should not overturn the popular will absent a clear constitutional violation. Because it was impossible to enforce such a counsel of judicial restraint directly, states increased the number of justices who had to agree for a law to be struck down, on the assumption that an argument of unconstitutionality that convinced an extraordinary majority of judges was more likely correct than one that persuaded only a bare majority. Further, the requirement did not threaten judicial independence because judges remained free to vote as they believed the law required. Although Ohio abolished its requirement in 1968, Nebraska and North Dakota continue to require a super-majority for rulings of unconstitutionality, and in Nebraska the requirement "has saved several important pieces of legislation."[128]

Nonpartisan Judicial Elections

Both conservatives within the legal profession and many progressives favored replacing partisan election of judges with nonpartisan elections, in which candidates would run in nonpartisan primaries and the two top vote-getters would run without party label in the general election. For progressives, the shift to nonpartisan elections promised to reduce the influence of political parties, and it was consistent with their support for nonpartisan elections for other offices as well. For the legal profession, such a shift promised to enhance its influence in judicial selection, as endorsements by the organized bar were expected to replace party endorsements as the primary influence on voter choice. According to Defenders, nonpartisan elections would promote judicial independence because judges would no longer owe their positions to party support. Progressives also insisted that nonpartisan elections would ensure more effective accountability to the public because voters would be free to choose who would serve, rather than merely selecting among candidates anointed by party leaders. Thus, whereas mid-nineteenth-century supporters of judicial elections had emphasized that judges having a separate base of power contributed to judicial independence, proponents of nonpartisan elections believed the key factor was insulating judicial candidates from the influence of political parties throughout the selection process. Finally, the organized bar expected that nonpartisan elections would reduce "violent and frequent changes" in the composition of the bench and ensure that, in the words of Chief Justice John Winslow of the Wisconsin Supreme Court, "a sitting judge who has performed his duties faithfully [would] be retained during his years of usefulness, regardless of his opinions."[129]

With the support of legal conservatives and progressives, North Dakota in 1910 became the first state to shift to nonpartisan judicial elections, and by 1920 eight other states had also done so.[130] The ease of shifting to nonpartisan elections contributed to the success of the reform. Although state constitutions mandated popular election of judges, most did not specify that the elections be partisan affairs, so nonpartisan elections could be instituted through changes in electoral laws rather than constitutional amendment.[131]

Yet nonpartisan elections disappointed many reformers. Progressives discovered that they reduced voter participation in judicial races and hence accountability. After Ohio enacted the Nonpartisan Judiciary Act of 1911, voting in judicial elections declined almost 50 percent from 1912–20, in comparison with the preceding decade.[132] Defenders found that without gatekeepers to exclude the unqualified, the scramble for position under nonpartisan elections attracted the wrong sorts of lawyers, and so—in the words of reformer Albert Kales—"the top men of the bar are seldom to be found on the bench in states operating under this system."[133] In addition, nonpartisan elections did not eliminate the influence of party leaders, who discovered new ways to dominate the electoral process, nor did it enhance the quality of the bench because voters purportedly lacked the knowledge to choose wisely among competing candidates. Thus, as early as 1913, William Howard Taft, the leader of the legal conservatives, concluded that nonpartisan elections had failed to secure judicial independence, and he and his allies sought an alternative.[134]

Merit Selection

The alternative that legal conservatives embraced was "merit selection."[135] Albert Kales, the architect of the merit plan, insisted that judicial elections were only nominally democratic because party leaders—"politocrats" in his terminology—determined who was nominated, so "the voter only selects which of two or three appointing powers he prefers."[136] Nonpartisan elections reduced the direct influence of party leaders, but the necessity of having to seek their support gave them undue influence over judges. The only way to insulate judges from external pressures, Kales argued, was to eliminate the input of political parties and the populace altogether in selecting judges, substituting a system of professional—and therefore, in his view, nonpolitical—appointment.[137] More specifically, Kales proposed that a commission drawn from the legal community screen potential judges and forward a list of qualified candidates to the state's chief justice, who would appoint from that list. In 1920 the American Judicature Society endorsed merit selection, and in 1937 the American Bar Association likewise did so, providing powerful institutional support for reform efforts. In 1940 Missouri became the first state to institute merit selection for all its judges, albeit substituting the governor for the chief justice as the appointing authority.[138] Kansas followed suit in 1958, and from 1960–90 seventeen more states embraced merit selection.

Kales included a system of retention elections in his original proposal, under which the public would periodically vote in an uncontested election on whether an incumbent judge should remain in office. But this was not fundamental to the plan. As Glenn Winters, the longtime president of the American Judicature Society, acknowledged, "The device of tenure by non-competitive election . . . was originally offered only to quiet the fears of . . . devotees of the elective method."[139] In the long run it was expected that such elections would be eliminated altogether. We shall have much more to say about merit selection and retention elections in Chapter 5.

Outcomes

The conflict over judicial independence and accountability during the Progressive era resulted in an almost complete victory for Defenders. Few states adopted the recall of judges, the recall of judicial decisions, the requirement of extraordinary majorities for invalidating statutes, or other reforms championed by proponents of judicial accountability. Even in those states, the direct effect of these reforms was minimal. Few judges were recalled, court rulings robbed the recall of judicial decisions of its effectiveness, and the requirement of extraordinary majorities hardly limited the police power rulings of state supreme courts. By contrast, the measures favored by Defenders enjoyed considerable success. Several states moved from partisan to nonpartisan judicial elections during the Progressive era, and a large number shifted to merit selection later in the century, so that currently fifteen states use merit selection to choose their supreme court justices, fourteen use nonpartisan election, and nine use a combination of merit selection and other processes.[140]

These results reflect, at least in part, the differing perspectives of proponents of judicial accountability and proponents of judicial independence. Those calling for greater accountability were interested primarily in the substance of judicial rulings. They espoused greater accountability in order to reorient the rulings of the courts, which they viewed as distorted by political ideology and class loyalties. As John Ross put it, "Their advocacy of various quixotic proposals to curtail judicial power often was intended merely to dramatize their grievances and remind the courts that an angry public possessed the means of curbing judicial power."[141] Once the rulings of the courts shifted, once they ceased to invalidate social and labor legislation, the reformers lost interest in the very reforms they had championed. In contrast, most Defenders had broader institutional concerns unconnected to the substance of particular decisions. Although they may have applauded the courts' rulings invalidating interferences with the liberty of contract, they were primarily interested in eliminating partisan and popular pressures on the courts. Making the courts responsive to professional norms rather than external forces would, they believed, contribute to the rule of law and ultimately enhance the standing of the courts. As a result, they continued to push for nonpartisan election and then merit selection even when popular distrust of the courts had abated, and in this less heated atmosphere they enjoyed considerable success.

The Past as Prologue

Fast forward to the present day, and what is striking is how closely the current debate over judicial selection and judicial performance mirrors the conflict of a century ago. The vocabulary of the current debate—"judicial activism" and "politicization"—may be new, but the complaints are not. Today, as they did then, Bashers complain that judges are frustrating popular government by reading their own ideological predilections into the law and that merit selection is "a masquerade to put political power in the hands of the organized bar and other members of the elite."[142] Today, as then, Defenders counter that unfair ideological attacks on the courts, combined with political efforts to influence judicial rulings, are undermining public respect for the courts and threatening the rule of law. As in the past, those advocating merit selection and retention elections find themselves on one side of an ideological divide, viewing the problem less in terms of the substance of judicial rulings and more in terms of the quality of the bench and its insulation from political influences.

Three differences are important. The first is an ideological reversal. Today it is political conservatives who are most critical of the courts and want greater judicial accountability, while it is liberals, now allied with the organized bar, who are most supportive of the courts and most alarmed by perceived threats to their independence. The second difference is that the view of mechanical jurisprudence that was first challenged during the Progressive era is now largely discredited, so that alternative justifications for judicial independence are now required. The third difference is that we now have the benefit of a half-century or more of experience with nonpartisan elections and merit selection, the reforms successfully championed by legal conservatives, so we are in a position to assess their actual effectiveness in safeguarding judicial independence while ensuring appropriate judicial accountability.

3 The Changing Face of State
Judicial Selection

FOR ALMOST A CENTURY, THE BATTLE OVER JUDICIAL INDEPEN-
dence and accountability in the states has focused on judicial
selection. The organized bar and other judicial reformers have pressed for
merit selection of state court judges: gubernatorial appointment of judges
from a list prepared by a (theoretically) apolitical commission, after which
judges periodically run in retention elections in which neither party labels
nor competing candidates appear on the ballot. By the early 1980s, the reformers could take considerable satisfaction in what they had accomplished. From
1960 to 1980, fifteen states switched from contested elections to merit selection
for choosing state supreme court justices (and usually other judges as well). In
addition, other states established judicial nominating commissions to prepare
lists of candidates for appointments to interim vacancies on their high courts,
and many judges in elective states first reached the bench in this manner.[1]
In some states these nominating commissions were established by constitutional amendment; in others, by statute or by gubernatorial order. Yet even
when governors instituted commissions, their successors, though not obliged
to do so, usually continued the practice, regardless of whether they shared
the political party of the governor who instituted the practice. Moreover, five
states that retained contested elections—Arkansas, Georgia, Kentucky, Mississippi, and North Carolina—switched from partisan to nonpartisan elections, and Illinois and Pennsylvania retained partisan elections for vacant
seats but instituted retention elections for incumbent judges.[2]

Even in the absence of reform, for most of the twentieth century state judicial elections—whether partisan or nonpartisan, contested or retention—tended to be de-politicized, low-key affairs. Incumbents often ran unopposed for reelection: from 1980–95 incumbent justices on state supreme courts were challenged only 61 percent of the time in partisan elections and only 44 percent of the time in nonpartisan elections.[3] When elections were contested, incumbents rarely faced serious challenges. According to one estimate, "of the total number of judicial elections held in the 50 states [during the 1970s], closely contested, partisan 'unjudicial' judicial elections probably constitute no more than 5 to 7 percent of the total."[4] Judicial campaigns themselves tended to be tepid, issueless affairs. Candidates did not raise substantial campaign funds, advertise in the media, or mount sustained attacks on their opponents.[5] Neither did groups supporting judicial candidates. Judicial campaigning largely consisted of "the judicial candidate [speaking] to any group willing to hear a dull speech about improving the judiciary or about judicial qualifications."[6] This was by design. Rules promulgated in the states, as well as guidelines established by the American Bar Association and state bar associations, prohibited candidates for judicial office from saying anything controversial, lest their statements compromise judicial independence or create an appearance of bias.[7] One commentator aptly described these judicial campaigns as about as exciting as a game of checkers played by mail.[8] Not surprisingly, such low-spending, low-conflict campaigns attracted little attention from the press, organized interests, grassroots organizations—or from anybody else. For Defenders, the absence of controversy and competition was a cause for celebration. If judicial elections could not be eliminated altogether, the hope was that they could be tamed, insulated from the passions and partisanship that characterized elections for other offices, in the hope that diminishing the electoral connection would safeguard judicial independence.

In recent decades the situation has changed.[9] The progress of merit selection has ground to a halt—since 1994, no state has adopted merit selection (although no state with a merit system has yet replaced it).[10] During the last three decades, legislators in North Carolina, Texas, and elsewhere have considered merit selection, only to reject it. So have voters. In 2000, voters in every county in Florida defeated a constitutional amendment that would have allowed for a local option as to merit selection, with an average affirmative vote of just 32 percent. Voters also rejected constitutional amendments instituting merit selection in Oregon (1978), Ohio (1987), South Dakota (2004), and

Nevada (2010). Although Defender organizations continue to advocate merit selection, the lack of progress has prompted them to explore other options as well.[11]

Even more dramatic have been the changes in judicial elections themselves.[12] Incumbents today are far more likely to face electoral competition: from 1996–2004, incumbents were challenged 93 percent of the time in partisan elections and 67 percent of the time in nonpartisan elections.[13] Judicial races have become, in an oft-repeated phrase, "noisier, nastier, and costlier."[14] This transformation extends to partisan and nonpartisan races, to contested and retention elections. Indeed, recent judicial elections have shown that retention elections and nonpartisan elections can rival partisan elections in terms of campaign expenditures, rancorous television ads, and interest group involvement.[15] This means that Defenders can no longer ensure their version of the proper balance between independence and accountability just by switching from partisan or nonpartisan elections to retention elections.

Given the efforts of reformers to de-politicize state judicial selection, why have state judicial races become so politically charged? Why do states now confront, according to Defenders, "judicial election and retention election campaigns drowning in dollars and misleading advertisements"?[16] Is this politicization merely a temporary phenomenon, or is it a more permanent shift?

State Judicial Elections Today

As of 2012, nine states selected their state supreme court justices in partisan elections, thirteen in nonpartisan elections, and fifteen through a system of merit selection in which justices run in retention elections after their initial appointment.[17] In addition, justices in California were appointed but ran in retention elections, and justices in New Mexico were appointed with the use of a nominating commission but ran for their initial reelection in partisan races.[18] It is estimated that 89 percent of all justices face elections at some point during their service on the bench.[19] How have these elections changed?

Money

Judicial elections campaigns are far more expensive than in the past, even the recent past. In 1991–92, candidates for state supreme courts nationwide raised $9.5 million in campaign funds. By 1999–2000, the amount had almost tripled, to $27.4 million. From 2000–2009, supreme court candidates raised $206.9 million nationally, more than double the $83.3 million raised in the preceding decade."[20] The largest contributors to judicial campaigns have been businesses and lawyers/lobbyists, each of whom contributed more than $50 million from 2000–2009. These figures actually underestimate the total expenditures in state supreme court races because interest groups, political parties, and individuals also independently spend substantial sums to elect justices. The exact amounts are difficult to determine because those who make independent expenditures to influence judicial races are not obliged to report their spending.[21] Nonetheless, Justice at Stake, a leading Defender organization, estimated that from 2000–2009, independent groups and political parties spent more than $39.3 million on television time, about 42 percent of the total cost of televised ads. In 2009, for the first time noncandidate groups outspent candidates in judicial elections.[22]

Expenditures vary considerably from state to state and sometimes from election to election. Open-seat races tend to be more expensive than incumbent-challenger contests.[23] According to Justice at Stake, partisan races are more expensive than nonpartisan: the top six states in candidate spending from 2000–2009—Alabama, Pennsylvania, Ohio, Illinois, Texas, and Michigan—were all partisan-election states.[24] However, when controlling for the size of the voting population and other variables, political scientists concluded that partisan elections were cheaper than nonpartisan contests.[25] Whichever analysis one finds more persuasive, the heavy expenditures by candidates and independent groups in the nonpartisan races in Mississippi in 2008 and in Wisconsin in 2008 and 2010 reveal that states with nonpartisan elections do not thereby avoid costly campaigns.

Some races have attracted particular attention. In 2000, the US Chamber of Commerce and its Ohio affiliates spent $4.4 million on supreme court elections in that state. In 2004, the Illinois Democratic and Republican parties, with support from (respectively) plaintiffs' lawyers and business groups, spent $2.8 million and $1.9 million on a single state supreme court race. And in 2004 Don Blankenship, the chairman and CEO of Massey Energy Company, personally spent $3 million to help elect Brent Benjamin to the West Virginia Supreme Court. His contributions and expenditures, which exceeded the total amount spent by all other Benjamin supporters and by Benjamin's own campaign committee, occurred while his company was appealing a $50 million jury award to a competing coal company. When Justice Benjamin refused to recuse himself and cast the deciding vote to overturn the award against Massey Energy, the case was appealed to the US Supreme Court, which ruled that Blankenship's expenditures created such an appearance of conflict of interest that Benjamin's participation in the case amounted to a denial of due process of law.[26]

Yet these striking examples stand out precisely because they are atypical. Spending by candidates in judicial races increased dramatically during the 1990s, but since then it has leveled off. Through the first decade of the new millennium, expenditures in state supreme court races varied less than $1 million in the (more expensive) biennia in which presidential elections occurred (2000, 2004, and 2008) and rose less than $6 million during non-presidential biennia.[27] The level of fund-raising and spending in particular races depends on the electoral threat a candidate faces. Heavy spending by one candidate triggers heavy spending by his opponent, if the opponent can raise the funds. The same holds true for expenditures by outside groups. For example, in 2008 Wisconsin Manufacturers & Commerce contributed $8,100 to supreme court candidates but spent more than $2 million in addition on television advertising. This prompted independent expenditures by liberal groups: the Greater Wisconsin Committee, which was linked to labor unions and the Democratic Party, spent almost $1.5 million on television ads during the same election.[28]

Yet the threat need not come from an opposing candidate. Although incumbents are almost always retained in retention elections, the absence of opposing candidates is no guarantee that those elections will be uncontested. In fact, just the opposite. Whereas opposing candidates must file for candidacy, thereby making known their intention to contest a race, groups seeking to defeat a sitting judge need not tip their hand as early. For example, those who unseated Justice Penny White in Tennessee and Chief Justice David Lanphier in Nebraska in retention elections launched their attacks only two months prior the elections, when it was too late for the incumbents to raise the funds necessary to mount an adequate response.[29] Given the potential for opposition, justices facing retention elections may build up a campaign war chest, both to discourage efforts to unseat them and to ensure that if they are targeted, they will have the resources available to respond to attacks. In 1998, for example, fearful of opposition by antiabortion groups that ultimately did not materialize, California Chief Justice Ronald George raised $886,936 and Justice Ming Chin $710,139 for their retention elections.[30] Thus uncertainty about opposition in a retention election may lead to the same sort of fund-raising and campaigning found in contested elections, even when incumbents are unchallenged.

Incumbents typically can raise and spend more than challengers. It may be that potential contributors, especially attorneys who appear before a court, are reluctant to support candidates challenging incumbent judges because if the incumbents win, they may remember who supported their opponents. Whatever the reason, spending differentials in incumbent-challenger races reinforce the advantages that accompany incumbency.[31] Yet this is not always the case. When in 2008 challengers unseated three incumbent justices in non-partisan elections in Mississippi, all the challengers outspent their opponents. Also, the fact that incumbents can raise more money than challengers does not guarantee electoral success, so long as challengers raise funds sufficient to mount a competitive campaign. Thus in 2008 Chief Justice Clifford Taylor of Michigan, who spent $3.1 million in his reelection bid, lost by ten points to challenger Diane Hathaway, whose total spending was $1.9 million.[32] It is the level of challenger spending, not of incumbent spending, that most affects vote margins in incumbent-challenger races.[33]

Defenders view the escalating cost of judicial campaigns as a threat to judicial independence. Having to raise money may create a sense of obliga-tion, and a concern not to alienate potential contributors to future campaigns might also affect judicial decisions. Highly qualified persons may decline to serve on the bench because they do not wish to sully themselves with fund-raising. As one judge ruefully described it, "I never felt so much like a hooker down by the bus station . . . as I did in a judicial race. Everyone interested in contributing has very specific interests. They mean to be buying a vote."[34] Furthermore, Defenders worry that "the time and effort expended by judges in fundraising can be a serious distraction from the work of the court that the judge is employed to perform."[35] In addition, expensive campaigns may undermine respect for the judiciary because of the perception that contribu-tors are "buying justice." Both poll and experimental data confirm that cam-paign contributions adversely affect public perceptions of judicial impartial-ity and the institutional legitimacy of state courts.[36]

Most Bashers view the increased expenditures in judicial races as posi-tive, bringing judicial elections more into line with elections for other offices. Chris Bonneau and Melinda Gann Hall have summarized the Basher argu-ment: "The more money candidates spend, the more information they can provide to voters; and the more information the voters have, the more likely they are to participate."[37] Higher expenditures reduce voter roll-off. Far from being "alienated by costly campaigns, citizens embrace highly spirited expensive contests by voting in much greater proportions than in more mundane contests."[38] Greater involvement by a better informed electorate enhances accountability. Thus, Bashers tend to describe what has occurred as "democratizing" the courts rather than "politicizing" them.[39]

Television and Campaign Ads

Campaigning for the bench has not only gotten more expensive; it has also changed in character. Campaigns have not abandoned traditional means of communicating with voters, such as public appearances, posters, and leafleting.[40] But candidates have supplemented these traditional appeals with a reliance on mass media, especially television. So too have independent groups. Thus whereas in 2000 only 22 percent of the states with contested supreme court races had televised ads, by 2007–8, 87 percent did. This increased use of television helps explain why judicial races have become more costly. More than $93 million was spent on air time in supreme court contests from 2000–2009, and in 2008 alone, there were more than 58,000 airings of ads in state supreme court races.[41]

Although judicial candidates are responsible for a bare majority of televised ads, increasingly interest groups and political parties have purchased airtime to support their favored candidates or, more frequently, to attack their opponents. In 2008, for example, candidates spent more than $9.5 million on televised ads, with more than 31,800 airings; but groups and political parties spent more than $10.3 million on ads, with more than 27,000 airings.[42] In fact, in Mississippi in 2008, an out-of-state group, the Law Enforcement Alliance of America, spent more on televised ads than did all the candidates and other groups combined.[43]

In a study of state supreme court campaigns in 2006, Scott Peters found that the ads put out by judges and candidates for judicial office "focused primarily on image and qualifications, the traditional form of communications for judicial campaigns, rather than on issues."[44] Although judges or candidates for judicial office may broadcast ads attacking their opponents, they may feel constrained by the canons of judicial ethics or the threat of judicial discipline. For example, in Wisconsin in 2008, a controversial ad by lower-court judge Michael Gableman distorted Justice Louis Butler's involvement in a criminal case, attacked him for "putting criminals back on the street," and questioned whether "Wisconsin families [can] feel safe with Louis Butler on the Supreme Court." After Gableman defeated Butler in a close race, the Wisconsin Judicial Commission charged that Gableman had violated the code of judicial conduct, triggering a protracted inquiry that ended only when the Wisconsin Supreme Court by a 3–3 vote deadlocked on the charges.[45]

Yet if most candidates feel constrained, noncandidate groups—the so-called attack dogs of state supreme court elections—do not.[46] So accompanying the increasing involvement of interest groups in political advertising has been a shift in tone, as harsh television ads attack the character, integrity, and rulings of incumbent judges. Defenders have for years denounced these attack ads as "pernicious rhetoric," "relentless negativity," and "dirty politics, even gutter politics," but with little effect.[47] Thus, an ad in Michigan in 2000 accused Democratic candidates of freeing killers and rapists; one in West Virginia in 2004 accused Justice Warren McGraw of freeing child molesters; another in Michigan in 2008 accused Chief Justice Clifford Taylor of falling asleep on the bench. Often attack ads highlight rulings that allegedly show a judge is "soft on crime," and some groups have used this tactic even when their objections to judges had nothing to do with criminal cases. For example, the accusation against Justice McGraw was leveled by For the Sake of the Children, a front group created and totally funded by Don Blankenship, the chairman of the Massey Energy Company, who wanted a more sympathetic justice to hear his company's appeal in a civil case. Similarly, the Chamber of Commerce used crime-control ads to attack justices sympathetic to plaintiffs in tort cases.[48]

Defenders view attack ads with alarm because they encourage voters to cast their ballots based on their agreement or disagreement with judges' rulings on "hot-button" issues rather than on whether judges adhered to the law. They worry that this may tempt judges to base their rulings on what is popular rather than what the law requires. Claiming that the attacks ads distort judges' records, Defenders contend that they may lead to the defeat of excellent judges because voters lack the information necessary to counteract the exaggerations and misrepresentations in the ads. Beyond that, Defenders worry that the allegations in the ads encourage cynicism about judges and judging, and their similarity to ads used in other political campaigns creates the impression that judges are no different from other officials. Even if attacks focus on individual judges, Defenders insist that their impact is general and magnified because "the public makes little distinction among judges (or even among different jurisdictions)."[49] Finally, Defenders believe that instead of promoting democracy, the relentless negativity of the ads is likely to disgust voters and discourage them from voting.

Bashers dismiss these concerns. In the absence of ads that publicize controversial rulings, they argue, voters would lack the sort of information they need to make well-informed choices. That ads are negative in tone does not mean that they lack substance—indeed, studies of political commercials suggest that negative ads often convey more information than do positive ones.[50] Far from deterring voter participation, negative ads spark voter interest and increase participation in elections.[51] Bashers do not believe that voters are actually uncomfortable with the attack ads or, indeed, any aspect of contemporary judicial campaigns because, as James Pozen has explained, "all of the new features of judicial elections are features that we have come to expect, if not entirely embrace, in our legislative and executive races."[52] If the ads undermine respect for the judiciary, Bashers conclude, it is less the ads than rulings highlighted in them that are to blame.

Why Have Judicial Elections Changed?

State judicial selection does not occur in a political vacuum; the same factors that have influenced American politics and law have also affected judicial selection. Thus, as the character of American politics and law has changed in recent decades, so too has state judicial selection. Several developments should be highlighted.

Partisan Shifts

Among the most dramatic changes during the latter half of the twentieth century was the spread of two-party competition throughout the nation. Many states that once were dominated by a single party, particularly in the South and in New England, now regularly conduct competitive elections.[53] This is important because the level of partisan and group conflict in the selection of judges is affected by the overall level of partisan and group competition within a state. In states where a single party predominates, conflict and competition in judicial elections—as in other elections—tends to be muted, although it may flare up in primary elections when there are intraparty divisions. But in states in which party competition is intense, that intensity spills over into judicial elections, particularly in partisan contests. In Pennsylvania, for example, Republicans and Democrats vigorously compete for the governorship and control of the state legislature, and they compete just as vigorously for control of the state's courts. From 1979–97, there were elections for nine vacant seats on the Pennsylvania Supreme Court, all hotly contested races, with Republicans winning five seats and Democrats four.[54] In 2007 alone candidates for the Pennsylvania Supreme Court spent $9.5 million in primary and general elections.[55] When in 2009 Republican Joan Orie Melvin defeated Democrat Jack Panella, 53 percent to 47 percent, in a race for an open seat on the Pennsylvania Supreme Court, a race in which the candidates spent $5.4 million, it gave Republicans a 4–3 majority on the court.

Politicization of judicial races is particularly likely when a state shifts from single-party dominance, as the emerging political party seeks to capture control of all the institutions of state government, including the courts. Texas has since 1876 elected supreme court justices in partisan elections, but prior to 1980, while the Texas Democratic Party dominated, judicial elections tended to be low-key affairs. But the rise of the Texas Republican Party changed that.[56] The emergence of the Republicans as a viable political alternative encouraged vigorous party competition for all offices, including seats on the state bench. As a result, six incumbent justices of the Texas Supreme Court and several lower-court judges were defeated in their reelection bids from 1980–98.[57] Republican control of the Texas judiciary became a real possibility. No Democrat was elected in the eighteen statewide judicial races in 2000, and in 2002 and 2004 Republicans won all eight races for the Supreme Court.[58] But the shift to uncontested one-party control has not yet occurred. In 2008, with a popular Democrat running for president, Democrats fielded candidates for all three supreme court races, and although the Republican incumbents won in each instance, all three races were decided by fewer than 10 percentage points. Even were a shift to Republican dominance to occur, this would not necessarily eliminate contested races: in 2010, for example, both Republican incumbents seeking reelection faced serious primary challenges.

Alabama underwent a similar transformation. Judicial candidates had run in partisan elections since 1867, but until 1994, no Republican had been elected to the Alabama Supreme Court for over a century.[59] However, in that year Perry Hooper, a Republican whose campaign was managed by Karl Rove, defeated incumbent chief justice "Sonny" Hornsby by 262 votes. In 1996 Republican Harold See won election to the court, and in 2003 he fought off a major challenge by a Democratic opponent. In 2004 the Republicans captured all three open seats on the court, winning more than 55 percent of the vote in each race, and as a result occupied all nine seats on the Alabama Supreme Court. Indeed, the most hotly contested race in 2004 occurred in the Republican primary, where Tom Parker defeated an incumbent justice, Jean Williams Brown, who had voted to remove Chief Justice Roy Moore after Moore refused to take down a courtroom display of the Ten Commandments. By 2005 only one of Alabama's nineteen appellate judges was a Democrat. However, general elections for the Supreme Court remain competitive: in 2006 Sue Bell Cobb, a Democrat, won the chief justiceship, and in 2008 another Democrat, Deborah Bell Paseur, barely lost in her bid for an open seat on the Court.

A shift in the partisan balance of power in a state can also increase the level of political conflict between a state legislature and the state supreme court beyond the normal friction inherent in a system of separation of powers. The partisan and ideological composition of a state legislature can change quickly, given the relatively short terms legislators serve. However, appellate judges tend to serve longer terms and often multiple terms, so turnover on the bench is more gradual. Thus, when a major political shift occurs in a state, the state's judges may be perceived—whatever their mode of selection—as out of step with the state's newly regnant political forces. Thus, after they gained control of the state legislature in 1996 and the governorship in 1998, Republicans in Florida tended to view the Florida Supreme Court, even though selected by merit selection, as a "remnant of the heyday of Democratic dominance" in Florida, and they introduced measures designed to increase political control of its composition.[60] This temptation to attribute a partisan cast to merit selection is hardly new—after Missouri created the first merit selection system in 1940, critics characterized it as "a self-perpetuating Democratic political system."[61]

Accompanying the increased partisan competitiveness of recent years has been a shift in the ideological distance separating Democrats and Republicans.[62] When the Democratic Party controlled the "solid South," conservatives from that region tempered the liberalism of the party nationally. But with both parties competitive throughout much of the country, liberals have gravitated toward the Democratic Party and conservatives toward the Republican Party, thus strengthening the ideological identity of each party and accentuating the lack of common ground between them. This is reflected in the increased party-based voting in Congress, as well as in poll data documenting an opinion gap between Democrats and Republicans on a wide range of issues.[63] As Gary Jacobson has observed, "Partisan polarization in Congress reflects electoral changes that have left the parties with more homogeneous and more dissimilar electoral coalitions."[64] This political polarization has sharpened interparty conflict, and thus the politicization of judicial elections replicates the increasingly rancorous partisan and ideological conflict present in the nation as a whole.

State Supreme Court Involvement in Public Policy

A second major development affecting state judicial selection is the increasing involvement of state supreme courts in addressing legal issues with far-reaching policy consequences, such as school finance, tort law, abortion, capital punishment, the rights of defendants, and same-sex marriage. The shift in the courts' agendas can be traced to institutional and legal developments within the states. The changing size and character of state supreme court caseloads is one important factor.[65] During the late nineteenth century, state supreme courts struggled with overwhelming caseloads, dominated by minor disputes and private law (primarily commercial) cases. Typically the state supreme court, as the sole appellate court in the state, exercised no control over its docket and so found itself facing a severe backlog of cases. Given such caseload pressures, justices had little time to concern themselves with the development of the law of the state. But in the twentieth century, most states created intermediate appellate courts to handle routine cases, thereby reducing the burden on state supreme courts. The establishment of intermediate appellate courts not only diverted less important cases but also encouraged a reduction in the mandatory jurisdiction of those courts.[66] When states gave courts more control over their dockets, this provided the opportunity, although not necessarily the incentive, for greater activism. State supreme courts became "less concerned with the stabilization and protection of property rights, more concerned with the individual and the downtrodden, and more willing to consider rulings that promote social change."[67] The reduction in caseload pressures also freed justices to concentrate on shaping the law of the state, both common law and constitutional law.[68] Indeed, "the architecture of the system [told] the judges of the top court to be creative."[69]

This creativity expressed itself initially in the field of tort law. Historically, state courts have had the responsibility for shaping the common law of the state. Since the end of World War II, state supreme courts have revolutionized the field of tort law, transforming standards for determining liability, abolishing long-standing immunities, eliminating common law limitations on causes of action, and generally making it easier for plaintiffs to pursue their claims. Writing in 1969, one scholar observed that the "most striking impression that results from reading the weekly outpouring of torts opinions is one of candid, openly acknowledged, abrupt change."[70] Beginning in the 1980s, state legislatures attempted to rein in these court-initiated changes by enacting "tort-reform" statutes that sought to restrict recovery and shift the law in ways favorable to defendants in tort cases. The plaintiffs' bar responded by challenging the constitutionality of some of these statutes. It argued that statutory limits on punitive or noneconomic damages violated state constitutional guarantees of jury trial because they limited the discretion of jurors in awarding damages, and that statutes of limitations and statutes of repose violated the "open courts" provisions of state constitutions, which guarantee that the courts be available for the redress of injuries.[71] These arguments enjoyed considerable success; during the 1980s and 1990s, as supreme courts in twenty-six states struck down more than ninety tort-reform statutes.[72] The success of these constitutional challenges and the ensuing conflict between state legislatures and supreme courts, as well as between proplaintiff and prodefendant interest groups, provided a major impetus for the politicization of judicial races. In fact, the increases in the costs of judicial campaigns correlate with the level of tort cases as a percentage of a state supreme court's docket.[73]

Equally important in providing opportunities for state supreme courts to shape state law was the emergence of the new judicial federalism—that is, the reliance by state courts on state declarations of rights to provide protections unavailable under the US Constitution.[74] This new judicial federalism emerged in the early 1970s, following the appointment of Chief Justice Warren Burger to succeed Earl Warren on the US Supreme Court. Civil-liberties and social-reform groups, anticipating a major shift in orientation on the US Supreme Court, began to look to state courts as a new arena in which to pursue their goals. Success in some states encouraged litigation in others, and the new judicial federalism became a national phenomenon.

Initially, most claims under the new judicial federalism involved the rights of defendants in criminal cases, and this has remained a major focus. But soon the range of controversial issues brought before state supreme courts expanded to include public school finance, abortion, the death penalty, same-sex marriage, and tort reform. In part this occurred because state constitutions included distinctive provisions that imposed obligations on state governments, "requir[ing] lawmakers to effectuate highly specific social goals, such as the provision of free public schools and the regulation of corporations, banks, and railroads."[75] In part too, state guarantees of a right to privacy and of gender equality encouraged litigation in state courts. Even when there were analogous provisions in the federal Constitution, distinctive language in state provisions provided the basis for novel claims.

In ruling on these hot-button issues, state supreme courts often upset prevailing policies and practices within their states. For example, since 1973, fifteen state supreme courts have invalidated the system of school finance in their states, requiring a major increase in state funding for education, often through new statewide taxes, and a redistribution of those funds among school districts.[76] The courts' controversial rulings have upset and activated important groups within state populations. Sometimes these groups responded by amending state constitutions to overturn judicial rulings, as occurred when California and Massachusetts reinstated the death penalty.[77] But more often groups sought to punish the "offending" justices by replacing them with others more sympathetic to the group's views. Thus, the leader of Iowa for Freedom, a group that helped to defeat justices who struck down the state's ban on same-sex marriage, stated, "This isn't just about gay marriage. It's about a court attempting to legislate and amend the Constitution from the bench, which endangers all of our freedoms. That's tyranny. What you're gonna see is the people of the heartland hold an activist court in check by voting three justices off the bench."[78]

Group Involvement in Judicial Selection

Another key development has been the increased involvement of interest groups in judicial selection. Traditionally, groups whose interests might be affected by judicial rulings had sought to influence decisions by filing *amicus curiae* briefs, developing test cases, and funding litigation. However, in recent years they have recognized that one of the best ways to shape the development of the law is by affecting who sits on the state bench, and they have increasingly sought to influence its composition no matter what the selection system. As the president of Ohio Bar Association explained after a particularly expensive election, "The people with money to spend who are affected by court decisions have reached the conclusion that it's a lot cheaper to buy a judge than a governor or an entire legislature, and he can probably do a lot more for you."[79]

In some instances, groups form in response to specific judicial rulings or to oppose particular candidates. For example, a group calling itself Alabama Voters against Lawsuit Abuse played a major role in defeating a Democratic candidate for the Alabama Supreme Court in 2008. Democracy Rising Pennsylvania formed in 2006 to defeat two Pennsylvania justices after the state's supreme court upheld a "stealth" pay increase voted by the Pennsylvania Legislature, and in 2004 in West Virginia a group called For the Sake of the Children was organized to defeat Justice Warren McGraw. These groups may not survive following the election—in Georgia, for example, the Safety and Prosperity Coalition was formed in 2006 to defeat Chief Justice Carol Hunstein, spent $1.7 million in the effort, and then disappeared.[80]

In other instances, preexisting groups are activated by adverse rulings or the threat of such rulings. Some of these groups are state-specific. For example, after the Florida Supreme Court in 1990 struck down a state law requiring minors to get parental consent before obtaining abortions, the Florida Right to Life Committee sought to defeat Chief Justice Leander Shaw, the author of the majority opinion. The Business Council of Alabama/Progress PAC was a heavy contributor to seven of the nine Republican justices who ran for election in Alabama from 2000–2009.[81] However, some apparently election-specific state groups may be merely covers for national groups with a longstanding interest in state supreme court elections. For example, Citizens for a Strong Ohio was heavily backed by the US Chamber of Commerce, and Iowa for Freedom was linked to the American Family Association and the National Organization for Marriage.

Most often, national groups have become involved because of tort-law issues, pitting business and insurance groups against plaintiffs' attorneys. As early as 1999, one commentator described judicial elections in Alabama as "a battleground between businesses and those who sue them."[82] In 2000 the US Chamber of Commerce spent more than $4.4 million in Alabama, Michigan, Ohio, and other states to support judicial candidates. The chamber's president Thomas Donohue explained the chamber's involvement as a response to "a small group of class-action trial lawyers [that] is hellbent on destroying other industries," which created a need "to elect pro-legal reform judicial candidates."[83] From 2000–2009 the chamber, in conjunction with other Republican and conservative groups, spent more than $26 million on state supreme court races. Plaintiffs' lawyers, together with Democratic and union groups, countered with expenditures of almost $12 million.[84] Sometimes groups whose

primary concern is tort law focus their advertising on judges' rulings in criminal cases in order to mobilize voters. For example, the Illinois Civil Justice
League sponsored ads portraying felons praising Justice Thomas Kilbride for
"sid[ing] with us over law enforcement or our victims," even though its main
aim was to curb awards to plaintiffs in medical malpractice and other tort
cases.[85]

Of course, interest groups are not always successful in unseating justices—in 1990, despite the opposition of prolife groups, Chief Justice Leander Shaw was reelected with 59 percent of the vote, and in 2000 Justice Alice
Resnick of the Ohio Supreme Court, despite being targeted by the Chamber of
Commerce, won with 57 percent of the vote. But groups have sometimes been
able to change the orientation of state supreme courts. Thus Joe Turnham,
the chairman of the Alabama Democratic Party, concluded, "People lamented
10 to 15 years ago about tort hell in Alabama. It's now consumer hell. Big corporations and big oil have bought control of the Supreme Court."[86] Moreover, interest group opposition to candidates has changed the intensity and
character of the reelection process because those groups have the resources to
increase the salience of the judicial races and because they are not bound by
the ethical restrictions that limit the campaign messages of judges and judicial candidates.

The interplay of politicians and interest groups is important as well. Politicians may seek to court groups by seizing upon a single controversial ruling as a weapon to attack judges, regardless of the legal merits of the ruling.
As Justice Hans Linde put it, "Voters are invited to feel angry at a decision
and to vent that anger against any judge who participated in it."[87] In addition to using court-bashing to score points with voters, politicians may seek
to enhance their political prospects by placing themselves in the forefront of
efforts to deny judges reelection. This has occurred most often with rulings
on the death penalty and the rights of defendants. Thus, Governor Don Sun-
dquist allied himself with the Tennessee Conservative Union and with victims'
rights groups in opposing Justice Penny White because of an opinion that she
joined, holding that rape was not in all cases an aggravating factor in murder
cases. And Mississippi politicians joined with the state prosecutors' association
in publicizing an opinion by Justice James Robertson that the death penalty
could not be imposed on rapists whose victims survived the attack.

One important effect of this increased group involvement in judicial elections appears to be a convergence among electoral systems, such that state

supreme court justices running in retention elections may face the same expensive, vituperative challenges that were previously confined to other judicial races. The 1986 race in California, in which Chief Justice Rose Bird and two associate justices were defeated, pioneered the practice of groups organizing to target sitting justices in retention elections, but it is hardly unique. In 1996 interest groups successfully targeted Justice David Lanphier in Nebraska and Justice Penny White in Tennessee; in 2005 they fueled the voter anger that defeated Justice Russell Nigro in Pennsylvania; and in 2010 they led the fight against three Iowa justices who invalidated restrictions on same-sex marriage. But not all such challenges have succeeded: Florida Chief Justice Leander Shaw in 1990 and Pennsylvania Justice Sandra Newman in 2005 survived well-funded campaigns to unseat them.

Although interest groups' intervention in retention elections has been episodic, it has had effects beyond occasionally unseating sitting justices. Such group involvement has warned sitting judges that they can never be sure whether they will face an organized effort to defeat them when they seek retention, and this in turn has encouraged them to take preemptive steps to avoid such opposition.

The increased involvement of interest groups in state judicial elections is likely to continue because, whereas a change in a single seat in the state legislature may have only a minimal effect, the effects of replacing a single justice may be dramatic. Were the supreme courts in Alabama, Michigan, Texas, and other states to cease issuing rulings on tort law, one suspects that the plaintiffs' bar and business groups would no longer offer huge campaign contributions to candidates for seats on those courts. But so long as those courts—and others—continue to address legal issues that are simultaneously contentious policy issues, they will attract the attention and involvement of interested groups.

US Supreme Court Rulings

The legal context within which judicial campaigns and elections are conducted has also changed. In *Republican Party of Minnesota v. White* (2003) the US Supreme Court upheld a challenge under the First Amendment to the "Announce Clause" of the Minnesota Code of Judicial Conduct, which prohibited judicial candidates from announcing their views on contested issues that might come before the courts.[88] Before *White*, state codes of judicial conduct severely restricted what those seeking or holding judicial office could say in judicial campaigns. Candidates in both contested and noncontested elections were prohibited from commenting on pending cases, taking positions that appeared to commit them on issues that might come before the court, appearing at political functions, or making promises of conduct in office.[89] Such restrictions meant that candidates could not convey relevant information about themselves or their opponents, "systematically depriv[ing] voters of the exact information we typically pine for them to have," and thereby making informed voter choice more difficult.[90] However, from the perspective of judicial candidates, particularly sitting judges, these restrictions could actually be an advantage because when questioned about their decisions and their values, they could plead that they were legally prohibited from discussing their views. In the wake of *White*, candidates could no longer make that claim, so groups could more effectively press them to announce their views on disputed legal and political issues.

Although *White* was a 5–4 decision, it fit comfortably within the court's jurisprudence on elections. As Justice Antonin Scalia noted for the Court, "We have never allowed the government to prohibit candidates from communicating relevant information to voters during an election."[91] Even commentators unenthusiastic about the ruling recognized that the Announce Clause was anomalous, "not simply a modification of traditional campaign speech rules designed to accommodate a distinctive institutional setting [but] a complete repudiation of these rules' cardinal tenet: that candidates should be encouraged to articulate positions on the issues that matter to voters so that voters can know what they are selecting for, prospectively, and can reward or punish performance, retrospectively."[92] Many of those who criticized the ruling were either opposed to judicial elections altogether or favored a highly circumscribed electoral process. They insisted that because the judicial office differed from political offices, the character of the selection process should likewise differ. *White* in their view "open[ed] the door, as both a practical and jurisprudential matter, to forces seeking to benefit from highly politicized courts."[93]

Eventually *White* may lead to the elimination of most restrictions on judicial campaigning. The court majority expressly distinguished the Announce Clause from provisions prohibiting judges from making pledges or promises of conduct in office, so it is possible that such pledge-or-promise limits could survive judicial scrutiny. However, lower courts have already relied on *White* to invalidate several code provisions, including prohibitions on "making false and misleading statements," bans on partisan political activities by judges, and restrictions on judicial solicitation of campaign contributions.[94] As one survey concluded, "Lower courts will continue to deregulate judicial election speech; [and] few trends point in the other direction."[95]

In practice, this might mean that judicial campaigns would be more like other political campaigns. By striking down the Announce Clause, the Supreme Court gave judicial candidates greater freedom of speech, and interest groups have demanded that they exercise that freedom, seeking to elicit their views through questionnaires and in public forums and publicizing those views to the electorate. Thus, a survey of state supreme court candidates in 2006 found that they on average received eighteen questionnaires and completed almost two-thirds of them.[96] Moreover, once a candidate responds to questions about her views, the pressure on other candidates to be similarly forthcoming can be intense because groups can highlight a candidate's failure to respond and use it to rally opposition against her. As the Nevada Judicial Information Committee urged voters, "Look for candidates who are courageous enough to answer the NVJIC questionnaire and not hide behind the . . . judicial canon prohibiting speech on issues of interest to voters."[97] These candidate views, then, will often become the basis on which campaigns for judicial office are waged.

Yet in the short term *White*'s effects have been limited. Penny White, a former Tennessee Justice who was defeated in a retention election, concluded that "the decision has transformed state judicial elections, attracting the attention and resources of special interest groups and prompting a financial arms race."[98] However, political scientists have "found no statistically discernible influence in state supreme court elections of the *White* decision on the propensity for challengers to take on incumbents, the willingness of citizens to vote, or the actual costs of campaigns."[99] An experimental study found that judicial candidates taking positions on issues and attacking their opponents' views did not alienate the electorate, perhaps because this new candidate speech did not markedly differ from the messages already put forth by independent groups not associated with the candidates. It thus concluded that "to the extent that the state judiciaries are threatened today by campaign activity, it is not because the U.S. Supreme Court awarded judicial candidates free speech rights in its 2002 decision."[100]

If the effects of *White* were less dire than its critics feared, it also did not trigger a reaction against politicized judicial campaigns. Some Defenders speculated that "the Court [in *White*] was not trying to normalize the practice of judicial elections so as to comport with minimal constitutional requirements; it was trying to accelerate the radicalization of judicial elections so that their defects would finally become apparent to all."[101] Certainly if that was the court's intention, there is no evidence that *White* had that effect.

Another major US Supreme Court ruling affecting judicial elections is *Citizens United v. Federal Elections Commission* (2010), in which the Court held that the First Amendment prohibited bans on corporate and union expenditures for the communication of political messages during federal elections.[102] Writing for a five–member majority, Justice Anthony Kennedy concluded that "if the First Amendment has any force, it prohibits Congress from fining or jailing citizens, or associations of citizens, for simply engaging in political speech."[103] At the same time, the court reaffirmed its early holding in *Caperton v. A. T. Massey Coal Co.* (2009) that a judge may be disqualified when a litigant's campaign expenditures have "a disproportionate influence in placing the judge on the case."[104]

Although *Citizens United* did not involve a judicial election, critics were quick to predict dramatic effects on judicial races. In his dissenting opinion, Justice John Paul Stevens noted that the decision came at a time "when concerns about the conduct of judicial elections have reached a fever pitch."[105] In a *New York Times* editorial, Dorothy James depicted *Citizens United* as "Hanging a 'For Sale' Sign Over the Judiciary," and the Brennan Center for Justice, a leading Defender group, concurred in a report entitled "Buying Justice: The Impact of *Citizens United* on Judicial Elections."[106] It is too early to tell whether these gloomy predictions will be vindicated. Certainly, as noted previously, the limitations that states had imposed prior to *Citizens United* had done little to stem corporate and union spending in state judicial elections. And just before the 2010 elections, the Supreme Court in *Minnesota Citizens Concerned for Life v. Swanson* (2010) declined to issue an injunction barring Minnesota from enforcing a law enacted in the wake of *Citizens United* that required nonprofit and profit-making corporations to do their political spending through an independent fund, thereby leaving unclear how broadly to read its decision in *Citizens United*.[107]

Public Perceptions of Courts

The politicization of judicial elections has both influenced and been influenced by changing public perceptions of law and of judges. Within the legal community, the critiques of the Legal Realists and their progeny have broken down the consensus about how one interprets the law or, indeed, what constitutes interpretation as opposed to judicial law making.[108] Indeed, they may have undermined the notion of judicial impartiality itself. For there is a temptation, not often resisted, to move from the descriptive to the prescriptive, from recognizing the influence of judicial values on judicial decisions to concluding that judicial decision involves nothing more than the promotion of those values and that it is legitimate for judges to decide cases on that basis.[109] This is implicit in the confirmation hearings for US Supreme Court justices, and the lessons learned in those proceedings likely affect assessments of state judges as well. As William Marshall has observed, "In a world where law is seen as driven by the individual ideologies of particular judges, the power to choose who is elevated to the bench becomes the power, in effect, to decide constitutional questions," and "the corresponding pitched battles that attend judicial [selection] are unlikely to end so long as politicians, academics, and judges themselves accept the notion that constitutional law amounts to little more than political spoils."[110]

This realism—some would say cynicism—about judicial decision making has influenced public opinion as well; indeed, "it is an ingrained aspect of our political and legal culture."[111] Although most Americans have never witnessed state judges in action nor read judicial opinions, poll data reveal a deep skepticism about the impartiality of state courts and their ability to administer justice even-handedly. Thus, in a 2005 Maxwell School poll, a majority of respondents agreed with the view that "in many cases judges are really basing their decisions on their own personal beliefs," and 82 percent believed that the partisan background of judges influenced their rulings a lot or at least some.[112] A poll for Justice at Stake reported similar findings: 64 percent of respondents agreed that "there are too many activist judges who make rulings that follow their own views rather than the law," and 60 percent thought "too many judges are legislating from the bench and making laws instead of interpreting the laws."[113] In a poll conducted by the Annenberg Public Policy Center in 2006, 75 percent of respondents believed that judicial rulings were influenced to "a great extent" or "a moderate extent" by judges' personal political views, and 68 percent criticized this as "not appropriate."[114]

As Keith Bybee has noted, public perceptions that the judicial process is infused with politics coexist rather uneasily with public expectations of impartial decision making, but despite this most polls show public confidence in judges and courts higher than that for other officials and institutions.[115] Nonetheless, the perception that judicial decisions reflect judicial ideology or idiosyncrasy rather than the legal merits of the case may encourage the conclusion that judicial decisions are not fundamentally different from those made by other political actors. If one accepts this, one may well conclude that judges should be evaluated on the basis of their political orientations and judicial decisions on the basis of whether one agrees with the outcomes. Such conclusions, of course, justify the politicization of judicial selection.

What Does the Future Hold?

Justice Felix Frankfurter once observed that "it is because the [US] Supreme Court wields the power that it wields, that appointment to the Court is a matter of general public concern and not merely a question for the profession."[116] The same holds true for the selection of state supreme court justices. Thus one can expect that the factors that have encouraged the politicization—or democratization—of state judicial selection in recent years will continue to operate for the foreseeable future. Even a switch to merit selection, were such an unlikely event to occur, would not shield judges from these "noisier, nastier, and costlier" judicial campaigns because the causes of the politicization of judicial selection in recent years are tied to factors that operate independently of the mode of judicial selection.[117]

Defenders will of course continue to decry the changes in the character of state judicial elections, arguing that the shift to competitive and politicized elections promotes a false accountability, while threatening judicial independence, the rule of law, and the quality of the state bench. But not everyone shares their concern. For Bashers the escalation in the costs of judicial campaigns is a positive development because it signals that races for judicial office have become more competitive, and greater competitiveness translates into more meaningful choices for voters. If the fear of electoral defeat induces candidates to spend more money on campaigns, this should make judicial elections more salient and ensure that more information is transmitted to voters. If the rules governing campaign speech are relaxed, this too should ameliorate the flow of information and encourage more informed voter choice. So should greater involvement by interest groups in judicial races.

We shall address the Defender and Basher views of judicial elections in Chapter 5. But before doing so, one needs a better understanding of judicial independence and judicial accountability. It is to this task and to a scrutiny of the Defender and Basher perspectives in light of this analysis that we now turn.

4 Analyzing Judicial Independence and Accountability

T HIS CHAPTER SEEKS TO CLARIFY THE TERMS OF THE DEBATE OVER
judicial independence and accountability. It also considers how
various mechanisms designed to secure judicial accountability affect judicial
independence. It then assesses how Defenders and Bashers propose to ensure
an appropriate balance between decisional independence and accountability.
What emerges is a surprising consensus between Bashers and Defenders as
to how judges should decide cases, albeit one that virtually guarantees dis-
appointment because it rests on an inadequate understanding of judicial
decision making. Finally, the chapter considers how a more adequate understanding of judicial decision making would alter the debate about judicial
independence and judicial accountability.

Definitions and Perspectives

Judicial independence has individual and collective aspects as well as decisional and institutional aspects. *Decisional independence* refers to the insulation of judges from undue or improper influence by other political institutions, interest groups, and/or the general public. Judges are not independent
if they respond to pressures from those who hold power or if they decide by
guessing what will please them. But one must "distinguish the arbitrary,
impertinent influences from those that are not," for as Stephen Burbank
has observed, "judicial independence is [not] served by the perception of

unaccountability."[1] Decisional independence obviously does not extend to a judicial freedom to decide cases whimsically or arbitrarily, on the basis of personal preferences or antipathies. Rather, it allows judges to render impartial judgments based on law. Decisional judicial independence thus is instrumental, a means to ensure impartial justice and to effectuate the rule of law, rather than an end in itself.[2] As a further benefit, by safeguarding the rule of law, judicial independence may also enhance public confidence in the integrity of the judicial branch.

Defenders identify the main threat to decisional independence as the pressure that external forces can exert on judicial decision making. Often, this pressure involves threats to the position or pay of sitting judges—in that sense, it is tied to the individual judge's self-interest. However, the threat may be to the operation of the judiciary as a whole, in that another branch of government might refuse to provide the assistance or resources necessary for the judiciary to function effectively. For example, the legislature might refuse to fund the judiciary at even minimum levels or the executive might purposely frustrate judges' efforts to carry out their responsibilities. Judges thus have both a self-interest and an institutional interest that may be subject to external threats or reprisals.

Perhaps surprisingly, Defenders seldom inquire why these pressures on judges should succeed in changing judicial behavior. Calls for the impeachment of judges because of their rulings almost never result in removal from office, and with the exception of elections, other means of penalizing judges for their decisions have also largely failed.[3] Judicial rulings may produce threats of retribution, but the threats have usually proved empty. Beyond that, judges take an oath to administer justice impartially, without fear or favor, and this commitment should encourage them to ignore pressures to bend the law or to favor particular litigants. Certainly the pressures put on American judges pale in comparison with those visited upon judges in authoritarian systems and fledgling democracies.[4] Moreover, other officials in the United States at least on occasion take unpopular actions that could jeopardize their continuation in office, and they regularly suffer criticism that is even more severe than that visited on judges. Nevertheless, judges do perceive the pressures on them to be real, and research suggests that these pressures sometimes improperly influence judicial decisions.[5]

Complementing the decisional independence of the judiciary is *institutional independence* or autonomy. Separation-of-powers principles require recognition of the autonomy of the judicial branch as a coequal partner of government. This means that the judicial branch, like the legislative and executive branches, must have the authority to govern and manage its internal affairs, free from undue interference by the other branches of government, although subject to the scrutiny of those other branches and the general public.

Judicial Accountability

Judicial accountability imposes constraints on judges by holding them legally or politically responsible for their behavior.[6] As Ruth Grant and Robert Keohane put it, accountability "implies that some actors have the right to hold other actors to a set of standards, to judge whether they have fulfilled their responsibilities in light of these standards, and to impose sanctions if they determine that these responsibilities have not been met."[7] The assumption is that actors will anticipate the retrospective judgments of those holding them to account and act accordingly. This holding to account thus is designed not merely to correct misbehavior by individuals but also to deter wrongdoing more generally—the penalty imposed on one malefactor is meant to influence the behavior of other potential malefactors.[8] Judicial accountability therefore fits within a broader pattern in American government of holding public officials responsible in order to prevent corruption, usurpations of power, or other abuses, and in order to ensure that governmental policy reflects the values and interests of the populace. The ability to call to account and sanction behavior is as necessary in the case of judges as it is for other public officials because judges too may be tempted to abuse their power or evade their responsibilities. However, the form that this accountability takes must respect the distinctive functions that judges perform. Judicial accountability therefore should address itself to instances of wrong-doing but should not interfere with the impartial resolution of disputes or impose pressure to depart from adherence to the law. As David Frohnmayer has insisted, "The judicial process cannot operate as simply another constituency driven political arm of government."[9]

Judicial accountability focuses on three aspects. Individual judges may be held accountable for the decisions they render (*decisional accountability*). This extends not only to case outcomes but also to the grounds for judges' decisions because judges are obliged to justify their rulings on the basis of accepted standards for the interpretation and application of law. In addition, the judicial branch as a whole may be held accountable for its performance as a separate branch of government (*institutional accountability*). Among the matters subject to scrutiny under institutional accountability are the judicial branch's management of the funds appropriated to it and its use of its rule-making and disciplinary powers.[10] Thus, these first two forms of accountability correlate with the two aspects of judicial independence—decisional independence and institutional independence—identified earlier. Finally, individual judges may be held accountable for behavior, whether on or off the bench, unrelated to the merits of their decisions that "is prejudicial to the effective and expeditious administration of the business of the courts" (*behavioral accountability*).[11] In the courtroom, inappropriate behavior might include exhibiting racial or gender bias, failing to treat attorneys and witnesses with appropriate respect, engaging in *ex parte* communications, or otherwise acting in an arbitrary fashion. It might also include failures to act—for example, neglecting cases or failing to conduct court proceedings in a timely fashion. Off the bench, judicial misbehavior might involve inappropriate political activity or other conduct—violations of the law, excessive drinking or gambling, sexual improprieties, and the like—that could undermine respect for the courts.

Although there may be borderline cases, behavioral accountability seldom raises concerns about judicial independence. The same cannot be said about institutional accountability, which is inevitably in tension with the judicial branch's institutional autonomy/independence. Drawing a line can be difficult here. At what point, for example, do specificity and detail in appropriations to the judiciary interfere with its authority to allocate funds internally to ensure an effective administration of justice? Does the creation of an inspector general, who will oversee the operations of the federal courts and report to Congress, impinge upon the autonomy of the judiciary as a distinct branch of government?[12] Because these often are matters of degree rather than issues of principle, they lend themselves to the give-and-take of negotiation and are usually resolved on that basis. Matters of principle regularly arise only when one turns to decisional independence and decisional accountability.

Mechanisms for Enforcing Accountability

Tables 4.1 and 4.2 identify various formal mechanisms that American federal and state governments employ—or have employed—to enforce decisional, behavioral, and institutional accountability. Four points should be highlighted at the outset. First, formal mechanisms are not the only means for enforcing accountability. This is particularly true for behavioral accountability. Allegations of judicial misconduct may come to authorities within the judicial branch by means other than formal complaint, and informal mechanisms may be used to address the misbehavior. In fact, informal action by supervisory judges "remains the judiciary's most common response to episodes of judicial misconduct."[13] These informal mechanisms include forwarding reports of misconduct to the erring judge, the threat of formal action, persuasion, and appeals to institutional loyalty. The effectiveness of such measures depends in part on the implicit threat of formal disciplinary proceedings should the judge not respond to the informal intervention. "Indeed, it is in part because a formal disciplinary mechanism is in place that informal means of discipline are so successful."[14]

Second, whereas some forms of accountability target individual judges, others may target a multimember court or the judiciary as a whole. Threats to decisional independence typically single out a particular judge rather than a court or the judiciary as a whole, although legislators on occasion target a court or the judiciary as a whole in order to register their dissatisfaction with the rulings of particular judges. For example, Congress has used its control over the judicial budget to make known its dissatisfaction with Supreme Court rulings.[15]

Third, mechanisms designed to promote behavioral or institutional accountability can sometimes be used to retaliate against judges for their rulings. This may have occurred in the 1990s in New Hampshire. When the New Hampshire Supreme Court invalidated the state's system of school finance, its ruling aroused a strong reaction in the state legislature because it forced legislators to enact a statewide property tax in order to equalize school funding. Thus, when reports surfaced of violations of the court's recusal policy in the context of a divorce case involving a sitting justice, the legislators seized on the impropriety and initiated impeachment proceedings against Chief Justice David Brock.[16] Brock was impeached by the New Hampshire House of Representatives but was not convicted by the state Senate, although the New Hampshire Supreme Court Committee on Judicial Conduct formally admonished him.[17] The New Hampshire episode is hardly unique. Legislators in several states have threatened to reduce funding for the courts to signal their displeasure with judicial decisions, although there is little evidence that they have carried out these threats.[18]

Fourth, the tables purposely omit overturning judicial decisions via statute or constitutional amendment as a mechanism of accountability. Changing

TABLE 4.1 Mechanisms of Accountability*

Self-Enforced Accountability	Accountability to the Law
	Oath of Office
Accountability within the Judicial Branch	Appellate Review
	Judicial Disciplinary Commissions
	Judicial Performance Evaluations
Accountability of the Individual Judge to Another Branch	Impeachment
	Removal by Address
	Removal upon Criminal Conviction
	Reappointment of Incumbents
Accountability of the Court to Another Branch	Budgetary Appropriations
	Creating or Eliminating or Replacing Courts
	Jurisdiction Stripping
	Program Oversight
	Selection of Judges in the Absence of Incumbents
Accountability of the Individual Judge to the Populace	Voting on Incumbents
	Recall of Judges
Accountability of the Court to the Populace	Selection of Judges in the Absence of Incumbents

* Some weapons for enforcing accountability—for example, voting on incumbents—may be in the hands of another branch of government or of the populace, depending on the law within the political unit.

the law does not hold judges accountable; it merely ensures that when future judges "say what the law is," they arrive at a different result. The relevant concern is judicial independence, not judicial supremacy, although the two may sometimes be confused in popular debate and even in judicial opinions.[19] Thus, when voters in California adopted an initiative amendment to overturn the California Supreme Court's ruling on same-sex marriage, they were not threatening judicial independence because the justices were neither pressured to change their interpretation of the state constitution nor penalized for that interpretation.[20] Although lawmakers may initiate legal changes because they believe that a court has misinterpreted or misapplied the law, legal changes may also reflect a view that law needs to be revised, regardless of whether it was correctly interpreted by the court.[21]

TABLE 4.2 Availability of Accountability Mechanisms

Mechanism	Target	Type of Accountability	Where Found
Accountability to the Law	Judge	Decisional	FS1
Oath of Office	Judge	Decisional/ Behavioral	FS1
Appellate Review	Court/Judge	Decisional	FS1
Judicial Disciplinary Commissions	Judge	Behavioral	FS1
Judicial Performance Evaluations	Judge	Behavioral	S2
Impeachment	Judge	Behavioral	FS1
Removal by Address	Judge	Decisional/ Behavioral	S2
Removal upon Criminal Conviction	Judge	Behavioral	S2
Voting on Incumbents	Judge	Decisional/ Behavioral	S2
Budgetary Accountability	Judicial branch	Institutional	FS1
Creating/Eliminating/ Replacing Courts	Court/Judicial branch	Decisional/Institutional	S2
Jurisdiction Stripping	Court	Decisional	FS2
Program Oversight	Judicial branch	Institutional	FS1
Selection of Judges in the Absence of Incumbents	Court	Decisional/Behavioral	FS1
Recall of Judges	Judge	Decisional/Behavioral	S2

Key: FS = federal and state courts; S1 = all state courts; S2 = some state courts.

Let us elaborate briefly on the mechanisms for enforcing accountability identified in the tables, before turning to a more detailed discussion of the Defender and Basher perspectives.

Self-Enforced Accountability

Both accountability to the law and the judicial oath of office assume that legal obligations bind judges, even in the absence of external enforcement, and judges regularly testify to their effect. However, whether a sense of obligation to the law binds judges, or equally binds all judges, or binds judges in all cases, is disputed. Moreover, at most the mechanisms of self-enforced accountability only guard against deliberate evasions of judicial responsibilities. If judges incorrectly believe that they are acting in accordance with the law, these forms of accountability have no effect. As noted in Chapter 2, early in the twentieth century a few states sought to ensure fidelity to the law in constitutional cases by requiring an extraordinary majority in order to invalidate a law. Underlying this requirement was the assumption that unless almost all judges agreed that a law violated the constitution, either the meaning of the constitution was unclear or judges were not adhering to that meaning, and in neither instance should the will of the people's representatives be struck down.

Intrabranch Accountability

The judicial branch can institute its own measures for enforcing behavioral accountability. Some state judiciaries use judicial performance evaluations to solicit feedback from attorneys, jurors, and members of the public, and these surveys inform individual judges and their superiors of problems that need to be addressed. Such surveys are particularly useful in the case of trial judges, who regularly interact with the public.

The responsibility for ensuring behavioral accountability may also be delegated to the judiciary by statute or by constitutional provision. Within the federal government, the movement over time has been from congressional supervision of the federal courts to its providing the tools for intrabranch governance and supervision.[22] Steps along this same path have been taken in the states, with the creation of administrative offices of the courts and of judicial disciplinary commissions to monitor judges' nondecisional behavior. These disciplinary commissions investigate, prosecute, and adjudicate allegations of judicial misconduct. As one expert has noted, "It is striking to note how *little* threat to independence is implicit in most instances that seem to call for accountability."[23] As with removal by address (discussed in Chapter 1), the commissions can take account of misconduct that does not rise to the level of an impeachable offense, but unlike under removal by address, the commission ensures due process for the accused judge, requiring a specification of charges and an opportunity for the judge to respond to them. In contrast to removal by address or impeachment, judicial disciplinary commissions employ a range of sanctions for enforcing accountability beyond mere removal from office, such as private reprimands, public reprimands, and suspension from office. This enables them to address a wider range of misconduct, with punishments proportionate to the offense. Also unlike removal by address or impeachment, the body that is enforcing behavioral norms is situated within the judicial branch rather than in a coordinate branch, thus obviating concerns about institutional independence.

Appellate review enforces decisional accountability within the judicial branch through the correction of legal error by lower courts. This form of accountability operates at the level of the court, not the individual judge; however, since appellate courts are often reviewing the rulings of a trial judge, in practice they may be one and the same thing. The idea of a judicial error in interpretation implies that the law can—or should—be read only in one way or, at least, that there is a single authoritative reading. The appellate court is deemed correct in its interpretation because its rulings are more authoritative, given the hierarchical structure of the court system. It may also be that the greater authority of the appellate court is rooted in a presumption that it is more expert in its judgment. We shall have much more to say about appellate review shortly.

Accountability of the Individual Judge to Another Branch

Both federal and state constitutions provide for the impeachment of judges. Some states also authorize removal by address, and others either by constitutional mandate or statute require removal from office when a judge is convicted of a serious crime. Impeachment enforces accountability on the individual judge for his or her behavior. This will most likely be nondecisional behavior, such as corruption or other malfeasance because the prevailing norms of judicial independence discourage the use of impeachment to punish judges for the substance of their rulings. However, at both the federal and state levels, these norms developed only gradually, and even today legislators may threaten impeachment when they disagree with court rulings.[24] Moreover, as the dispute in New Hampshire involving Chief Justice Brock illustrated, the line between decisional and nondecisional behavior can become (sometimes purposely) blurred. Nonetheless, as even Defenders note, "the threat posed by idle calls for impeachment should not be overstated. No federal judge has ever been removed from office for rendering an unpopular decision."[25]

Removal by address enforces accountability on individual judges for their behavior, authorizing the governor to remove them upon address by two-thirds of the state legislature, with the gubernatorial role typically more ministerial than discretionary. Provisions for removal by address were included in early state constitutions to address conduct that did not rise to the level of an impeachable offense but nonetheless warranted removal. The "address did not have to allege willful or criminal misconduct. It needed only a favorable vote by both houses, not an investigation or trial."[26] Thus, removal by address came quite close to service during the pleasure of the legislature, although the guarantee of tenure during "good behavior" did imply that some misconduct had to be alleged. Although this mechanism has fallen out of fashion, it remains in several state constitutions.

Finally, whereas Article III federal judges serve during good behavior, few state judges do.[27] Although most states use retention or contested elections to determine whether incumbents should continue in office, some assign reappointment authority to those responsible for the initial appointment—the governor, the legislature, or both. Control over whether to reappoint enforces accountability on the *individual judge* for his or her behavior, whether decisional or nondecisional. For trial courts, this control is more likely to be related to nondecisional behavior, both because trial judges are in contact with members of the public on a regular basis and because decisional irregularities can be corrected via appellate review. For appellate courts, decisional as well as nondecisional behavior may provide a basis for nonreappointment.

Accountability of the Court(s) to Another Branch

Legislatures ensure the institutional accountability of the judicial branch through their control over court budgets and through their oversight over court operations and programs. They control the number of judgeships, the salaries of judges, and to some extent the structure of the court system. For example, the US Constitution creates the US Supreme Court but authorizes Congress to create and empower—and therefore to eliminate or replace—all other federal courts. Some state constitutions, such as Maine's, follow this federal model by entrenching only a single court in the state constitution. But most state constitutions establish various trial and appellate courts, although they vary as to whether the state legislature can add other courts.

Legislatures can use their power to eliminate or replace courts to enforce accountability at the level of the court, although of course individual judges are displaced when the legislature abolishes a court. The abolition of judgeships may be final, as when Congress in 1802 abolished the circuit judgeships after Thomas Jefferson's inauguration, or it may be a prelude to creation of a new court with the same jurisdiction, as when Kentucky in 1823 eliminated the Court of Appeals and replaced it with the Supreme Court. The elimination or replacement of courts may be motivated by disagreement with decisions, as in the Kentucky case, or by concern about the partisan complexion of the court, as in the Jeffersonian assault on the circuit courts. It may also occur as part of a general reform of the state's court system unrelated to account-ability concerns—for example, a desire to reduce costs in the administration of justice—as occurred when New Jersey in 1978 abolished its county courts.

Complementing legislative control over the structure of the court system is control over the jurisdiction of the courts. The US Constitution grants Congress broad authority here, as the power to create inferior courts includes the power to define their jurisdictions. The Constitution prescribes the original and appellate jurisdiction of the Supreme Court, but its appellate jurisdiction is subject to "such exceptions, and under such regulations as the Congress shall make."[28] Most state constitutions narrow the legislature's authority by prescribing in detail the jurisdiction of various courts, and most define appellate jurisdiction to at least some extent. Like the power to create or abolish courts, control over jurisdiction can serve ends unrelated to accountability. However, legislators can use their control over jurisdiction to deal with disfavored decisions or the prospect of disfavored decisions by prohibiting courts from ruling on cases in a particular area. This somewhat resembles overruling judicial decisions by statute or amendment, in that judges are not directly held accountable for their decisions.

Accountability of Individual Judges or the Judiciary to the Populace

"Elections have been a key component of Anglo-American conceptions of public accountability ever since the founding of the American constitution."[29] Judges who are elected to office periodically stand for reelection, and those selected via merit selection are subject to retention elections. Roughly 89 percent of state judges stand for election at some point in their careers.[30]

Voting on incumbents enforces accountability on the *individual judge* for his or her behavior, both decisional and nondecisional.[31] The same holds true for accountability to the populace as to another branch. For judges on trial courts, accountability is more likely related to nondecisional behavior, both because trial judges are in contact with members of the public on a regular basis and because decisional irregularities can be corrected via appellate review. For judges on appellate courts, decisional behavior is more often the focus.

Voting in the absence of incumbents enforces accountability at the level of the court, not the individual judge. This is a crucial but often overlooked distinction. Discussions of decisional independence and accountability on appellate courts typically ignore the implications of having multimember courts, but in considering judicial independence, one should think in disaggregated terms. What one is seeking is that individual judges are free from external pressures that interfere with their impartial decision making. In seeking judicial accountability, however, it makes more sense to think of a court as a whole, as an aggregate. For on multimember courts, no single judge can determine the outcome, and it is the outcome, not the vote of the individual judge, that is key. Thus, a system of judicial selection and tenure that maximizes the opportunity for each individual judge to decide without fear or favor is crucial, but it is less important that the court as a whole be free to pursue whatever legal course it deems best.

Voters can indicate their verdict on the overall direction of a court by the sort of judicial candidate they choose when a vacancy occurs. In an appointive system, they can also do so in electing those who will appoint judges, particularly when those appointing authorities—presidents or governors—have made the decisions of a court a major campaign issue, as did Richard Nixon in 1968 and George W. Bush in 2000 and 2004.[32] Appointing authorities can indicate their own views of the overall direction of the court by those they nominate to fill vacancies. These retrospective judgments on the work of a court in no way interfere with judicial independence, as individual judges remain free to decide as they believe the law requires. The aim is judicial independence, not judicial supremacy.

The recall enforces accountability on the individual judge for either decisional or nondecisional behavior. The recall originated in the late nineteenth century and now exists in nineteen states, although only ten authorize the recall of judges.[33] In theory, long terms of office combined with the recall might serve as an alternative to short judicial terms and frequent elections. In practice states rarely employ the recall against judges, and when they do, it has almost always been for egregious behavioral lapses rather than for judicial rulings.

Defenders on Judicial Accountability

Insofar as Defenders favor decisional accountability for judges, they prefer that the accountability be self-imposed or that it remain within the judicial branch (appellate review). The same holds true for behavioral accountability and institutional accountability: Defenders prefer judicial disciplinary

procedures over impeachment or removal by address, and they have ada-
mantly opposed a proposal that an inspector general be appointed to report
to Congress on the federal courts.

Accountability to the Law

Defenders emphasize accountability to the law as fundamental to decisional
accountability. Yet accountability to the law is not really accountability at all;
it is merely a reformulation of the rule of law, the idea that the obligation to
decide according to law eliminates—or at least constrains and channels—the
exercise of choice by judges. Accountability to the law fails as true accountability because implicit in the very idea of accountability is the notion of
answer-giving, of providing an account of oneself. This in turn implies that
there must be *someone* to whom the account is given, by whom one is held
accountable. The fact that appellate judges write opinions explaining their
decisions is insufficient because there is no person or institution that can
hold the judge to account—in H. L. Mencken's memorable phrase, "a judge
is a law student who marks his own examination papers."[34] Defenders insist
that judges will enforce that standard against themselves, that their professional training and the obligations of office will lead them to decide cases in
accordance with their understanding of what the law requires, rather than
on the basis of their personal preferences, their ideological commitments,
or other nonlegal factors.[35] As a description of judges' self-understanding,
this may be accurate, although an impressive body of social science research
casts doubt on the adequacy of that self-understanding. Undoubtedly, many
judges recognize an obligation to adhere to the law, an obligation fortified
by their oath of office, and many strive to behave accordingly, but that is
better understood as self-restraint or as professionalism rather than as
accountability.

Moreover, even striving to decide according to law does not mean that
judges will always succeed—failures to achieve impartiality or fidelity to the
law need not be deliberate. And should a judge depart from the requirements
of the rule of law, whether from error or by design, accountability to the law
affords no mechanism for punishing or correcting the departure. Other public officials take oaths of office, yet this does not prevent us from devising
mechanisms for holding them accountable. If this is true, it is hard to see why
one would rely on the good faith of judges any more than on the good faith of
presidents or members of Congress.[36]

There are additional problems as well. In championing accountability to the law, Defenders typically rely on an understanding of law that cannot withstand critical scrutiny. The idea of accountability to the law, at least as presented by most Defenders, suggests that the law is settled and knowable, not unclear or contingent, and that it precludes the exercise of discretion or judicial will. One is unfortunately reminded of Justice Owen Roberts's oft-derided claim in *United States v. Butler* (1936): "When an act of Congress is appropriately challenged in the courts . . . the judicial branch of the Government has only one duty—to lay the article of the Constitution which is invoked beside the statute which is challenged and to decide whether the latter squares with the former."[37] Put differently, it appears that underlying the notion of accountability to the law is the assumption that the law supplies a single right answer. For if judges can decide a case for either plaintiff or defendant, prosecutor or defendant, and still claim fidelity to the law, then it is hard to see how accountability to the law provides a meaningful constraint. Yet the understanding of law as settled and accessible is at odds with legal scholarship over the last century. Legal Realism revealed the inevitability of judicial discretion and policy-making; political science research on judicial behavior documented the connection between judicial attitudes and case outcomes; recent legal theory has emphasized the indeterminacy of law and the necessity of choice; and political science has shown how strategic considerations and nonideological personal goals affect the exercise of that choice.[38] Although most legal scholars concede that some interpretations of the law are indisputably wrong, arguments for such interpretations are seldom before the bench. Rather, both sides in a dispute typically can advance plausible legal arguments for their positions, and the judge is therefore obliged to *choose* between those positions. Yet if legal indeterminacy permits judges to exercise discretion in at least some cases, then the notion that they are accountable to the law seems to break down. At a minimum, a defensible version of accountability to the law must incorporate a considerably more sophisticated understanding of judicial decision making than Defenders currently advance.[39]

From a somewhat different angle, accountability to the law implies rule-bound behavior: the rule of law requires a law of rules in Justice Antonin Scalia's felicitous phrase. If one examines discussions of accountability outside the judicial context, however, the emphasis on rule-bound behavior becomes more problematic. Thus, in the public administration literature, the notion of a Weberian bureaucracy of rule-bound administrators has given way to more explicit recognition of the necessity and desirability of choice by civil servants.[40] Similarly within the judicial sphere, legal scholars have recognized that not all judicial behavior is rule-bound. This need not be a matter of judicial choice: even when there are rules or norms, as Ruth Gavison has noted, "the more general and abstract the norm is, the greater the need for creativity in judicial application."[41] State judges elaborate the common law, and many scholars argue that judges should contribute to evolution of the law in other areas as well, in their interpretation of constitutions and even in their interpretation of statutes.[42] Moreover, judges regularly confront cases of first impression, in which the law is unclear or indeterminate. Finally, law may be couched in broad standards rather than rules, giving judges considerable opportunity to create legal doctrine that will guide current and future decision making.[43] The question for judges, as for administrators involved in the interpretation and application of law, may not be whether discretion will be exercised but how it can be channeled and guided so as to serve the public good.

Accountability via Appellate Review

Defenders also claim that appellate review enforces decisional accountability. Appellate review resembles accountability to the law in that the standard for accountability is the same—namely, fidelity to the law—and judges remain insulated from pressures coming from other branches or the general public. However, this is a more promising form of accountability. Judges are held accountable by other judges, so there are established procedures for enforcing accountability and specific persons charged with reviewing lower-court decisions and enforcing fidelity to law. Moreover, the problem of legal indeterminacy is reduced because there is a single authoritative version of the law, namely, that propounded by the appellate court, although the law thus propounded may be unclear or difficult in application.

Accountability via appellate review is attractive in several respects. First, it is most likely to come into play in situations in which oversight of judicial rulings is appropriate or necessary. Where the law is clear or where little is at stake, the losing litigant is unlikely to appeal, so the cases in which accountability is enforced are more often those in which more is at stake or the law is unclear. As John Ferejohn and Larry Kramer have noted, "The more controversial the decision, the likelier it is that a great amount of judicial review will follow," and hence (one would assume) the greater likelihood that the eventual outcome would reflect the law rather than idiosyncratic or ideological judgment. Thus, "appeals reduce the risk posed by wayward judges by ensuring that multiple judicial voices are heard before any particular judgment becomes final": they lessen the damage a single judge can do.[44]

Second, those holding judges accountable are themselves legal professionals, who therefore presumably have the expertise necessary to assess judicial rulings according to the standards that should govern them and engage in error correction. Judges recognize the legitimacy of those above them in the legal hierarchy passing judgment on their work, whether they agree with the appellate court's ruling, and acknowledge their obligation to conform to the higher court's rulings. As a Wisconsin Supreme Court justice once put it, "We are bound by the results and interpretations . . . in these high court rulings. Ours not to reason why; ours but to review and apply."[45]

Third, accountability via appellate review is corrective but not punitive. If the ruling of a lower-court judge is reversed, the appellate court explains the basis for the reversal, thereby enabling the judge who is reversed—and other judges as well—to avoid the same error (and reversal) in the future. Doubtless, lower-court judges do not enjoy having their rulings reversed, but reversal does not threaten the judge's position or salary. Moreover, the correction is typically administered without invective, in contrast to many popular attacks on courts and judges. Instead of imputing bad faith to the judge being reversed, the appellate court usually presumes in its opinion that the error demanding reversal was an honest one, even when there might be reason to suspect otherwise. From the Defender perspective, this is all to the good: "If the objective is to preserve the rule of law as best we can, it would seem that the dichotomy between honest and dishonest error needs to be preserved, and that in the case of honest error, accountability should be limited to corrective measures and exclude punitive ones."[46]

Fourth, although accountability via appellate review is public, in that appellate decisions are published, it is typically of low visibility, so that judges who are reversed are not subjected to broader public condemnation. Accountability via appellate review, like the accountability of officials within a bureaucracy, is largely invisible.

Finally, there is reason to believe that appellate review yields better decisions. In some instances, errors at trial may reflect the charged environment in which the trial is conducted, but appellate courts are distanced from that environment and better able to take a balanced view. Having a multimember court also reduces the likelihood that rulings will reflect personal idiosyncrasy. Moreover, when multiple interpreters reach the same outcome in a case, this increases confidence that the result is rooted in law rather than will.[47] Indeed, the prospect of appellate review, even without its exercise, may improve the quality of judicial rulings. Insofar as judges recognize that their rulings are subject to review, they may strive to avoid rulings that are likely to be overturned. Thus, just as congressional oversight need not always be exercised in order to keep administrators in line, so also the threat of appellate review may be enough to promote adherence to the law.

Despite these advantages, which are real and important, appellate review is not fully adequate for enforcing judicial accountability. For one thing, relatively few judicial decisions undergo appellate review. In part, this reflects the limited resources of time and energy available for overseeing the decisions of lower courts. Take, for example, the review conducted by courts of last resort. In its 2008 term, the US Supreme Court received more than seventy-five hundred petitions for certiorari but decided only 78 cases with full opinions. During that same period, federal courts of appeals decided almost 30,000 cases on the merits, so less than 1 percent was reviewed by the Supreme Court.[48] Precise figures are unavailable for state courts, but the available data are suggestive. During 2007, state appellate courts decided more than 255,000 cases.[49] Only a miniscule percentage of rulings by state intermediate courts of appeals were reviewed by state supreme courts, and an even smaller percentage of state supreme court rulings scrutinized by the Supreme Court. These data thus raise questions about how effective the threat of reversal really is, about whether the extremely unlikely prospect of appellate review is sufficient to constrain lower-court judges. Some commentators have also suggested that the sting of reversal is overrated. "Judges who concur with the reviewing court's perspective will strive to follow its lead even in the absence of review, but those who believe that their reviewing court's judges are in error will generally not be shamed by review."[50] Indeed, they may continue to press their own interpretation of the law, knowing that the likelihood of review and reversal is negligible.

One must also remember that not all judicial rulings are subject to appellate review. This holds true for both trial and appellate court rulings. The unjustified acquittal of a defendant in a criminal trial is not subject to appellate review because no person can be tried twice for the same offense. When the parties to a case arrive at a settlement that is endorsed by a trial judge, that settlement is typically not subject to appellate review because there may be no party to challenge the outcome. Even when appellate review does occur, appellate courts are generally bound by the factual determinations made at the trial level.[51]

Even less accountability exists for appellate court rulings. State supreme court rulings are not susceptible to federal review if they rest on "adequate and independent state grounds."[52] Thus, state rulings based on state statutes, the common law, or state constitutions are altogether immune from federal judicial scrutiny, unless a "federal question" is raised or unless the case falls within the federal courts' diversity jurisdiction. This is important because in recent decades state supreme courts have based many of their most controversial rulings on state constitutions and state declarations of rights. Other high-profile rulings have been rooted in the common law. Similarly, there is no way to appeal rulings of the US Supreme Court with which one disagrees. Thus, for the decisions that most exercise Bashers, rulings by the US Supreme Court or by its state counterparts, appellate review seldom ensures accountability, and these rulings establish the precedents upon which lower courts will rely.

Accountability via Elections

Defenders oppose judicial elections as a mechanism for enforcing account-ability, and since the early twentieth century, they have coalesced behind efforts to replace competitive elections with merit selection. Indeed, the reform movement's support for even the retention elections that are part of merit selection has been begrudging at best.[53] Thus the American Bar Asso-ciation's Commission on the 21st Century Judiciary recently concluded that "the preferred system of state court judicial selection is a commission-based appointive system" and that judges, once appointed, "should not be subject to reselection processes."[54] We examine judicial elections in detail in Chapter 5, but it is worth noting here that many of the concerns voiced by Defenders do not involve decisional independence. Defenders contend that because voters lack the knowledge to choose wisely, the overall quality of the judiciary will suffer, even if the judges selected are independent. In addition, they fear that judicial elections undermine popular respect for the judiciary.[55] The funding of campaigns creates the appearance that justice is for sale, because it appears that special interests use campaign contributions to secure special treat-ment in the courts. In addition, campaigns that sacrifice civility and trade in personal attacks may sap public confidence in the judiciary, regardless of who wins. Furthermore, campaigns encourage judicial candidates to portray themselves in ways—for example, tough on crime—that appear to undermine judicial impartiality. These may be legitimate concerns, but they have little direct relationship to decisional independence.

Criticism of Judges and Judicial Independence

Defenders are concerned not only with efforts to remove judges but also with harsh criticism of sitting judges by officials and members of the general public.[56] This too, it is claimed, threatens judicial independence. While conceding that judges are not above criticism, Defenders seek to distinguish between "fair" and "unfair" criticism, between legitimate criticism and illegitimate "judge-bashing" and "attacks on the judiciary."[57] "Irresponsible criticism," Defenders insist, does not merely injure its target, it also encourages "unfounded cynicism and reduces respect for the judiciary."[58] Indeed, they fear that the relentless drumbeat of criticism in recent years has created the impression, by repetition rather than by persuasion, that courts are no different than other political institutions. This in turn has eroded the diffuse support necessary to maintain public acceptance of—or at least acquiescence in—judicial rulings with which it disagrees. If, as Alexis de Tocqueville maintained, the power of the courts in America ultimately depends on public opinion, then courts need to cultivate that opinion, but attacks on the courts serve to undermine it.[59]

One may well question whether attacks on the courts have quite the effect that Defenders claim. The US Supreme Court's ruling on *Bush v. Gore*, for example, provoked bitter criticism of the justices, but these attacks have had no appreciable long-term effect on overall support for the Supreme Court.[60] In fact, courts generally rank higher than other institutions in public estimation.[61] Moreover, insofar as one does find diminished respect for the courts, an issue of causality remains. Is the decline in support caused by highly publicized judicial rulings on controversial issues such as abortion, same-sex marriage, and the pledge of allegiance, or is it caused by unfair criticism of the courts? As former justice Hans Linde, a strong advocate of judicial independence, has acknowledged, "Courts give up their defense against the charge that law is nothing more than politics when they explain their decisions as a choice of social policy with little effort to attribute that choice to any law."[62]

Even if attacks on the courts do undermine their legitimacy, Defenders acknowledge that any attempt to police irresponsible criticism would run afoul of the American commitment to public scrutiny of the actions of government—of all government institutions. Judges cannot claim a pass on such scrutiny, merely because vigorous criticism might jeopardize support for the judiciary. It may be that other officials who are attacked are free to respond to criticism of their actions, whereas the canons of judicial ethics prohibit judges from doing so. These regulations do restrict judges' ability to comment publicly on the decisions they have reached, although Canon 5A(3)(e) does permit judicial candidates to "respond to personal attacks or attacks on the candidate's record." Furthermore, as a result of *Republican Party of Minnesota v. White* (2002), judges have the opportunity to present their judicial philosophy and their personal views in campaigns. Judges can also use election campaigns to defend the importance of judicial independence, and as Chief Justice Shirley Abrahamson of Wisconsin (among others) has suggested, this can be quite an effective stratagem.[63] Finally, what judges cannot say, their allies can. With the American Bar Association and its local chapters, national court-friendly organizations such as the American Judicature Society, and proponents of the particular decisions that are under attack, there are plenty of potential spokespeople for judges.[64] Indeed, the Constitution Project's Task Force on the Distinction between Criticism and Intimidation of Judges recommended the creation of state and local coalitions to respond to unfair criticism of judges.[65] One cannot guarantee the emergence of such groups, but it does allay the concern that judges are unable to defend themselves.

A further problem concerns the putative distinction between fair and unfair criticism. No one likes to be criticized, and the harsher the criticism, the greater the resentment. But, as Monroe Freedman has suggested, "much of the judicial hand-wringing about criticism of judges has more to do with judicial vanity than judicial independence."[66] Certainly, on a practical level, there is never likely to be a consensus on the line between fair and unfair criticism. One Defender NGO proposed that "when public discourse on any court decision swerves from issues to demagoguery, then the line [on inappropriate criticism] has been crossed." More specifically, it condemned "attacks that imply or outright state that a judge has made a ruling merely to follow a political agenda," because they "lower public trust in the fairness and impartiality of our courts."[67] Yet attributions of inappropriate motives are a staple of political discourse, and in some instances they might even be accurate. Moreover, any attempt to limit allegedly unfair criticism of government officials and government action is incompatible with our "profound national commitment to the principle that debate on public issues should be uninhibited, robust, and wide-open, and that it may well include vehement, caustic, and sometimes unpleasantly sharp attacks on government and public officials."[68] This may be particularly true in the case of officials who are not elected or who enjoy lifetime or extended tenure, as the inability to exact electoral retribution makes it all the most important that their behavior be scrutinized for usurpations of power or derelictions of duty. Of course, reasonable people might well disagree as to whether such abuses have occurred, but the opportunity to debate this is at the heart of self-government. Indeed, our system does not permit government—or any other entity—to censor comments about officials or public policy merely because they are deemed mistaken, or even vindictive. Vigorous, even intemperate, criticism is fundamental to popular government. To quote once again from Justice Brennan's opinion in *New York Times v. Sullivan*, "Criticism of official conduct does not lose its constitutional protection merely because it is effective criticism and hence diminishes official reputations."[69]

Bashers on Judicial Accountability

The Basher perspective is far more difficult to analyze than the Defender perspective because Bashers have focused on denouncing instances of alleged judicial misbehavior rather than on elaborating a detailed vision of what good judicial behavior entails. In addition, Bashers lack an institutional base: most Basher organizations have been state-level ad hoc operations, formed to address particular perceived abuses and disappearing thereafter. Democracy Rising Pennsylvania, formed to unseat incumbent justices in 2005, and JAIL4Judges, formed in South Dakota to support a 2006 initiative to eliminate judicial immunity, typify the sort of ephemeral political action groups that dominate the Basher cause. Political figures and legal popularizers have typically served as the leading spokespeople in the Basher cause, so political rhetoric has often substituted for sustained analysis. There is no Basher equivalent to the American Bar Association or the American Judicature Society, addressing issues of judicial independence and judicial accountability on a sustained basis. Perhaps the closest equivalent is the Landmark Legal Foundation, whose president Mark Levin, formerly chief of staff to Attorney General

Edwin Meese, is a talk-radio host. There has likewise until recently been virtually no Basher presence in the scholarly debates on judicial independence and accountability and no body of literature elaborating the Basher perspective. In the absence of alternative sources, we rely in this chapter primarily on Mark Levin's best-selling *Men in Black*, which—although illustrative of the Basher perspective—is focused on the US Supreme Court and does not systematically address judicial independence and accountability.

Public Opinion and Judicial Rulings

Some Bashers, particularly those who focus on state courts, insist that judges should be denied reelection for rulings that conflict with popular sentiments and overturn expressions of the people's will. Condemnations of judicial interference with the people's will are particularly prominent in those states in which judges have struck down popular referenda or initiatives. Thus a Montana antitax activist characterized the state supreme court as "seven black-robed terrorists" who had "overturned the wishes of 176,000 voters."[70] The assumption appears to be that in a system dedicated to popular rule, judges should not interfere with direct expressions of the popular will.

Taken literally, this understanding of democratic government is untenable. The idea of popular sovereignty does not require that judges decide cases on the basis of popular prejudices or public opinion. The people of the various states, in adopting their state constitutions, chose to differentiate functions, and they mandated that judges serve as more than mere mirrors of public opinion, so when they do so, they are conforming to popular wishes, not frustrating them. Some state constitutions expressly authorize judges to strike down popular enactments that conflict with the constitution, eliminating whatever taint of illegitimacy might attach to the power of judicial review. Others include provisions—for example, that initiatives be confined to a single subject—that imply enforceable limits on the popular will. And even in states that do not expressly authorize judicial review, long unchallenged practice has confirmed its legitimacy. Furthermore, state constitutions indicate that the role of judges in the administration of justice is not a representative one.[71] As confirmed by their oaths of office, which are oftentimes contained within the constitution itself, judges are obliged to decide cases on the basis of the law and the facts, not on the basis of what is politic or popular. Although there might be a basis for giving a presumption of constitutionality to popular enactments, it is hard to square the support of some Bashers for judicial subservience to public opinion with judicial independence or, indeed, with the idea of fidelity to the law.

Comparison with the jury helps to clarify the point. Trial by jury is central to ensuring popular participation in the administration of justice, but this popular participation is channeled rather than free-wheeling. Jurors are not instructed to decide based on their likes and dislikes; rather, they take an oath to decide based on the facts and the law, to deliberate and to exercise judgment. They of course do not always succeed in this, and their rulings are not above criticism. Yet popular criticism of jury decisions is typically limited to the outcome of the individual case, not to the jury system as a whole, to how jurors exercised their responsibilities in the particular case rather than to the character of those responsibilities. The same should apply to judges as well.

The Rule of Law

Because both Defenders and Bashers claim to champion the rule of law, their positions share certain commonalities. Both acknowledge that judges should not be punished for following the law—if one is dissatisfied with outcomes when judges follow the law, the solution is to change the law, not the judges. Both further concur that appellate review should be available to ensure that legal errors are corrected and justice done in individual cases. Finally, both agree that judges who refuse to follow the law should be held accountable for their actions.

The "refuse" is crucial here. Defenders insist that judges should not be punished for good-faith mistakes in their interpretation of the law.[72] If judges were removed every time they made a mistake, soon there would be no more judges and no one willing to serve on the bench. Defenders also assume that the vast majority of judicial departures from the law involve honest mistakes. The law may be unclear or in flux, or a case may raise novel questions for which legal guidance is limited, or other problems may frustrate honest efforts to follow the law. Thus, when it is claimed that judges have failed to adhere to the law, Defenders believe that the presumption should be that this was the result of honest mistake, and the burden should be on those challenging this presumption to present direct evidence of intentional misbehavior.[73]

Bashers disagree. When judges depart from what the law requires ("judicial legislation"), Bashers insist that they typically do so intentionally ("judicial activism"). In attributing bad faith to judges, Bashers imply that the law is clear and knowable. For example, Levin in *Men in Black* insists that judges should be bound by the "plain language of the Constitution" and "the plain meaning of the law."[74] The more difficult one sees the task of legal interpretation, the more inclined one is to view errors in interpretation as mistakes. Conversely, the clearer the law is, the more likely it is that judicial willfulness explains departures from the law. Like the Legal Realists, Bashers acknowledge the prevalence of judicial choice, but unlike the Realists, they deny that this is an inevitable part of judging. There are right answers to legal questions, and conscientious judges can (rather easily) discover them, so their failure to do so is itself indicative of bad intention. Indeed, were there not right answers, Bashers would lack a legal basis for criticizing disfavored judicial rulings as illegitimate. For Bashers, then, the culprit is judicial manipulation of legal materials to achieve predetermined results, not legal indeterminacy. Thus, Levin attributes disfavored judicial rulings involving the Equal Protection Clause to "the Supreme Court tak[ing] the *clear language* of the Fourteenth Amendment and twist[ing] it like a pretzel."[75]

The Basher perspective thus suffers from the same failure to acknowledge jurisprudential complexity that mars the Defender perspective. In fact, the Basher failure is even more complete. Whereas Defenders insist that judges' special expertise in the law, developed through specialized training and years of legal practice, equips them to discern what the law requires, Bashers imply that such background is not essential. Even public officials and ordinary citizens without legal training can readily detect when judicial rulings are not faithful to the law and can enforce accountability to the law. Otherwise they would not be qualified to determine when judges are misbehaving and to hold them accountable by impeaching them or denying them reelection.

For many Bashers, the analysis—problematic though it is—stops there. However, at least some Bashers recognize that not all law is immediately clear, that judicial interpretation of the law is a necessity rather than a choice. This admission undoubtedly complicates the task of detecting and combating judicial willfulness. The Bashers' preferred solution is to constrain judges by designating a single approach, variously described as either originalism or textualism, as the only valid approach to interpretation of the law in general and of constitutions in particular. Reliance on a single interpretive approach, Bashers argue, prevents judges from switching among approaches in order to achieve their desired results, or at least makes it easier to detect whether judges are remaining faithful to the law or are using it to disguise the pursuit of their personal preferences. Beyond that, reliance on text and history better comports with the idea of law, which implies a fixed written standard for the resolution of disputes. "Too many judges," Levin maintains, "consider the Constitution a document of broad principles and concepts, one that empowers them to substitute their personal beliefs, values, and policies for those enumerated in the Constitution."[76] Moreover, the legal doctrines these judges develop to give specificity to these "broad principles"—Levin in particular mentions "implicit in the concept of ordered liberty" and "deeply rooted in this Nation's history and tradition"—are themselves "mere window dressing," because they can be manipulated to achieve whatever outcome a judge desires.[77] Finally, reliance on text and history generally leads to support for long-established practices and minimizes opportunities for judicial innovation. As the extended jurisprudential debates on originalism and textualism attest, the viability and desirability of the Basher solution is hotly contested.

Levin insists that judicial adherence to originalism does not preclude judicial invalidation of statutes—it is judicial legislation, not judicial review, that is the problem.[78] Indeed, he identifies several cases in which the Supreme Court should have struck down laws—*Plessy v. Ferguson*, *Wickard v. Filburn*, and *Kelo v. City of New London* among them—but failed to do so. Nevertheless, given the "relentlessly power-hunger judiciary," he cautions that judges should only strike down laws that are plainly unconstitutional, and he would hold accountable those who engage in "social engineering."[79] However, judges who seek to adhere to Levin's standard of the clear mistake may find it difficult to apply. For example, whatever one's ultimate view of its constitutionality, few legal scholars would conclude, as Levin does, that the McCain-Feingold Act is "obviously unconstitutional."[80]

The Basher endorsement of originalism and textualism is of course a popularized version of the jurisprudential approach espoused by Justices Antonin Scalia and Clarence Thomas and by conservative constitutional scholars who champion a jurisprudence of original meaning.[81] What may be less obvious is its connection to the accountability to the law proposed by prominent Defenders. These justices and scholars accept the notion that fidelity to the law is both possible and desirable and that accountability to the law is effectual in curbing judicial willfulness. Because they are concerned with jurisprudence rather than with independence and accountability, those who espouse textualism and/or original meaning typically do not propose alternative mechanisms for ensuring judicial fidelity to the law. Nor do their allies. Bashers may rage about judicial legislation, but they have few solutions to offer for the problem other than better judges.

Enforcing Accountability

The limited terms of most state judges mean that Bashers concerned about state judicial activism can enforce accountability through the reselection or nonreselection of individual judges. There is, perhaps surprisingly, some agreement between Defenders and Bashers even here. Both acknowledge that holding judges accountable for their *overall record* does not threaten judicial independence, particularly when that record indicates that the judge either does not understand the law or refuses to follow it. Chief Justice Rose Bird of California is the acknowledged poster child for the problem of judicial defiance of the law. Following a constitutional amendment that reinstituted the death penalty in California, Bird voted to strike down the death sentence in every capital punishment case that came before the California Supreme Court. This refusal to apply the law led to her removal from office, and whether one is a Defender or Basher, it is hard to detect a threat to judicial independence in the voters' rejection of her.[82]

Yet defiance of the law is seldom so blatant, and Bashers and Defenders would likely have difficulty agreeing on other instances of judicial defiance. But the principle of holding judges accountable for their overall record can be applied in other instances as well. Suppose, for example, that a judge's rulings are reversed far more frequently than those of his peers. Those evaluating whether the judge should continue in office might reasonably conclude that this indicates either judicial willfulness or judicial incompetence. Whichever the cause, Defenders should concur with Bashers that the judge can be held accountable for this failing either by being denied another term in office, if the judge does not serve during good behavior, or by being denied advancement within the judiciary. Thus, when Judge Harold Carswell was nominated to fill a Supreme Court vacancy, opponents quite appropriately pointed to the frequency with which his decisions were reversed by the court of appeals in urging a vote against his confirmation.

Where Bashers and Defenders part ways is over whether judges should be removable for a single disfavored decision. Defenders insist that it is inappropriate to remove a judge based on a single ruling. However, it is difficult to see why this is so because neither of the principled arguments supporting this position bear scrutiny. Such a position could rest on the belief that a single instance of judicial failure to follow the law is not sufficiently serious to warrant removal. Yet if a single instance of serious misconduct would justify impeachment, it is hard to see why it would not similarly justify removal by nonreelection. If a judge took a bribe in only one case, that would suffice for removal. Deliberate failure to adhere to the law in even a single case would violate a judge's oath of office and seem an equally serious form of misconduct.

Moreover, in insisting that judges be evaluated on their overall record rather than their ruling in a single case, Defenders assume that failure to adhere to the law in a single case does not justify an inference of a propensity to do so in other cases or that one cannot draw conclusions about the overall record from the particular instance. Yet this is precisely what voters do in other elections. Faced with incomplete information and the difficulty of acquiring additional information, voters generalize based on the information they have. As Paul Sniderman and his colleagues have noted, "Citizens can frequently compensate for their limited information about politics by taking advantage of judgmental heuristics. Heuristics are judgmental shortcuts, efficient ways to organize and simplify political choices: efficient in the double sense of requiring relatively little information to execute, yet yielding dependable answers even to complex problems of choice."[83] Why this should be less reliable or less defensible in a judicial election than in other elections is unclear. It may be, as some commentators have complained, that state judicial races are "drowning in dollars and misleading advertisements."[84] But this hardly distinguishes judicial elections from elections more generally.

What actually appears to underlie the Defenders' insistence on evaluating the judge's overall record is a prudential concern that judges not be penalized for honest mistakes in their interpretation of the law. Focusing on a single ruling facilitates voters choosing based on the outcome of the case, rather than on the legal correctness of that outcome. Beyond that, Defenders recognize that setting the bar so high on what constitutes legitimate voter behavior in effect is equivalent to condemning judicial elections altogether, to asserting that those who would remove judges are unqualified to determine whether the judges have properly interpreted the law. "Judicial elections might technically be democratic, but they are a type of dangerous democracy."[85] Bashers would emphatically disagree.

Judicial Independence in an Era of Legal Realism

Judicial accountability requires both someone to whom the judge is answerable and norms to which the judge is held to account. In the debate over decisional independence, Bashers and Defenders have largely focused on who should hold judges accountable. Perhaps because they both endorse fidelity to the law as the standard that should govern judicial decision making, they have devoted less attention to analyzing what constitutes fidelity to the law or explaining how one determines when judges have met or failed to meet that standard. While a fully elaborated treatment of these matters would require a book of its own, some comments about what an adequate treatment would look like might be helpful.

The idea of the rule of law implies that there is a right answer, or at least that there are wrong answers, in legal interpretation—"claims of fidelity and fallibility presuppose that the [law] means something in and of itself."[86] If the law is altogether unintelligible or if it imposes no constraints on judicial choice, then the notion of holding judges accountable to the law has no meaning, and with it falls the defense of judicial independence as a means of promoting decision according to law.

Most legal scholars reject what has been called the strong indeterminacy thesis ("in every possible case, any possible outcome is legally correct"), arguing that there are clearly correct outcomes in many cases.[87] However, not in all. "The bell announcing Legal Realism cannot be unrung," so few scholars today deny the existence of legal indeterminacy, insisting that there is a single, clear right answer in all cases.[88] Even if there are correct answers to all legal questions, judges have manifestly failed to discover them, as the prevalence of dissent on multimember courts attests. Rather, skillful judges acting in good faith regularly reach different conclusions.

Such disagreement occurs for several reasons. Conflicting interpretations of the law may reflect the different approaches used to determine its meaning—contrast Justices Scalia and Thomas, with their textualist, original meaning approach, to Justice Breyer, with his more pragmatic approach.[89] In some instances, there may be no "unambiguous preexisting and preinterpretive legal norms" to be applied.[90] Often the differences among judges are rooted in the difficulty of the task: the law may be vague, or the situation to which it must be applied may be unprecedented; thus, saying what the law is may require the exercise of judgment rather than mechanical application of the law. Even when there are preexisting legal norms, it may not be clear what legal norm should be applied in a particular case or how the law applies to the facts in the case.[91] Perhaps unsurprisingly, the problem of indeterminacy seems to arise most often in controversial cases. "The extent to which there are determinately correct answers to legal questions is inversely proportional to the extent of leeway left to legal officials in arriving at concrete decisions"; issues on the frontiers of constitutional law and the common law are not only politically contentious but also tend to require judicial decision making in the absence of well-established legal norms.[92] Put differently, "the question of legitimacy arises most acutely around controversial decisions for which the law does not provide a clear answer, the kind of answer on which all competent lawyers are likely to agree."[93]

Given this lack of agreement, the fact that judges divide over the meaning of the law is not sufficient, in and of itself, to deny that they sought to remain faithful to it. Yet if one is to justify decisional independence based on the rule of law, there must be some basis for distinguishing the exercise of judgment from unbounded discretion, "decision making without recipes" from judicial caprice.[94] Not every decision is defensible. And there is a further difficulty. Even if there is a correct answer in a case and even if judges have arguably found that correct answer, it may still be impossible for them to demonstrate that it is indisputably the right answer.[95] Simply put, even "a determinately correct answer" may not be "demonstrable to the satisfaction of virtually every reasonable person who reflects carefully on the matter."[96] Moreover, as Defenders are quick to point out, when those responsible for holding judges accountable are not themselves lawyers, they may not be "reasonable" or may not "reflect carefully on the matter." (Bashers in response might point out that those defending judges may likewise be unreasonable.) Rather, "conservatives and liberals have their own views about the meaning of the Constitution and quickly declare activist those judicial decisions that differ from their personal policy preferences."[97] Thus the complexities of the task of judging make it more difficult to determine when judges are deciding appropriately, and this in turn raises the possibility of error on the part of whoever holds judges accountable.

What is to be done? One alternative, previously mentioned, is to seek to reduce legal indeterminacy by adopting approaches to interpretation that limit judicial discretion. Many of those who endorse textualism or a jurisprudence of original meaning do so in order to circumscribe judicial choice, as a means to cabin judicial discretion rather than as a means to discover an authoritative constitutional meaning. Yet this does not altogether solve the problem. History may not offer clear answers, and critics charge that "textualism simply reproduces the problems that arise from the uncertainty of multiauthored ancient texts."[98] So it is not surprising that even judges subscribing to the same interpretive approach sometimes find themselves at odds. Beyond that, to say that textualism and originalism help reduce judicial discretion is quite different from saying that they offer the best understanding of the law. Yet it is fidelity to the law, not the absence of judicial discretion, that is the standard to which judges are to be held accountable. Similar concerns have been voiced about using rules rather than standards as a way of curtailing judicial choice.[99]

Another proposed alternative is to shift the inquiry from the substance of judges' decisions to the way in which they reached those decisions—judges must be "reasonable," not "arbitrary." Thus, according to one legal scholar, "the rule-of-law requirement is that among the various possible decisions not ruled out by the relevant legal materials, the court chooses 'reasonably' rather than merely 'arbitrarily' (in the sense of 'willfully')."[100] Or as Ferejohn and Kramer have suggested, judicial independence "seeks first and foremost to foster a decision-making process in which cases are decided on the basis of reasons that an existing legal culture recognizes as appropriate."[101] Under this view, then, judges may legitimately come out on either side of a case, so long as they can offer a satisfactory legal justification for their decision. The adequacy of this alternative is questionable, however, for it does not claim to deal with how judges reach their decisions but rather with their ability to advance a rationale within parameters established by the legal community. In addition, because there are multiple approaches to legal interpretation, the pertinent parameters are themselves so broad and nebulous that even willful judges would likely be able to frame their decisions within those parameters and thereby escape accountability.

It has also been proposed that the focus be shifted from whether the judges' decisions were correct to whether, if they were not, they were the result of "dishonest error." As Charles Geyh has argued, "If the objective is to preserve the rule of law as best we can, it would seem that the dichotomy between honest and dishonest error needs to be preserved, and that in the case of honest error, accountability should be limited to corrective measures and exclude punitive ones."[102] Moreover, in enforcing accountability, Defenders insist, the burden of proof should be on those asserting "mistake" and "intentional mistake."[103] For it is but a short step from disagreement with a ruling to challenging the good faith of the judge who issued it. Yet there are problems with this approach as well. As a practical matter, serious inquiry into whether judges willfully substituted their own views for what the law required "would necessarily require a probing inquiry into the judge's subjective mental state that could itself threaten the values of judicial independence."[104] More generally, shifting the focus to judicial willfulness transforms the nature of judicial accountability, from the substance of judicial decisions to the process by which judges reached those decisions. In addition, the shift in the burden of proof, with the strong presumption that judges have acted appropriately, merely reverses the potential for error. Judges who have wrongfully departed from what the law requires will escape accountability for their actions unless they can be proved to have done so intentionally.

Indeed, Bashers can turn this argument on its head. If more than one possible interpretation of the law is possible, why should judges choose which one will prevail? Why should not the people, through the recall or their votes on sitting judges, provide input into which defensible interpretation they believe courts should follow? In doing so, of course, voters would not be engaging in legal analysis. Rather the idea would be that legal experts have concluded that the law is unclear, and therefore political rather than legal considerations will be determinative. In such circumstances, Bashers argue, community sentiment should decide because the alternative is not the rule of law—the law points in more than one direction—but the rule of judges. Yet complications arise when one attempts to put this into practice. For how is one to determine whether legal indeterminacy exists? Absent such a determination, the danger remains that voters may choose to remove judges based on their votes in cases in which the law was clear and was followed by the judges.[105]

As William Marshall has observed, "The notion that law reflects the philosophical views of those empowered to decide cases is no longer a mere abstraction or a matter discussed only in the hallowed halls of academia. It is an ingrained aspect of our political and legal culture."[106] Faced with this reality, some Defenders have largely abandoned the effort to distinguish between fidelity to the law and the rationalized "preferences of self-willed and doctrinaire judges, arguing for deference to judicial decisions, even controversial constitutional rulings."[107] Some assert that judges possess special qualities or attributes—for example, superior knowledge of and expertise in the law—that justify deference to their rulings. Yet, as Christopher Eisgruber tartly observed in discussing constitutional litigation, "this argument holds only if the Constitution is indeed a technical document, like a will, contract or statute."[108] Others base their argument for deference on the institutional position of judges, contending that their (relative) insulation from politics enables them to render impartial and objective decisions. Yet the claim that judges are separated from politics is at best controversial, for decisions about the values and standards that will govern a society are inherently political. And even if judges are insulated from partisan politics, that is no guarantee of impartiality and objectivity. In fact, several decades of social science research on judicial decision making have documented the influence of judges' pre-judicial attitudes on the decisions they render, essentially demolishing the claim that judges are above politics.

Conclusion

Thus one is left, as one began, with the idea of holding judges responsible for decision according to law. A balance must be struck between judicial independence and accountability, recognizing the difficulties in adherence to that standard and in determining when judges have failed to meet the standard. On the one hand, the complexities of the task of judicial decision caution against attributing bad faith to all decisions that one finds wrong-headed. Judicial independence requires that judges have some breathing space. There may be more than one legally defensible outcome in a case, and even when a decision is not legally justified, one cannot assume that judges are consciously departing from the law in pursuit of personal or ideological agendas. Yet this cannot justify abandoning the task of holding judges accountable for their decisions because judicial decisions can have broad social consequences. The fact that mistakes will occur, that judges will sometimes suffer for decisions that either were correct or were good-faith efforts to interpret the law, is no reason to give up on accountability. Nor is the fact that judges have greater expertise in the law than do those holding them accountable. Judicial independence is valuable as a means toward securing impartial decisions, but judicial accountability is likewise essential as a check on those wielding power.

5 Reconsidering Judicial Elections

"**M**ORE SWEAT AND INK HAVE BEEN SPENT ON GETTING RID of judicial elections than on any other single subject in the history of American law."[1] So claimed Roy Schotland in 1998, and in the years since, the literature condemning judicial elections has proliferated. Not that these efforts have enjoyed much success—no state since 1985 has abandoned contested judicial elections.[2] In 2010 voters in Nevada handily defeated a proposal to institute merit selection, despite a high-powered campaign led by former Supreme Court Justice Sandra Day O'Connor. Public opinion polls continue to register strong popular support for electing judges, even as they reveal public concern about the influence of wealthy interests on judicial elections. Approximately 89 percent of state judges face election at some point.[3] For Defenders the issue of judicial elections has taken on increased urgency in light of the "new politics of judicial elections," with its soaring spending, unprecedented interest-group involvement, rancorous political advertising, and hotly contested races.[4] But in recent years the professional consensus against judicial elections been challenged by some political scientists and legal scholars. They deny that "judicial elections are going wild," insisting rather that "they are going normal" by more closely resembling races for other political offices, and they claim that these more competitive and contentious judicial elections enhance judicial accountability.[5]

In this chapter we consider the contemporary debate over judicial elections. Because so much energy has been expended attacking such elections, we focus on the Defenders' arguments against such elections and the evidence underlying those arguments, scrutinizing them in light of what social science tells us about elections.[6] Two preliminary points deserve emphasis. First, judicial elections take a variety of forms—contested partisan elections, contested nonpartisan elections, and uncontested retention elections—and some types of elections may be better at safeguarding judicial independence while ensuring judicial accountability. Second, even if the Defenders' case against judicial elections proves unpersuasive, that does not prove that states should elect their judges; it merely shows that they should not dismiss elections as a possible mode of judicial selection.

Judicial Elections Provide an Illusory Accountability

Some Defenders deny that judicial elections promote meaningful accountability to the public. They note that low turnout in judicial elections means that only a small percentage of voters may determine outcomes.[7] They also maintain that judicial races often are uncompetitive, so that voters lack an effective choice, and when no opposing candidate runs in a partisan or nonpartisan election, they lack a choice altogether. As Charles Geyh framed it in his "Axiom of 80," roughly 80 percent of the electorate does not vote in judicial elections, and roughly 80 percent cannot identify the candidates for judicial office.[8] Finally, Defenders note that in partisan elections in particular, the selection of what candidates will appear on the ballot may be dominated by party leaders, so that voter choice is highly circumscribed.[9]

However, social science research reveals that Defenders have exaggerated ballot roll-off and underestimated the quality of competition in judicial races. The overall roll-off rate in state supreme court elections from 1990–2004 was 22.9 percent, which is comparable to that in other less publicized races, and this roll-off rate has remained stable over time.[10] Moreover, this figure is not indicative of a consistent lack of voter interest, as roll-off rates in judicial elections vary dramatically, from 1.6 percent to 65.1 percent across elections, and from 12.5 percent to 59.2 percent among states.[11] Some judicial races thus attract widespread voter interest and participation, whereas others do not—the fact that a judicial office is at stake is not decisive. In general, roll-off declines when races are contested and when candidates run with party labels. These factors may be interrelated: partisan elections are more likely to be contested than are nonpartisan elections (and of course retention elections are by definition uncontested). Thus, an early study found that in state supreme court elections outside the South from 1948–74, 87 percent of partisan elections were contested as compared to 49 percent of nonpartisan elections.[12] More recent data are similar: from 1990–2004, only 59.9 percent of incumbents on state supreme courts were challenged when they sought reelection in nonpartisan election states, but 82.4 percent were challenged in partisan election states.[13] Changes in the South, presumably tied to its transformation to a two–party region, are particularly pronounced.[14] Over the last two decades, perhaps as a result of the "new politics of judicial elections," electoral challenges have become more frequent. In 1990, incumbents were challenged in only 37.5 percent of nonpartisan races and in 70.6 percent of partisan races, but by 2004 the figures had risen to 72.0 percent and 90.9 percent respectively.[15]

Nevertheless, for voters to hold judges accountable, elections must be not merely contested but competitive—there has to be a real possibility that incumbents will lose. Overall, incumbent justices fare very well in state supreme court elections, but there are important differences among partisan, nonpartisan, and retention contests. Judges rarely taste defeat in retention elections. A study of retention elections from 1942–78 found that only thirty-three judges were not retained in office.[16] A more recent survey of retention elections for supreme court justices from 1980–2000 showed that less than 2 percent were defeated.[17] The most comprehensive study of retention elections, examining trial and appellate court races in ten states from 1964–2006, found that only 56 of the 6,306 judges running in retention elections were not retained (less than 1 percent).[18] More than half of the defeated judges from 1964–2006 were in Illinois, which requires a 60 percent affirmative vote for retention, and the super-majority requirement has proven crucial: only one of the judges who were not retained received a positive vote of less than 50 percent.[19] Moreover, the outcomes of retention elections are rarely close: the mean yearly average positive vote has ranged from a low of 69 percent in 1990 to a high of 85 percent in 1964 and over the last decade it has not been fallen below 75 percent.[20]

But if retention elections usually fail to provide meaningful accountability, the same need not hold true for partisan and nonpartisan elections. Partisan elections for state supreme courts are almost always contested, and nonpartisan elections are increasingly contested. These contested races tend to be competitive: from 1990–2004, incumbent justices received only 57.9 percent of the vote in contested nonpartisan races and 55.7 percent in contested partisan races.[21] And partisan races in particular provide real opportunities for turnover: whereas only 1.3 percent of incumbents were defeated in retention elections and 5.2 percent in contested nonpartisan elections, 31 percent of incumbents were defeated in contested partisan elections.[22] Comparison with other elections underscores the competitiveness—and hence the potential for meaningful accountability—in judicial elections. From 1990–2004, partisan elections for state supreme courts had lower reelection rates for incumbents than did races for the US House of Representatives, the US Senate, and state governorships. Even nonpartisan races for state supreme courts during this period were as competitive as House races and almost as competitive as Senate contests.[23]

If a partisan or nonpartisan election is uncontested, there is of course no way for voters to render a verdict on a candidate. In such circumstances retention elections provide greater accountability, because voters can vote for or against an incumbent judge. However, given the deficiencies of retention elections in promoting accountability, this is less an argument for retention elections than for greater electoral competition. And if one wishes electoral competition, then partisan elections are preferable to nonpartisan ones, so the movement of states from partisan to nonpartisan elections and from contested to uncontested elections has reduced electoral accountability. Also, states with contested elections might change their electoral laws so that when there is no challenger in a race, the election could be conducted as a retention election. If the problem is lack of electoral competition in judicial races, the solution is not to abandon such elections but to make them more competitive.

Voters Are Not Qualified to Elect Judges

Defenders' main concern is that voters are not qualified to select judges. This is so because (1) voters lack the expertise necessary to assess whether a judge's decisions are legally defensible; (2) they lack expertise in the law and do not understand the judicial process; (3) they lack sufficient information about the candidates; (4) the information they receive is often unreliable or distorted, coming as it does from interested sources; (5) voters in choosing between incumbents and challengers inappropriately focus on isolated cases rather than on judges' overall performance in office; and (6) even in assessing those isolated cases, voters tend to decide based on whether they like or dislike their outcomes rather than on whether the judge decided them in accordance with the law.

This is a daunting inventory, to put it mildly. If Defenders are correct, then the argument against judicial elections is irrefutable. Yet some skepticism may be warranted. For one thing, the logic of the Defenders' argument could easily be extended to condemn all elections. Voters seldom have detailed knowledge about the other branches of government or about those seeking legislative or executive office. Does this mean that they should not choose their governors or representatives? Or is there something, never elaborated, about why detailed knowledge is particularly necessary in judicial elections? In addition, the Defenders' argument would seem to extend to other modes of judicial selection as well. It is unlikely that governors and others involved in the appointment of judges possess the detailed knowledge demanded by Defenders and that they ignore what decisions prospective judges are likely to render. If this is true, then do the criticisms of judicial elections apply to appointment as well? Who then is really qualified to select judges? With these provisos in mind, we turn to the Defenders' arguments.

Lack of Expertise to Assess the Legal Adequacy of Judicial Rulings

Some Defenders argue that what distinguishes judges from other public officials and makes electing them problematic is that the task of judging requires professionals with a distinctive expertise. As one Defender put it:

> The judge is in fact less akin to the political executive and legislator than he is to the medical doctor, engineer, professor, military leader, or scientist. He must be, in the highest sense, an expert. There is little more 'democratic' necessity to choose a public expert called a judge by direct popular election, open to all comers having the minimum or formal requirements, than there is to choose another kind of expert such as an admiral or university president.[24]

We do not select surgeons or auto mechanics by popular vote because we lack the knowledge necessary to assess the competence of those operating on people or on cars. Similarly, ordinary citizens should not elect judges because they lack the legal knowledge necessary for assessing whether judges have adhered to the law in their rulings. Indeed, Defenders insist, voters rarely even try to do so. Instead, judicial elections all too often become referenda on judges' "voting records": if you like the outcomes, you support the judge; if not, you oppose the judge; and the quality of legal reasoning supporting the rulings plays no role in voter choice.[25]

Even most Bashers concede that voters lack legal expertise. But if one accepts the judge-as-legal-technician argument, it follow that judges should be selected and assessed by legal professionals because only they have the requisite legal expertise. In fact, that was what the earliest version of merit selection proposed: a commission dominated by legal professionals choosing a list of candidates, with the state's chief justice appointing from that list.[26] However, merit systems today include nonlawyers on the nominating commissions—in most states attorneys constitute a minority on the commission—and the governor, who may lack legal training, makes the appointment.[27] Thus today's merit-selection systems share the defect ascribed to elective systems.

There are other reasons to be skeptical of the Defender argument. For one thing, those advocating selection by legal experts are often the very persons empowered by such a system. Beyond that, the Defenders' argument rests on the assumption that "law and politics are distinct universes," a proposition that, as Paul Carrington has observed, was debunked by the Legal Realists, and "was unconvincing even before that."[28] Yet once one acknowledges that judging involves more than the exercise of technical expertise and that judges' values may influence their rulings, the analogy between judges and mechanics collapses. This of course does not prove that voters are qualified to select judges, merely that their lack of technical expertise does not disqualify them.

Lack of Sufficient Information about Candidates and the Judicial Process

The broader argument against electing judges is that voters lack the knowledge necessary to do the job well. Several studies have documented that voters may lack even the most rudimentary information about judicial candidates, and voters themselves have complained about their lack of information.[29] But it is worthwhile to consider what sort of knowledge voters need.

According to Defenders, those selecting judges need to understand the judicial process and the responsibilities of the judge within that process because only then can they assess whether a prospective judge has the requisite knowledge, temperament, and other qualities essential for office. They must also have some expertise in the law, so that they can determine whether a prospective judge has the appropriate legal knowledge or whether the rulings of an incumbent represent defensible interpretations of the law. Furthermore, they must be aware of the full range of decisions rendered by incumbent judges, as well as of the experience of nonincumbents and of their reputation

in the legal community. Finally, they must have knowledge of other qualities that make a good judge, and this knowledge typically comes from direct
observation or personal interaction.

Few voters possess this information. Public understanding of the law is
limited, and voters often lack detailed information about those running for
office.[30] As one commentator put it, "When it comes to politics and political
information, most Americans are severely undernourished."[31] This is especially
true for non-top-of-the-ticket races, like judicial elections. When judicial elections are ill-financed, low-visibility affairs, with sparse coverage by the media,
voters seldom have much information about judicial candidates prior to voting.[32] Even when races are hotly contested, with extensive advertising, voters
may ignore or tune out the messages and so may not learn much about the
candidates. For many voters apparently, the realization that there are judicial
contests on the ballot first occurs in the voting booth; thus, they must choose
based on information available on the ballot itself.[33] Once their ballots are cast,
voters may not even recall the names of the candidates for whom they voted.

Whether these gaps in information are sufficient to condemn judicial
elections, however, depends on whether they prevent voters from competently
choosing among candidates. Many experts in voting behavior believe they do
not. "Asserting that limited information precludes reasoned choice," Arthur
Lupia and Matthew McCubbins insist, "is equivalent to requiring that people
who want to brush their teeth recall the ingredients of their toothpaste."[34] The
criterion is not the quantity of information voters have but whether voters'
electoral choices accurately reflect their views, whether they "cast the same
votes they would have cast had they possessed all available knowledge about
the policy consequences of their decision."[35] Voters can make reasoned choices
even with limited information, if they can compensate for their informational
shortfalls by taking advantage of judgmental shortcuts (cues) to clarify and
simplify political choices. These cues "requir[e] relatively little information to
execute, yet yield dependable answers even to complex problems of choice."[36]
The key to good voter choice, then, is not to demand levels of civic virtue that
are beyond the reach of most citizens but to "offer them instead cues and signals which connect their world with the world of politics."[37]

Distorted or Unreliable Information about Candidates
Given Defenders' concerns about voter ignorance, one might expect they
would welcome the greater salience of recent state supreme court elections,

in which groups and candidates have spent substantial sums on television ads and other political appeals to publicize views and criticize opponents. But Defenders uniformly condemn these developments and have tried to combat them.[38] For example, after a campaign to defeat Justice Richard Teitelman of the Missouri Supreme Court in a 2004 retention election, the first serious effort to unseat a justice in decades, the Missouri Bar Association formed a special committee to determine how to respond to what it termed "inaccurate and intemperate" attacks on the justice and to prevent such attacks in the future.[39] In part, the bar's reaction reflected a concern that politicized elections, with their hefty campaign contributions and attack ads, undermine respect for the judiciary.[40] But Defenders more generally worry that "voters in [judicial] elections are especially vulnerable to high-tech media manipulation" through negative ads that unfairly attack judges, distort their rulings, and slander their character.[41] They note that televised ads in judicial campaigns focus voter attention on one or a few judicial rulings rather than on the judge's overall record and urge voters to choose judges based on their agreement or disagreement with sensationalized accounts of those rulings, rather than on whether a judge followed the law. Television ads may also invite voters to cast their ballots based on antipathy to a group or individual involved in a case—for example, pedophiles or murderers—rather than on whether the judge followed the law.[42] Finally, Defenders fear that potential voters may become disgusted by the relentless negativity of these ads and refrain from voting.

To take the last point first, there is no evidence that negative ads reduce voter turnout. A 1999 metastudy of fifty-two separate studies on negative advertising and turnout concluded that "participatory democracy may be on the wane in the United States, but the evidence reviewed here suggests that negative political advertising has relatively little to do with it."[43] A more recent study found that negative campaign ads actually stimulated turnout, presumably because exposure to ads of any sort makes citizens more familiar with who is running and hence more likely to vote.[44] Other recent studies found that negative ads did not affect turnout, but none indicated that negative ads reduced it.[45]

Yet in fairness most Defenders are concerned less with turnout than with the threat that groups or candidates might use ads to manipulate voters and the electoral process. This is a legitimate concern, but Defenders tend to overestimate the negative effects of aggressive campaign ads and underestimate their positive potential, perhaps because such ads have appeared in judicial campaigns only recently, even though they are an established part of campaigns for other offices.[46] Voters often select candidates on the basis of their character, and in low-information races in particular, they tend to support incumbents absent negative reports about their character or performance in office. Thus, attacks on one's opponent are vital for ensuring effective competition for office and informing voter choice. Certainly some attacks are tasteless and misleading. And those who launch the attacks are engaged not in public service but in seeking to advance their own interests and ideas. Nevertheless, as Justice William Brennan reminded us in *New York Times v. Sullivan* (1964), we share "a profound national commitment to the principle that debate on public issues should be uninhibited, robust, and wide-open, and that it may well include vehement, caustic, and sometimes unpleasantly sharp attacks on government and public officials."[47]

Even so, Defenders worry that negative campaign ads substitute manipulation for reliable information and thereby distort voter choice. There is no research addressing whether this happens in judicial elections. But because negative campaigning and attack ads are not limited to judicial races, more general studies of these phenomena may help in assessing the Defenders' concerns.

Defenders charge that attack ads are designed to create outrage and hostility. As Justice Hans Linde put it, "Voters are invited to feel angry at a decision and to vent that anger against any judge who participated in it."[48] Underlying this criticism is the assumption that "if there is anything worse than an uninformed voter, it is an emotional voter."[49] But few attack ads are fact-free appeals to emotion and prejudice. Indeed, some research suggests that negative ads typically have more factual content than do positive ads.[50] Even former Chief Justice Thomas Phillips of Texas, an opponent of judicial elections, has conceded that "while roundly deplored, `the ritualized scandals of political spending' in Texas judicial elections have given many voters enough information to cast something more than a random vote."[51] So attack ads may provide sustenance to information-starved voters.

Yet Defenders insist that the information transmitted is self-interested and unreliable. Certainly those who disseminate the ads have a point of view and are seeking to persuade voters—that is simply the nature of political campaigns. But, as Lawrence Baum has noted, "voters should not be regarded as passive recipients of campaign messages," and they may "find proffered reasons to remove a judge from office insufficiently credible or significant to guide their vote."[52] Whether attack ads distort voter choice depends on whether voters are taken in by false claims and whether they rely on ads in deciding whom to support.[53] When no alternative sources of information are available, one might expect voters to be affected more by campaign ads. But if there are other bases for voter choice, presumably fewer voters will rely on the ads in casting their votes, so the key to reducing the influence of negative ads is providing alternative cues to guide voter choice.

Both Defenders and Bashers acknowledge this but differ as to what those alternative cues should be. For many Bashers, the most promising alternative cue is party affiliation because if there is one constant in studies of judicial elections and of elections more generally, it is the importance of party labels for voter choice. According to William Flanigan and Nancy Zingale, "Party-line voting becomes stronger for less visible offices, including Congress, because issues and personal attributes of the candidate are less likely to have an impact on the voter in less publicized races."[54] Partisans tend to cast their ballots for fellow partisans in the absence of other information. For example, Phillip Dubois found that in states with partisan elections in which both a state supreme court seat and the governorship were at stake, there was a .84 correlation between the percentage of the vote received by the gubernatorial candidate and the supreme court candidate of the same party on the county level.[55] Justice Fred Williams of Missouri noted how top-of-the-ballot races affect judicial contests almost a century ago: "I was elected to the state supreme court in 1916 because President Wilson kept the country out of war, but I was defeated in 1920 because the President did not keep the country out of war."[56] This is reasonable because "the party label can provide low cost, but valuable, information concerning electoral choices," particularly in low-visibility races.[57]

Defenders reject partisan judicial elections and hence the use of party affiliation as a voting cue, preferring nonpartisan elections. But voting research suggests that such elections impede informed voter choice because "nonpartisan ballots raise the information costs to citizens [and] result in less informed voting decisions."[58] For "where partisan labels are not available, voters must rely upon other kinds of short-cut guides to voting, such as the incumbency, name familiarity, or ethnic-religious affiliation of the candidate. And where none of these other nonparty cues are meaningful to the individual voter, votes may be cast on the basis of the sex, nickname, or ballot position of the respective candidates, truly arbitrary decision-making tools."[59] Indeed, there is anecdotal evidence of this in judicial races, of candidates being elected or rejected because they had names familiar to voters or names that led to stereotyping by voters.[60]

While Defenders prefer nonpartisan elections to partisan elections, they really favor uncontested nonpartisan elections (retention elections).[61] Such elections eliminate messages from opposing candidates from the information mix, and this encourages voters to rely on another low-cost voting cue, namely, incumbency. As a result, in more than 98 percent of retention elections, incumbent judges retain their seats. The overwhelming success of incumbents raises questions about whether retention elections promote informed voter choice. It is hard to believe that more than 98 percent of all appellate judges consistently decide cases based on law rather than their personal attitudes and "demonstrate scholarly writing and academic talent, and the ability to write to develop a coherent body of law."[62] It is likewise dubious that more than 99 percent of trial judges consistently exhibit "judicial temperament," "judicial management skills," and "courtesy to litigants, counsel, and court personnel."[63] It is far more likely that retention elections result in a large number of false positives, that incumbents enjoy a level of success that far exceeds what would be expected if voters made informed decisions on all judges.

Several factors are at work here. First, if voters tend to support incumbents in the absence of reasons not to do so, in most retention elections there is not enough information about judicial performance to generate a negative vote.[64] That is not, of course, the same as saying that the incumbent has performed well; it is merely saying that there is no evidence of poor performance or that such evidence has not reached the voters. In a contested election, one's opponent has an interest in publicizing negative aspects of one's performance in office. But in a retention election that incentive is lacking, and it is rare that others take up the responsibility of providing such information. Newspapers rarely do so: a study of local newspaper coverage of fifty-one state supreme court races in sixteen states from 2000–2004 found coverage of judicial elections very limited, and the absence of a race with competing candidates reduced coverage even more.[65] Only when organized groups have targeted particular judges and widely disseminated negative information about their performance in office have incumbents been defeated.[66] Of course, this is the very politicization that Defenders abhor.

In response, Defenders propose other sources of information to counter political advertising, replace party labels, and better guide voter choice. Specifically, they favor voters' guides, distributed by state governments, state bar associations, and other groups, with information on factors such as incumbents' experience, integrity, professional competence, judicial temperament, and record of dealings with the public.[67] They also urge states to distribute information about judicial performance prior to retention elections.[68] These performance evaluations would presumably be based on "objective, process-based criteria expected of any judge" and so prevent "one or two controversial issues [from becoming] the focus of the campaign," thereby "helping voters to cast an informed ballot."[69]

But judicial performance evaluations and voters' guides are hardly an adequate alternative. First off, relatively few states supply such materials: according to the American Judicature Society, only eight states provide voters' guides, and eight conduct retention evaluation programs, although in some other states the League of Women Voters, the state bar, or other groups provide voter guides.[70] In addition, the evaluations they offer may not be impartial. In a comprehensive study of retention elections, Larry Aspin found that "voters still routinely retain almost all judges, *which is what existing judicial performance evaluation systems usually recommend (e.g., Alaska, Arizona, and Colorado)*."[71] If the evaluations are uniformly positive, one wonders how stringent and how neutral they are. Finally, what limited evidence we have raises questions about whether the evaluations reach voters and are relied upon by them. For example, a study of the 1996 retention elections in Alaska revealed that only 58 percent of voters were aware of the judicial performance evaluation reports made available by the Alaska Judicial Council.[72]

Even if voters are aware of voters' guides and performance assessments, it is not clear that they guide voter choice in the most important cases, namely, in hotly contested elections and in uncontested elections in which there is an organized effort to defeat incumbents. In such elections, voter guides are typically competing for attention with television ads attacking sitting judges—and one suspects not competing very effectively. In part, this relates to the sheer magnitude of efforts to influence voters via political ads. In 2008, for example, in races that featured television ads, on average there were 2,803 spots per contest.[73] In part, too, this relates to the tone of the voter guides and to the information they convey. In marked contrast to televised ads, the guides do not deal with the substantive rulings of judges, and the blandness of judicial performance evaluations stands in marked contrast to the dramatic—albeit simplifying and sometimes misleading —claims of political commercials in judicial races.

Where does this leave us? Although party labels may offer an inexact indication of a judge's general orientation, they enable voters to base their decisions on the overall performance or expected performance of the judge. But when this cue is removed, voters are more "likely to cast ballots consistent with the balance of campaign messages they have received, giving a substantial advantage to the candidate best able to get his or her message out to voters."[74] Thus, the absence of party labels may make judges particularly susceptible to "electoral challenges based on narrow issues that arouse particular interest groups rather than the broad quality of their performance on the bench."[75] Partisan judicial elections thus appear to encourage more informed voting and to reduce voting based on potentially misleading campaign ads.

Inappropriate Criteria Influencing Voter Choice

Consider once again why Defenders champion voters' guides and performance evaluations: they are based on "objective, process-based criteria expected of any judge" and thus help prevent "one or two controversial issues [from becoming] the focus of the campaign," thereby "helping voters to cast an informed ballot." Thus what is crucial about such evaluations is not the quantity but the character of the information they provide. By choosing what information to convey about judges, voters' guides and performance evaluations seek not only to inform voters but also to influence the bases on which they cast their votes.[76] Defenders may concede that voters should have input, at least in retention elections, but that input should be of a particular sort. They believe that voters should not decide based on the ideology or political orientation of the judge. They should not decide based on their agreement or disagreement with the judge's rulings and in particular not on their reaction to specific controversial decisions. They should not decide whether the judge has remained faithful to the law, presumably because they lack the expertise necessary to render such a judgment. Instead, they should decide based on "process-based criteria." This is how Defenders understand informed—or at least appropriate—voter choice. So judicial performance evaluations typically do not convey information as to judges' sentencing behavior or their frequency of reversal by appellate courts—matters in which voters might be intensely interested—and they certainly do not highlight controversial rulings that judges have made.

A moment's reflection reveals how problematic this is. From a practical standpoint, as Charles Geyh has observed, "if we make voters go to the trouble of deciding whether a judge should remain in office, it is fatuous to suppose that they can be persuaded to bracket out their views on the merits of the judge's most important decisions and cast their ballots on the basis of an arid assessment of the incumbent's general fitness."[77] Beyond that, if fidelity to the law is the most important trait in a judge, then it should be a criterion in deciding whether an incumbent remains on the bench. And if voters do not assess whether judges have adhered to the rule of law, who will? Judicial disciplinary commissions are prohibited from inquiring into the substance of judicial rulings, and many state supreme court rulings are not subject to appellate review. For example, when state supreme courts base their ruling on independent and adequate state grounds, as they have in cases involving same-sex marriage, public school finance, the rights of defendants, and other issues, there is no mechanism other than the judicial election to assess whether those rulings represent faithful interpretations of the law. The choice seems to be between an assessment that may sometimes be done badly and no assessment at all.

A more radical argument also deserves mention. When judges divide on a legal question, each arguably giving his/her best interpretation of the law, this suggests that more than one possible interpretation of the law is defensible. As Richard A. Posner has noted, "Legalism does exist, and so not everything is permitted. But its kingdom has shrunk and greyed to the point where today it is largely limited to routine cases, and so a great deal is permitted to judges."[78] This in turn leads to two questions: Who should choose among these defensible interpretations, and on what basis should they make that choice? There is a vast jurisprudential literature addressing these questions that need not detain us here. The Basher argument for popular participation in judicial elections is—or should be—that where more than one interpretation of the law is possible, then the people should by their vote provide input as to which defensible interpretation they favor.[79] This popular vote assessing judges based on their rulings does not involve expert legal analysis, nor can it claim to do so. Rather, the argument is that legal experts have found that the law is unclear, and in such circumstances political rather than legal considerations, matters of public preference or public utility rather than legal necessity, must decide. Where the law is unclear, community sentiment should prevail. The alternative, according to Bashers, is not the rule of law, because the law points in more than one direction, but the rule of judges.[80]

Defenders insist that voters should assess judges based on their overall record rather than on their rulings in one or a few publicized cases. For if judges believe they will be removed based on a single decision or set of decisions, they might be tempted to make decisions that will be politically palatable rather than those required by the law. One might reasonably view this as an argument against judicial elections generally, since one can hardly regulate the bases on which voters make their choices. Yet the threat to decisional independence may be less substantial than Defenders fear. For if, as Defenders also contend, many voters lack even a rudimentary knowledge of judges and their rulings, then they are hardly in a position to hold judges accountable for those rulings. Studies of judicial elections also suggest the threat may be overblown. The overwhelming majority of incumbent judges in retention elections retain office, often by comfortable margins—if anything, voters overretain judges.[81] And studies of partisan elections reveal that party affiliation, not particular rulings, is the main determinant of voter choice.[82] Even in those instances in which judges have come under sustained attack for particular rulings, most have been reelected.

Turning from the empirical to the theoretical, it is unclear why voters should not make choices based on one or a few judicial decisions. If one generalizes from specific instances in other spheres of life, why can one not do so in judicial elections? Beyond that, consider the following thought experiment: Were there a single documented instance of corrupt behavior by a judge, would that be a sufficient basis for voting against his reelection? Yet those who challenge judges based on their alleged failure to adhere to the law in a particular case are making a similar claim, namely, that a betrayal of trust in a single instance is sufficient justification for voting against a candidate. Defenders might respond that corrupt behavior is easier to detect than judicial willfulness, but that is a prudential rather than a principled argument.

The Special Character of Judicial Elections

Even if voter knowledge and behavior in judicial elections resemble what is found in other elections, Defenders contend that the distinctiveness of the judicial office renders judicial elections problematic. Whereas legislators and executives are expected to be accountable to constituents, judges are not, and whereas legislators and executives are expected to be responsive, judges are supposed to be impartial and independent. In the florid prose of one Defender, "A judge has no constituency except the unenfranchised lady with the blindfold and scales, no platform except equal and impartial justice under law."[83] Participation in elections does not diminish political officials, but given the distinctive responsibilities of the courts, fund-raising and campaigning may have that effect on judges by raising questions about judicial impartiality.[84] Poll data confirm this: as "spending in judicial election campaigns has skyrocketed, between eighty and ninety percent of the public believes that judges are influenced by the campaign contributions they receive."[85] This led Justice Anthony Kennedy to conclude in his concurring opinion in *New York State Board of Elections v. Lopez Torres* (2008) that "when one considers that elections require candidates to conduct campaigns and to raise funds in a system designed to allow for competition among interest groups and political parties, the persisting question is whether that process is consistent with the perception and the reality of judicial independence and judicial excellence."[86]

During the twentieth century, states established legal rules designed to differentiate judicial elections from other elections. These included restrictions on fund-raising—in contrast with candidates for other offices, candidates for judicial office could not solicit funds directly—and on what judges and judicial candidates could say during their campaigns. But in recent years these efforts to distinguish judicial elections have come under attack. In *Republican Party of Minnesota v. White* (2002), the US Supreme Court ruled that the First Amendment prohibits states from restricting candidates for judicial office in both contested and noncontested elections from announcing their views on contested legal issues.[87] Before *White*, codes of judicial conduct protected judicial candidates, who were able to plead that they were legally prohibited from discussing their views, a rather bizarre restriction that, as one commentator noted, "systematically deprived voters of the exact information we typically pine for them to have."[88] But because after *White* they can no longer make that claim, groups can now pressure candidates to announce their views, sometimes by distributing questionnaires to all judicial candidates and publicizing their responses, or, if they fail to respond, questioning their lack of transparency. Indeed, in the wake of *White* the focus has shifted to whether judges can be prohibited from committing themselves during their campaigns on issues that might come before them. Other restrictions also have come under fire. For example, four federal courts—two district courts and two courts of appeals—have enjoined state judicial canons prohibiting judicial candidates from personally soliciting campaign contributions.[89] Finally, the lifting of restrictions on campaigning and spending for other elections have been understood to apply to state judicial elections as well.[90]

Put simply, if states choose to elect their judges, they can no longer insulate those elections from the hurly-burly of electoral politics. For Bashers, the removal of restrictions on campaign speech increases the information available to voters and therefore improves voter choice and judicial accountability. For Defenders, these changes threaten judicial independence and judicial impartiality. Yet even prior to *White*, the character of state judicial elections had changed, and so *White* and subsequent rulings removing restrictions on campaigning by judicial candidates have not fundamentally altered the political landscape. Indeed, several of the dire effects predicted as a result of *White* and its progeny have failed to materialize. Thus, the most systematic assessment of *White*'s effects found "no statistically discernable influence in state supreme court elections of the *White* decision on the propensity for challengers to take on incumbents, the willingness of citizens to vote, or the actual costs of campaigns."[91] Other research supports this, at least with regard to removing restrictions on campaign speech: "The data are striking and compelling in revealing that making policy statements during campaigns does not seem to render a judge unable to make fair and impartial decisions on the bench, at least in the eyes of ordinary people."[92]

The Cost of Judicial Elections May Adversely Affect Judicial Decision Making

The cost of judicial campaigns has escalated in recent decades, leading Defenders to conclude that of the "many threats to judicial independence, one of the most pervasive problems is the nature and cost of running for the bench."[93] The cost of campaigns threatens to distort judicial decision making in two ways. First, because success in judicial elections requires substantial campaign expenditures, raising such funds may place those elected to the bench in debt to their campaign contributors, and as a result they may feel obliged to decide cases in the interest of those who financed their campaigns. Second, judges approaching the end of their term of office may alter their rulings so as to enhance their reelection prospects. They may forestall potential voter backlash by deliberately mirroring public sentiments rather than making the difficult decisions that adherence to law sometimes requires.[94] Trial judges may seek to avoid being accused of being "soft on crime" by sentencing those convicted more harshly. Appellate judges may seek to avoid the soft-on-crime label by upholding convictions in criminal appeals, particularly in capital cases and in cases involving heinous crimes. Beyond that, judges may seek to attract funds for their reelection campaigns by pandering to particular groups, or they may rule so as to preclude opposition from groups that could be mobilized against them, or they may tailor their rulings to avoid giving primary or general-election opponents issues on which to attack them. Judges elected on partisan ballots may rule in such a way as to please—or at least not anger—party leaders. Even judges who try to avoid being influenced by the prospect of a reelection campaign acknowledge that it may subconsciously influence their judgments. Thus, describing a judge's predicament in deciding controversial cases while facing reelection, former California justice Otto Kaus compared it to "finding a crocodile in your bathtub when you go to shave in the morning. You know it's there, and you try not to think about it, but it's hard to think about much else while you're shaving."[95] Finally, judges who ignore the electoral consequences of their rulings may be defeated when they seek reelection. Let us consider these concerns.

Campaign Contributions and Judicial Decisions

No candidate in a hotly contested race can win or even stand a serious chance of winning without substantial funding.[96] As a former West Virginia justice observed, "I know that when I run for reelection for judge, I would rather have an impecunious Oliver Wendell Homes as an opponent than a well-financed Jack the Ripper."[97] Defenders claim that there is a danger that campaign contributions and independent expenditures in these elections may influence judicial decisions, that the cost of campaigns itself is a threat to judicial independence. Beyond that, they insist that contributions and expenditures create an appearance of impropriety. For example, a 2002 poll by the American Bar Association found that 72 percent of respondents felt that judges having to raise funds might affect their impartiality, and a poll the same year by the Justice at Stake Campaign showed that 76 percent of respondents believed that judicial decisions were influenced at least in part by campaign contributions.[98] As noted previously, other polls report similar findings.[99]

In considering Defenders' concerns, one should keep in mind the purpose served by spending in elections, namely, enabling candidates to convey information about themselves and their own views, about their opponents and their views, and about what (in general) they would do should they win office. Thus, candidates and groups use the funds they raise to inform and influence the electorate, and in so doing they contribute to the fund of information upon which voters rely. These are valid and important purposes. But do the large contributions and independent expenditures necessary for an effective campaign compromise judicial independence and encourage judicial partiality?

There is little evidence of judges being bribed by contributors and supporters, although some infamous instances have in recent years created an unappetizing appearance of corruption. In Illinois, for example, with an appeal in a $1 billion class-action suit against State Farm Mutual Insurance on its way to the Illinois Supreme Court, two candidates for an open seat on the court spent $9.3 million in the campaign, and the victor, Lloyd Karmeier, received more than $350,000 in direct contributions from State Farm employees, lawyers, and others involved with the company and more than $1 million more from groups affiliated with the company. Justice Karmeier refused to recuse himself in the case and ultimately cast the deciding vote in striking down the verdict against State Farm. In West Virginia, as noted previously, with a $50 million verdict against the Massey Coal Company awaiting review by the West Virginia Supreme Court, the president of Massey Coal, Don Blankenship, formed a nonprofit group, For the Sake of the Children, to which he contributed $3 million of his own money for television ads attacking incumbent justice Warren McGraw. After Blankenship's preferred candidate, Brent Benjamin, defeated McGraw, Benjamin refused to recuse himself and cast the crucial vote overturning the $50 million verdict against Massey Coal. On appeal, the US Supreme Court ruled that Justice Benjamin's participation in the case created an unacceptable potential for bias in violation of due process and overturned the West Virginia Supreme Court's ruling.[100]

Although these highly publicized cases are atypical, there is a real concern that judges will favor those interests or attorneys that have contributed to their campaigns, and in fact some studies appear to document this. For example, Stephen Ware's study of the Alabama Supreme Court reported a correlation between the sources of judges' funding and their votes in arbitration cases.[101] In studies of the Texas Supreme Court, Madhavi McCall found correlations between campaign contributions and the judges' votes, and in a study of tort cases in Alabama, Kentucky, and Ohio, Eric Waltenberg and Charles Lopeman likewise discovered that judges' votes correlated with campaign contributions.[102] Damon Cann found that justices on the Georgia Supreme Court were more likely to rule in favor of attorneys who contributed to their campaigns, and Aman McLeod reached a similar conclusion about the Michigan Supreme Court.[103] Yet other researchers have not detected such relationships—a study of contributions by attorneys to justices of Wisconsin Supreme Court from 1989 to 1999, for example, concluded that "for the most part" contributions "do not result in a greater likelihood that the vote of that judge will be influenced."[104] Moreover, one must be cautious in drawing conclusions from these studies. The fact that justices rule in ways that please contributors does not mean that they rule in that fashion *because of* those contributions: correlation does not indicate causation. It seems more likely that in most cases the known orientation of judges or their challengers attracts support from groups who share that orientation rather than that judges change their views because of the support they receive. It is hardly a coincidence that plaintiff's lawyers tend to support Democratic rather than Republican judicial candidates or that business and insurance groups tend to support Republican candidates. Candidates are more likely to attract campaign funds than to alter their behavior in response to them. This conclusion is supported by most studies that have examined the influence of money on policy-making in other arenas—for example, by looking at whether campaign contributions influenced voting by legislators. In a few instances, scholars have discovered that contributions had an effect.[105] However, most studies have concluded that how legislators voted attracted money rather than that the attraction of money determined how they voted.[106]

Yet if the fact that judges have received substantial contributions to attain office does not necessarily compromise judicial independence or integrity, the prospect of having to secure popular and financial support if they hope to remain on the bench might. So let us turn to running for reelection.

Reelection and Judicial Decisions

Defenders have warned that judicial incumbents may alter their rulings in order to make themselves more attractive when they run for reelection. As former Massachusetts Chief Justice Margaret Marshall put it, "Fair and neutral judges, knowing that each written opinion may be scrutinized as a statement of political partisanship by interest groups, may feel tremendous pressure to look over their shoulders, to abandon the principles of judicial neutrality, when deciding cases."[107] There is basis for this concern, as some judges have frankly acknowledged that the prospect of an election influences their decisions. In interviews conducted with judges who ran in retention elections from 1986–90, 15 percent indicated that as the election approached, they sought to avoid controversial cases and rulings, while another 5 percent indicated that they became more conservative in sentencing in criminal cases.[108] A more recent survey reported that only a small minority of judges facing retention elections considered themselves independent of voter influence, while a "very high percentage of judges . . . say judicial behavior is shaped by retention elections."[109] There is also evidence that at least some judges have modified their behavior prior to elections. Thus a study of Pennsylvania trial judges found that the sentences they imposed "become significantly more punitive the closer they are standing to reelection."[110] A more general analysis by Joanna Shepherd concluded that "elected state supreme court justices routinely adjust their rulings to attract votes and campaign money."[111]

Whether these findings are generalizable, they are troubling. Judges who deliberately ignore what they believe the law requires and instead issue rulings designed to curry popular favor are betraying their trust and violating their oath of office. Such perversions of justice are deplorable, and those who sacrifice impartiality for personal advantage do not belong on the bench. Yet one should be cautious about drawing conclusions about the desirability of judicial elections from what may be isolated instances of judicial misbehavior. Furthermore, if judges modify their behavior prior to an election, one cannot be sure whether they are departing from the law or embracing it. Recall the Basher claim: judges who are not electorally accountable tend to base their decisions not on the law but on their personal or ideological predilections, and only the prospect of facing the public impels them to adhere to the law. If that argument is correct—certainly a huge question—the judicial change in behavior as an election looms may be producing rulings more, not less, in accordance with what the law requires.

One must also question how widespread the problem of judges being affected by forthcoming elections really is. One can reasonably expect that most judges, however chosen, will have the strength of character to adhere to the law even when it is unpopular to do so. In *Bridges v. California*, the US Supreme Court overturned a finding of contempt against a newspaper that had published material critical of a judge's behavior in a highly publicized case.[112] In rejecting the claim that such criticism interfered with the administration of justice, Justice Hugo Black, writing for the court, argued that to assume that such articles would have a "substantial influence [on the judges' rulings] would be to impute to judges a lack of firmness, wisdom, or honor—which we cannot accept as a major premise."[113] One can expect similar fortitude in the judiciary of our day as well.

Insofar as there is a problem, it may lie not in the mode of selection but in the necessity of seeking further terms on the bench. In appointive as well as elective systems, those controlling judges' continuation in office may make their determinations based on agreement or disagreement with a judge's rulings, and judges appointed to the bench might be tempted to court the favor of those who control whether they remain in office. The potential for corruption, therefore, arises whether incumbents are seeking to retain their seats on the bench through reelection, through reappointment, or through election following initial appointment (as in merit-selection systems).[114] However, it arises only when incumbents are seeking to retain their seats—it does not arise when a vacancy is being filled, whether by appointment or election. Thus one could solve this problem by eliminating the process of reselection, whether by granting tenure during good behavior or up to a specified retirement age or by limiting judges to a fixed, nonrenewable term of office. We consider this last option in Chapter 6.

Judicial Elections Have Adverse Effects on Public Perceptions of the Judiciary

Defenders argue that in getting rid of judicial elections, one would also eliminate negative campaigning, campaign contributions, and other practices that undermine respect for the judiciary. In support, they can cite research which reports that "citizens in states using partisan elections to select judges have lower levels of diffuse support [for state courts] than citizens in states that appoint their judges."[115] Yet one should not necessarily conclude that campaigns and elections have compromised the institutional legitimacy of state courts. For one thing, the same public that expresses concern about campaign contributions also favors election rather than appointment of state judges. Moreover, despite concerns associated with the financing of judicial campaigns, the public has indicated greater confidence in state courts than in other institutions of state government.[116] One recent poll did find a significant decline in popular support for state courts, but it is impossible to determine whether that indicates a permanent or temporary shift in perspective.[117]

One must also ask whether it is the process of judicial selection that has most affected popular assessment of state judges. A comparison with the federal judiciary is revealing here. Federal judges do not run for office or solicit campaign funds, and they enjoy tenure during good behavior. Yet their selection is likewise highly politicized, and federal judges are probably accused of activism even more often than state judges are, which raises the possibility that judicial rulings, not the mode of selection, most affect popular assessments of the judiciary. In a 2005 Maxwell School poll, a majority of respondents agreed that "in many cases judges are really basing their decisions on their own personal beliefs," and 82 percent of respondents believed that the partisan background of judges influenced their rulings a lot or at least some.[118] A poll for the Defender organization Justice at Stake reported similar findings: 64 percent of respondents agreed that "there are too many activist judges who make rulings that follow their own views rather than the law," and 60 percent thought "too many judges are legislating from the bench and making laws instead of interpreting the laws."[119] In a poll conducted by the Annenberg Public Policy Center in 2006, 75 percent of respondents believed that judicial rulings were influenced "a great extent" or "a moderate extent" by judges' personal political views, and 68 percent indicated that this was "not appropriate." More than half of those expressing an opinion believed that it was "essential" or "very important" that there be a way to remove judges from office if they make "an unpopular ruling," and 65 percent favored popular election of judges (versus only 30 percent who favored commission-based appointment).[120] This last finding coincides with the findings in other polls. The respondents in the ABA poll mentioned above were more likely to trust elected than nonelected judges, and a 2005 Maxwell School Poll found that 75 percent of respondents rejected reducing the number of judges subject to election.[121] It also is consistent with popular rejection in state after state of proposals to eliminate contested judicial elections. Since 1994, proposals for merit selection have been rejected by state legislatures or by popular vote in Florida, Georgia, Idaho, Illinois, Louisiana, Nevada, Texas, and West Virginia.[122]

The relationship between politicization and popular skepticism about the impartiality of judges is likely more complicated than the survey results suggest. It may well be that campaign ads that accuse judges of "legislating from the bench" and "judicial activism" or that highlight the groups from which judges have received campaign contributions have fueled popular suspicions that judges are dependent and partial. Yet it is unlikely that campaign ads simply created these suspicions or that, absent politicized election campaigns, such skepticism would vanish. Thus, despite the arguments of Roscoe Pound and Albert Kales, reiterated by Defenders today, popular respect for the courts does not depend primarily on reducing attacks on judges.[123] These attacks have resonance because they seem to accord, at least in part, with how courts operate—or at least how they are perceived to operate. What we find here mirrors the divide between conservatives and progressives a century ago on what undermines faith in the judiciary. Yet in the interim the American public has been fed a steady diet of Legal Realism, has witnessed the evolution of federal judicial selection into "an ideologically-driven appointments process [that] legitimizes ideological judicial decision-making," and has seen courts become aggressively involved in a wide range of policy disputes, often striking down long-standing policies or practices.[124] Given these developments, one suspects that negative campaigning and accusations of judicial legislation have reflected, more than created, the current legal and political climate.

Judicial Elections Have Adverse Effects on the Quality of the Bench

Defenders contend that the requirement of running for judicial office dissuades highly qualified attorneys from seeking judgeships. Although this assertion does not directly implicate judicial independence, the implicit assumption appears to be that the more qualified the judges, the more likely they are to make well-considered decisions, and this will promote the rule of law. Yet there is little evidence that appointment leads to better judges.

Defenders note that in states with partisan elections, those who might make the best judges may not belong to the dominant party and thus stand no chance of election. Even if they have the "right" party affiliation, the party may use judgeships as patronage rather than nominating the most qualified persons, and well-qualified attorneys may lack the political connections necessary to secure nomination. In both partisan and nonpartisan races, those who might be the best judges might not be effective campaigners. Prospective judges may also be repelled by the necessity of getting involved in politics and by the tawdriness of campaigning and elections in general. They are likely to find fund-raising distasteful, and they may not relish the prospect of having their character assailed in television ads. Even if they should be elected, they might feel pressures from those who contributed to their campaign, and they could not easily ignore these pressures because, given their limited and uncertain tenure, they must remain aware of how voters and potential contributors to future campaigns might react to their decisions. In sum, Defenders argue that the uncertainty of the position and what must be done to obtain and retain it discourages desirable candidates from seeking judicial office.

There may be some basis for these concerns, but they are likely exaggerated. Certainly some prospective judges may be dissuaded from seeking office by the prospect of campaigning and fund-raising, yet these are merely, as one commentator observed, "pedestrian concerns."[125] It is more likely the politicization of the selection process and the potential attacks on one's character and views that render seeking a judgeship unattractive. However, such politicization occurs even outside the electoral arena. As one commentator noted in speaking of the appointment process for federal judges, "ideological scrutiny has embittered many nominees [and] discouraged individuals from enduring the confirmation process."[126]

Partisan elections do favor candidates from the dominant political party, but so do appointive systems. Most judges appointed by governors, whether in a merit system or not, are of the governor's party.[127] In Missouri, which pioneered merit selection, all but one of the justices appointed to the state's supreme court have shared the political affiliation of the appointing governor.[128] As federal judicial selection demonstrates, being well-connected politically is crucial in appointive, as well as in elective, systems. Furthermore, it is not only elective systems that fail to recruit the most prominent attorneys. Under all selection systems, attorneys who leave a prestigious law practice for a seat on the bench suffer a dramatic pay cut, and this is likely a more powerful disincentive than having to run for office. Finally, only a tiny minority of state judges serve during good behavior or until a specified retirement age; therefore, appointed as well as elected judges know that their tenure is uncertain and that future terms of office may be contingent on not alienating those who control their reselection.[129]

The question as to whether an appointive system produces a more qualified judiciary than does an elective system is easier to pose than to answer. One problem is defining judicial quality. Although there is a vast literature on the qualities desired in a judge, the list is so broad—a catalog of nearly every virtue known to humankind, plus the advantage of experience—that it offers little guidance.[130] Even were there a consensus on what qualities are desirable, it would be difficult to devise measures for determining whether prospective judges have those qualities or have them to a greater extent than do other candidates for the bench.

Defenders have sought to avoid these difficulties by focusing on the process of selection rather than its outcomes, arguing that removing politics from judicial selection allows choices to be made on the basis of professional qualifications, and this will enhance the quality of the bench. As the American Judicature Society insisted on the eve of the adoption of the first merit system, "The most important single step in improving judicial administration in a majority of the states is that of making judges independent of politics."[131] But even if this is true, there is no evidence that appointment, whether through merit selection or adoption of the federal model, eliminates politics from the selection process. The classic study of judicial appointment in Missouri, the state that pioneered the merit system, concluded that commission-based appointment transformed the politics of judicial selection but did not eliminate politics.[132] More recent accounts have documented partisan conflict and competition between elements of the bar—for example, between plaintiffs' attorneys and defense attorneys—in several merit selection systems.[133] Finally, those appointing judges regularly consider party affiliation in making their selections. The seven justices of the Florida Supreme Court who decided *Bush v. Gore* were all Democrats, even though Florida had merit selection, because they were all appointed by a Democratic governor.[134] Today there are Republicans on the Florida Supreme Court because Republican Governors Jeb Bush and Charlie Crist had the opportunity to make appointments.[135] Thus appointment may be no less partisan in its results than are judicial elections.

Several studies have sought to assess how the mode of selection affects judicial quality by focusing on the characteristics of those selected and their performance in office. The earliest research used the backgrounds of state supreme court justices as indicators of judicial merit, assuming that different selection systems would attract a different set of attorneys to the bench. However, these comparisons found no significant differences in the quality of law schools attended, in the career paths pursued, or in other characteristics of justices selected by appointment versus those selected by election.[136] Noting the crudity of these measures, Defenders have questioned whether they "capture those qualities that are most important to the enterprise of judging."[137]

But the only empirical study that purports to document the superiority of appointed judges is one by the American Judicature Society, which found that in states where some localities elected their trial judges and others appointed them, merit-selected judges were disciplined by judicial disciplinary commissions less often than were elected judges.[138] This likewise seems a crude measure of quality.

The most thorough recent examination of judicial recruitment via merit selection is James Gardner's study of the New York Court of Appeals.[139] Governor Hugh Carey by executive order established a judicial nominating commission for the Court of Appeals in 1975, and two years later voters ratified a constitutional amendment instituting merit selection for the court. However, the amendment produced merit selection in name only. Instead of an open process attracting highly qualified applicants from all legal backgrounds, New York's system "degenerated into a fundamentally closed competition among a very small number of sitting, experienced justices of the Appellate Division."[140] Of the eighteen judges appointed to the Court of Appeals since the advent of merit selection, sixteen had previously served on the New York Supreme Court or Court of Claims, but "only 4 had significant careers at the highest levels of private practice," and "only one was a prosecutor."[141] Moreover, "New York's switch to merit selection of its judges coincides with a decline in the Court's national reputation." Whereas in the past the Court of Appeals ranked at or near the top in terms of reputation and impact, a recent study ranked the Court of Appeals twenty-fourth.[142] Although one cannot generalize from a study of a single court, the New York experience cautions that a switch to merit selection does not automatically enhance the quality of the bench.

Some political scientists and legal scholars have directly compared the rulings of elected and appointed judges, with mixed results. Studies have found little difference between elected and appointed judges in their willingness to support plaintiffs in personal-injury litigation, in their sentencing in DWI cases, or in their rulings on racial-discrimination claims.[143] Other studies have found that appointed judges were more likely to uphold sex-discrimination claims, more likely to favor the defendant in criminal procedure rulings, and more likely to oppose imposition of the death penalty.[144] Yet even when the mode of selection correlates with different outcomes, it is hard to know what conclusions to draw from this. From a result-oriented perspective, one might prefer one set of outcomes to another, but there is no reason to believe that one set of results reflects greater knowledge of or fidelity to the law.

Recent research measuring the quality of judicial performance has found little difference between elected and appointed judges. Amanda Frost and Stefanie Lindquist compared the rate of reversal for judges based on their mode of initial selection and based on their method of retention, finding virtually no difference in either instance.[145] In the most ambitious study thus far, Stephen Choi, Mitu Galati, and Eric Posner began with the assumption that "the data would demonstrate that appointed judges are better than elected judges."[146] They measured the productivity of courts by the number of cases they decided, the quality of their judicial opinions by the frequency with which they were cited by out-of-state courts, and the independence of their judges by the frequency with which they deviated from the votes of their fellow partisans on the court. These authors discovered that elected judges wrote the most opinions, that appointed judges wrote opinions that garnered the most out-of-state citations (with partisan-elected judges and merit-selected judges ranking equally low on this measure), and that partisan-elected and merit-selected judges ranked equally high on their independence measure. They concluded that "it may be that elected judges are, indeed, superior to appointed judges. Or it may be that elected judges are superior to appointed judges *in small states only* and not necessarily in large states. At a minimum, the conventional wisdom needs to be reexamined."[147]

Concluding Thoughts

Implicit in the Defenders' critique of judicial elections is a model of a less rancorous, apolitical mode of judicial selection, one that focuses on professional competence rather than extraneous considerations. Leaving aside the desirability of this alternative, let us turn instead to its realizability. For the question is not whether there are problems with the popular election of judges—admittedly there are. The question rather is whether alternative modes of selection are less prone to those problems. For insofar as other modes of judicial selection exhibit the same flaws as popular election of judges does, changing the mode of section is not the solution. Moreover, if popular election of judges is no more problematic than other modes of selection, then there may be reason to prefer popular election. Such a system is an established element in state politics—since 1846, every state constitution that has been adopted has provided for some form of judicial election—and today the vast majority of state judges stand for election at some point. Beyond that, the American political tradition supports direct popular control over political officials—the right of the people to "cashier their governors"—absent strong reason to forgo it. Finally, there is a strong American tradition of popular input into the administration of justice, exemplified in reliance on the jury and on lay judges, and popular election of judges fits comfortably within that tradition.

It is true that with elections judges who adhere to what they believe to be the demands of the law will sometimes be removed from office. Yet the aim in judicial selection should not be simply to retain in office all judges who act in good faith and seek to adhere to the law, for in doing so, one may also retain many judges who do not merit retention. Like others who hold office at the discretion of the people, judges may be removed for good reasons or for bad, and electoral defeat is part of the risk of going before the public. To insist that judges should remain in office absent proof of wrongdoing is to claim that they have a right to their offices and that the burden lies on those who would remove them. But it is not clear why this should be so. Holding public office, including judicial office, is employment at will.

There is broad consensus about how we should choose governors and state legislators and about what they should do. But there is considerably less consensus about what we want our judges to do and therefore less consensus, both historically and currently, about how we should select our judges.[148] We want judges who are free from inappropriate external influences so that they can render impartial decisions according to law in the cases that come before them. Yet we also believe that those who wield power should be held accountable for its exercise, and state courts—particularly state supreme courts—clearly make decisions of broad societal import. Defenders believe that judicial elections threaten judicial independence and hence judicial impartiality, undermining the rule of law. Yet as our analysis has shown, most arguments against judicial elections cannot withstand scholarly scrutiny. Given this and "given democratic preferences for empowerment of leaders through the popular will, judicial election . . . nests easily inside democratic principles," and so there is much to recommend it.[149] At a minimum, election is one among several reasonable alternatives that states might choose for selecting judges.

Yet if a state does embrace judicial elections, it should consider what steps might be taken to remedy the flaws associated with judicial elections while securing the benefits of popular input. Chapter 6 addresses those questions.

6 Ensuring Judicial Independence and Accountability in the Twenty-first Century

IF THE ELIMINATION OF JUDICIAL ELECTIONS IS UNLIKELY AND MAY even be undesirable, then how does one promote both independence and accountability under an elective system? Several proposals have been advanced, including altering the standards and procedures for disqualification and recusal of judges, public financing of judicial elections, and limiting state supreme court justices to a single nonrenewable term of office. We assess each of these proposals and conclude with a consideration of the difficulties of controlling "judicial legislation" without invading judicial independence. We therefore offer as an alternative to judge-focused approaches a reinvigoration of popular constitutionalism in the American states.

Disqualification and Recusal

Canon 3 of the American Bar Association's Model Code of Judicial Conduct admonishes judges to conduct their personal and extrajudicial activities so as to minimize the risk of conflict with the obligations of judicial office.[1] Even so, conflicts of interest may arise. Defenders insist that the need to raise large sums of money to compete for judicial office aggravates conflict-of-interest problems. Because judges depend upon campaign contributions, their decisions could be influenced by gratitude for past contributions or by the hope of receiving future donations. This concern is particularly acute when "the principal sources of financial support are central stakeholders or counsel in cases pending before their beneficiary's courts."[2] Such situations run the risk of encouraging judicial partiality or bias; even when they do not, they create an unwelcome appearance of corruption. In addition, in the wake of *Republican Party of Minnesota v. White* and its progeny, which have struck down various restrictions on judicial speech during election campaigns, candidates for judicial office may make statements that raise questions about their impartiality on the bench. To counter such problems, states provide for the disqualification of judges when the potential for bias exists, and judges may, when requested, recuse themselves to avoid the appearance of impropriety. These mechanisms promote judicial independence, by insulating the administration of justice from inappropriate external influences, and they do so without interfering with judicial accountability because judicial disqualification or recusal does not limit popular input in the selection or retention of judges.

State law establishes standards as to when judges are disqualified from presiding over or participating in cases, and both state law and professional standards encourage judges to recuse themselves to avoid the appearance of partiality. In doing so, they seek to strike a balance between the need to avoid judicial impropriety and the desire to prevent the overuse of motions for recusal by lawyers engaging in forum shopping.[3] Rule 211 (A) of the ABA's Model Code of Judicial Conduct mandates that "a judge shall disqualify himself or herself in a proceeding in which the judge's impartiality might reasonably be questioned."[4] However, recent events—in particular, the notorious failure of justices in West Virginia and Illinois to recuse themselves despite substantial contributions and campaign expenditures by parties in litigation—raise questions about how effective this judicial self-policing is. As noted, in Illinois Justice Lloyd A. Karmeier refused to recuse himself in a case involving the State Farm Mutual Insurance Company despite the fact that individuals and entities closely associated with the firm contributed more than $1 million to his campaign. And in West Virginia, Justice Brent Benjamin refused to recuse himself in a case in which one of the parties had not only donated the $1,000 statutory maximum to his campaign but had also donated $2.5 million to a section 527 political organization formed to oppose the incumbent in the race. Indeed, the West Virginia case prompted the intervention of the US Supreme Court, which ruled that Justice Brent Benjamin's decision to participate in the *Caperton* case had the effect of denying due process to the opposing party in the case.[5]

These and other examples have led to a flood of proposals for reform designed to strengthen recusal procedures—as Judge Margaret McKeown of the Ninth Circuit put it, "The topic du jour is recusal."[6] Under the rules of the West Virginia Supreme Court of Appeals—and of many other courts as well—disqualification motions are addressed only "to the justice whose disqualification is sought."[7] This created a problem in *Caperton* and presumably in other cases as well because judges may be unwilling, for good reasons or bad, to recuse themselves when it would be appropriate to do so. Judges have a "duty to sit" absent strong reasons not to, and this makes judges loath to recuse themselves. Some observers insist that "recusal motions are not pejorative. A lawyer who requests judicial recusal is alleging only that the circumstances suggest to neutral observers a probability of bias; he or she is not accusing the judge of any wrongdoing."[8] However, it may not appear that way to the challenged judge because "the judge who disqualifies herself for bias in a given case concedes incapacity to be the impartial arbiter she has sworn to be."[9] This is confirmed by a survey of state judges that revealed a deep hostility toward disqualification motions and a reluctance to recuse.[10] Thus, one proposal is not to let judges judge in their own cases by taking the decision on contested motions for disqualification away from the challenged judge. One way to do this is by establishing bright-line rules governing the disqualification of judges. For example, more than one-third of the states have judicial peremptory challenge statutes, under which counsel can "strike" one judge per proceeding. Although this may multiply disqualifications, it has the advantage of being straightforward and inexpensive, and it avoids the unseemliness and retribution risk of a disqualification proceeding.[11] Another bright-line rule is the American Bar Association's recommendation for mandatory disqualification of judges who have accepted contributions from parties appearing before them that exceed a certain threshold amount. This rule reduces the incentive for groups or litigants or attorneys to seek favor through large campaign contributions, although they may contribute to judicial campaigns for a variety of reasons other than the hope of advantage. However, the ABA's proposal adds little to the existing law in those states that cap campaign contributions, and it may lend itself to gamesmanship, in that parties or lawyers could disqualify unfavorable judges by making contributions to their campaigns. Even without the ABA rule, candidates could agree to recuse themselves, if elected, in cases involving contributors. Perhaps for these reasons, no state has yet followed the ABA's recommendation.[12]

An alternative with better prospects of adoption is to provide for an independent adjudication of disqualification motions. For, as Steven Lubet has observed, "the great irony of the [*Caperton*] case is that a simple procedural change—the determination of disqualification motions by the entire court, instead of referring them to a single justice—would probably have obviated the need to address the Due Process Clause at all."[13] Some reformers have proposed that a judicial panel, rather than the challenged judge, rule on disqualification motions.[14] The panel might include the entire court on which a judge sits, or alternatively, as was proposed in West Virginia in the wake of *Caperton*, it might involve a judicial recusal commission comprised of acting or retired judges. Under the West Virginia plan, the panel would hold a hearing and then issue a written response to the motion for disqualification. Reformers have also proposed that contested disqualification motions simply be assigned to another judge, as is presently done in Texas under the Texas Rules of Civil Procedure.[15] Finally, they have encouraged judges to seek assistance before deciding on whether to recuse themselves, either from state-established recusal advisory boards, or, in the case of a challenged judge on a state appellate court, from the other members of that court.[16]

Disqualification and recusal seek to address the deleterious effects of politicized judicial elections rather than attempt to limit such politicization. Perhaps for this reason, many Defenders have placed less emphasis on them, insisting that other steps, such as campaign finance reform, are likely to be more effective.[17] Some Defenders also worry that frequent recusals might send the wrong message: if judges often cannot sit on the cases coming before them, this may undermine confidence in the impartiality of judges. In addition, some Defenders are concerned that frequent recusals might limit the available judicial workforce, which in turn might encourage a dilution of standards for impartiality in order to have judges available who could hear cases.[18]

The very real concerns raised by Defenders make clear that one must monitor the effects of recusal reform. But at this point the adverse consequences are simply speculative, and it is just as possible that strengthening disqualification and recusal will serve judicial independence without compromising judicial accountability. This would hardly solve all problems, but there is a place for modest reforms that achieve limited objectives without adverse consequences. Let us turn now to the broader alternative of campaign finance reform and, more specifically, to public financing of judicial campaigns.

Public Financing of Judicial Elections

Defenders have argued that if one must have judicial elections, they should be funded through public financing. As of 2012, four states—Wisconsin, North Carolina, New Mexico, and West Virginia—had adopted this reform. Wisconsin pioneered public financing for judicial races in 1976 as part of a program of partial public funding for candidates for all statewide offices, but it totally revamped its system in 2009 to provide full funding in judicial races following an escalation of expenditures and rancor in recent supreme court races.[19] In 2002 North Carolina established the first system of full public financing of state judicial elections as part of a package that also included a switch from partisan to nonpartisan judicial elections. This package was adopted in response to the 2000 election in North Carolina, which for the first time saw judicial candidates spend more than $1 million. New Mexico became the third state to introduce public financing for judicial elections in 2007. Although the reform was not prompted by any dramatic rise in campaign expenditures, judicial elections in New Mexico had become contested with incumbents facing challengers in 80 percent of partisan races and suffering defeat in 11 percent of the races, and this apparently played some part in the introduction of public financing.[20] Finally, West Virginia established a pilot program of public financing that extended only to supreme court races in the wake of the *Caperton v. Massey Coal* (2009). Thus, the politicization of judicial elections in individual states helps explain why and when those states adopted public financing.

The states with public financing select their judges in various ways: West Virginia conducts partisan elections; Wisconsin has nonpartisan elections; North Carolina switched to nonpartisan elections when it adopted public financing; and New Mexico has a hybrid system that includes commission-based selection, partisan elections, and retention elections. Despite these differences, their public-financing programs share some common features.[21] First, public financing is available for only some judicial races. North Carolina has instituted public financing only for general elections for its appellate courts, and West Virginia's pilot program of public financing covers only supreme court races. Candidates running for the trial bench or, in some states, in primary elections must therefore raise their own campaign funds. Second, to qualify for public financing, candidates must demonstrate the seriousness of their candidacy by raising a certain amount of "seed money" through small private contributions. To receive public funds in North Carolina, for example, Supreme Court candidates must raise between $40,050 and $80,100 in voter contributions during the primary election, with no contribution to exceed $500. Failure to abide by restrictions on how this seed money is raised may lead to a denial of public funds, as happened in 2010 in New Mexico, when an appellate court candidate was denied funding because he had exceeded the $5,000 limit on what publicly financed candidates could contribute to their own campaigns.[22] Third, once candidates accept public financing, they must accept no private campaign contributions and spend no money beyond the public funds. In North Carolina, West Virginia, and Wisconsin, if publicly financed candidates were outspent by a privately financed candidate or through independent campaign expenditures, they could receive additional public funds in order to ensure their competitiveness in the election. However, in 2011 the US Supreme Court ruled that such "rescue" provisions violate the First Amendment.[23]

Efforts to introduce public financing in other states have not succeeded. These failures cannot be attributed simply to a general opposition to public financing of election campaigns—looking beyond judicial elections, Peter Wallison and Joel Gora note that "depending on which study one consults, there are public funding programs of one form or another in sixteen to twenty-five states."[24] Doubts about the need for public financing in states with merit selection or nonpartisan elections help explain the reluctance to extend it to judicial races. So too may cost concerns. In addition, despite public concern about the influence of campaign contributions on judges, poll data reveal that the public continues to favor the election of judges and opposes public financing of judicial races.[25] Given the current precarious financial position of the states, it is unlikely many will take on the new expense of financing of judicial races in the near future. Indeed, the trend is in the opposite direction. In 2011 the West Virginia Senate killed a proposal to inject more money into the state's pilot public-financing program, raising questions about its viability, and Wisconsin's 2011 biennial budget altogether eliminated public funding for supreme court campaigns.[26]

Defenders have led the fight for public financing: the American Bar Association, Justice at Stake, and the American Judicature Society have all endorsed public financing for state appellate elections.[27] Those supporting public financing believe that it will ensure that judges are not beholden to campaign contributors, a concern that assumed increased importance in the wake of *Citizens United v. Federal Election Commission* (2010).[28] Thus Bert Brandenburg, executive director of Justice at Stake, claimed that the *Citizens United* ruling "pours gasoline on an already raging bonfire that will affect all federal and state elections. And it will pose an especially grave threat to the integrity of elected state courts."[29] Brandenburg's comments echoed Justice John Paul Stevens's dissenting opinion in *Citizens United*, which noted that states "may no longer have the ability to place modest limits on corporate electioneering even if they believe such limits to be critical to maintaining the integrity of their judicial systems."[30]

Yet Defenders who argue that public financing is necessary to guarantee judicial independence immediately encounter an embarrassing problem: their argument seems to imply that, absent such financing, judge's votes are for sale. For obvious reasons, Defenders are reluctant to say this, so they emphasize other justifications for public financing. They argue that even if contributions do not compromise judicial decision making, they create the *impression* that judgeships and judges' votes can be bought and thereby undermine popular respect for the courts.[31] Even a single instance of apparent judicial corruption, they note, can have far-reaching effects because the public rarely differentiates among judges or between levels of courts in forming their impressions of judicial conduct.[32]

There is some empirical support for this assertion. A national poll commissioned by Justice at Stake in 2004 found that 71 percent of respondents believed that judges' rulings were influenced by campaign contributions from interest groups.[33] More recently, based on a telephone survey of a representative sample of Kentucky citizens, James L. Gibson concluded that "the strongest effects on [the] institutional legitimacy [of courts] come from campaign contributions. When groups with direct connections to the decision maker give contributions, legitimacy suffers significantly."[34] However, Gibson cautioned against reading too much into these results, noting that "the assumption that public concerns about campaign contributions translates into a lack of confidence in the judiciary is not supported by the evidence."[35] In particular, he noted that the same ABA poll that found respondents concerned about campaign contributions affecting the impartiality of judges also found that 75 percent favored elections over appointment of judges and 74 percent expressed "a great deal" or "some" confidence in courts and judges.

Defenders further want to distance judges from the unsavory task of soliciting contributions for their campaigns, whether directly or through intermediaries. This not only serves to avoid the appearance or actuality of corruption but also helps recruit highly qualified prospective judges who may be dissuaded from serving on the bench because of the prospect of having to solicit funds.[36] As suggested in Chapter 5, this is a dubious argument. Finally, Defenders note that requiring judicial candidates to raise funds makes judicial campaigns similar to other political campaigns, undermining the sense of the distinctiveness of the judicial office in the minds both of the public and of those considering seeking judicial office.[37]

The Operation of Public-Financing Programs:
Wisconsin and North Carolina

Although it is too early to draw conclusions about the systems of public financing that New Mexico and West Virginia adopted in 2007 and 2010, the experiences of Wisconsin and in North Carolina offer some insight into the effects of public financing and the claims of its supporters.[38] Wisconsin introduced partial public financing in 1976 to supplement private fundraising, but the availability of public funds did not preclude private donations to judicial campaigns. The Wisconsin system relied upon a taxpayer check-off on the state income-tax form for funding. Although participation in the program did not increase tax liability, few taxpayers participated, and this chronic underfunding meant that public funds were very limited, so public funding provided only a small percentage of the funds spent by judicial candidates, and many candidates decided to forego public funding altogether.[39] Thus a 2001 study of Wisconsin judicial races found that public funds accounted for less than 5 percent of the money spent by judicial candidates.[40] Public funding also did not discourage an escalation of campaign costs. In 2007 three candidates for a seat on the Wisconsin Supreme Court raised $2,680,160 through private contributions, and in a 2008 race two candidates raised $1,196,436.[41] In that latter year challenger Michael Gableman unseated incumbent Louis Butler after a highly contentious campaign conducted largely through televised attack ads.[42] Total spending on Wisconsin judicial races in 2008 hit $8.5 million, with more than $2 million of that total coming from a business-backed group called Wisconsin Manufacturers and Commerce. In 2009, in response to these escalating costs and the changing character of judicial elections, Wisconsin enacted legislation providing full funding in judicial races, with funds from the state's general fund alleviating shortfalls from the taxpayer check-off.[43]

The initial experience under this new law suggests that it did not change the dynamics of judicial elections. The 2011 race for a seat on the Wisconsin Supreme Court pitted an incumbent, Justice David Prosser, against challenger JoAnne Kloppenburg. Although nominally a nonpartisan election, the partisan affiliations of the candidates were widely publicized—Prosser was a Republican and Kloppenburg a Democrat—and the race was seen in part as a referendum on the controversial policies of Republican governor Scott Walker. In addition, a victory by Kloppenburg would have given Democrats a 4–3 majority on the Wisconsin Supreme Court, which could have proved decisive were the court called upon to consider challenges to some of Governor Walker's initiatives. Given these unusual circumstances, one should not generalize too much from this race. Nonetheless, it is clear that Wisconsin's system of full public financing did not reduce interest group involvement; it merely diverted it to independent expenditures, as independent groups spent more than $3.5 million on television ads, a record for the state. Nor did public financing lead to a less rancorous election. Groups supporting Kloppenburg charged that as a district attorney Prosser had refused to prosecute a pedophile priest, that he was antiunion, and that he would be a rubber stamp for Governor Walker. Groups supporting Prosser dismissed the sexual assault ad as "sleazy and full of lies" and charged that Kloppenburg was soft on crime. The outcome was a narrow victory for Justice Prosser, confirmed only after a recount, with unprecedented voter turnout for a Wisconsin Supreme Court election.[44]

In 2002 North Carolina adopted a system of full public financing for judicial candidates, under which candidates for the appellate bench who qualify for public funding and forego private fundraising are eligible for substantial lump-sum payments from the Public Campaign Fund. This fund is supported by taxpayer check-offs on their state income tax, the same system employed in Wisconsin pre-2009. Although the level of public participation has hovered below 10 percent, for the 2008 election this check-off raised $2.1 million or about 51 percent of the Public Campaign Fund's total receipts. Additional funding has come from a $50 surcharge on the annual fee paid by attorneys to the State Bar, begun as a voluntary surcharge but changed to a mandatory one in 2005. Also, judicial candidates must return unspent funds to the Public Campaign Fund, and individuals can make voluntary contributions to the fund.[45] Taken altogether, the fund collects about $4.6 million per election cycle, and these revenues in recent years have provided each publicly financed candidate for the North Carolina Supreme Court with slightly more than $200,000 in public funds.

Defenders view North Carolina's system as "a model for judicial campaign financing in other states," and it is easy to understand why.[46] By providing full financing during general elections for candidates for appellate courts, North Carolina has eliminated reliance on private contributions, thereby addressing both the possibility and the appearance of corruption. It also has encouraged most eligible candidates in North Carolina to avail themselves of public funding: in 2004, twelve of sixteen candidates for appellate judgeships opted for public financing; in 2006, eight of twelve; and in 2008, eleven of twelve.[47] Finally, it has severed the connection between the ability to raise funds and election outcomes. In the four election cycles before public funding, the highest-spending candidate won 71 percent of the time, but with public financing that fell to 46 percent, and actual differences in expenditures among publicly funded candidates were minimal.[48]

Yet one thing that has made the North Carolina program attractive to candidates was the availability of "rescue funds." In 2006 a challenger to Supreme Court Justice Sarah Parker spent $155,000 more than the spending cap for publicly funded candidates, triggering a dollar-for-dollar disbursement of $155,000 in matching funds to Parker, and in 2008 Supreme Court Justice Bob Edmunds received almost $13,000 in rescue funds based on independent expenditures made by the state Democratic Party in favor of Edmunds's opponent.[49] The invalidation of such "rescue funds" by the US Supreme Court therefore raises questions about whether North Carolina's public-financing system will continue to be attractive to judicial candidates.

Skepticism about Public Financing

Many of the criticisms of public financing have focused on "rescue funds," with critics charging that they disadvantaged challengers, who were able to overcome the advantages incumbents enjoy only by outspending them and reducing the level of campaign communications. The Supreme Court's ruling in *Arizona Free Enterprise Club's Freedom Club PAC v. Bennett* allayed these concerns. However, opponents of public funding further point out that public financing may not reduce spending in judicial races. As David Schultz has suggested, in speaking of campaign finance reform more generally, "regulations that seek to limit money in politics do not seem to prevent contributors from giving; they simply shift their donations to another venue."[50] For groups and individuals interested in judicial races, the shift would be to independent expenditures. Reliable data on such expenditures are notoriously difficult to obtain, so there is no way to test directly whether public financing's prohibitions on direct contributions increase independent expenditures in judicial races.[51] Nevertheless, the infamous nonrecusal election in West Virginia and the Wisconsin race in 2011 suggest this is not an idle concern.

If public financing encourages potential donors to divert funds to independent expenditures, that could jeopardize the very aims that Defenders are seeking to achieve. Defenders wish to reverse the trend toward "noisier, nastier, and costlier" judicial campaigns, but television and radio ads financed by independent expenditures have tended to be more objectionable, from the point of view of Defenders, than those produced by the candidates themselves, who may be reluctant to be identified with some attack ads. So if one aim is raising the level of discourse in judicial races, public financing may not have that effect. Defenders also hope that public financing will buttress public faith in the impartiality of the courts, but it is not clear that public financing promotes this goal because it cannot prevent those making independent expenditures from engaging in "relentless negativity" and "dirty politics, even gutter politics."[52] But unless they eschew such appeals, the fact that candidates' campaigns are publicly funded is unlikely to prevent an undermining of respect for the judiciary because the public cannot be expected to differentiate between expenditures by candidates and independent expenditures against their opponents.

Public Financing and Judicial Accountability

Defenders argue that full public financing promotes judicial independence by providing funds without strings attached and by freeing judicial candidates from the burden of raising funds, at least once they have qualified for such financing.[53] It also severs the connection between judges and donors or potential donors, thereby eliminating possible improper influences on judicial decision making. But Defenders seldom address its effects on judicial accountability, and these too deserve attention.

In order to hold judges accountable, the public must have sufficient information about judges and their performance on the bench. Insofar as public financing reduces the funds available to candidates for communicating with voters, it may exacerbate what is already perceived as a problem. In North Carolina, overall expenditures in state supreme court races increased from

2002 to 2004, despite the institution of public financing, but this was an artifact of a larger pool of candidates; spending per candidate has declined since the advent of public financing.[54] This is hardly surprising, as reducing the sums spent in judicial campaigns was one of the aims behind the adoption of public financing. North Carolina has attempted to allay the problem of inadequate information by distributing a voters' guide that provides information about judicial candidates. In 2008, it posted the guide online and mailed four million copies to households throughout the state. An exit poll conducted after the 2004 election found that 38 percent of voters who received the guide identified it as their primary source of information for judicial races.[55] Yet whether voter guides can adequately inform voter choice remains unclear—the guides may not reach their intended audience, they may not be read, and even if they are, they may not contain the information voters believe they need.

Even with the distribution of the voter guides, voting in North Carolina's state supreme court races declined dramatically after the introduction of public financing. Comparing the vote in 2000 and 2004, both years in which a presidential race increased voter turnout, Bonneau and Hall found that average ballot roll-off under the partisan system was 4.9 percent, but roll-off after the institution of public financing and nonpartisan election was 23.3 percent.[56] Thus effective accountability suffered because fewer citizens participated in the election for supreme court justices. This increased roll-off cannot be attributed solely to the switch to public financing, as shifting from partisan to nonpartisan judicial elections also reduces participation by eliminating a valuable cue for voters. However, the effect is most pronounced when races are not contested, and when nonpartisan elections attract challengers and generate competitive races, roll-off is reduced.[57] In the case of North Carolina, where the state supreme court races in 2004 were competitive, one would not have expected the dramatic decline in turnout that occurred, which suggests that the shift to public financing may have contributed significantly to the reduced electoral accountability for judges.[58]

There is also the question of how public financing affects races for judicial office. For judges to be held accountable, there must be serious electoral competition: candidates must be willing to contest races, and challengers must have a real possibility of unseating incumbents. As one student of elections put it, "One of the goals of campaign finance reform should be to reduce or minimize the inherent advantages of incumbency, and thus make elections more competitive."[59] With regard to the willingness to contest, some

Defenders have cautioned that, by eliminating the need to raise funds, public financing may encourage candidates to seek election. Thus, Charles Geyh predicted, "To the extent that the availability of public money makes running for elective office more attractive, publicly financed judicial elections will tend to increase competition for judicial office. On the one hand, increased competition is salutary in that it expands voter choice. On the other hand, increased competition may undermine ongoing efforts to cool judicial campaign rhetoric and dissuade candidates and the electorate from compromising judicial independence by turning elections into referenda on the popularity of incumbent judges' isolated decisions."[60] This prediction has been borne out in North Carolina, at least when there is no incumbent in the race: in 2004 an open seat attracted eight candidates, and in 2006 an open seat brought out five candidates.[61] However, electoral challenges to judicial incumbents declined, although it is difficult to disentangle whether the shift to public financing or to nonpartisan election produced this effect.

With regard to the seriousness of electoral challenges, the effects of public financing are mixed. Judicial incumbents tend to attract more funding than do challengers and typically outspend them.[62] When challengers are able raise substantial funding, they can achieve greater name recognition and communicate to potential voters information about their backgrounds and their views, which usually increases their percentage of the vote. So if public financing has an equalizing effect on resources, reducing funding disparities between incumbents and challengers, this would seem to benefit challengers.[63] However, in order to unseat incumbents, a rough equality of funding is seldom enough. Challengers usually must outspend incumbents in order to defeat them because incumbents enjoy the advantages of office (name recognition, experience, and so forth). But public financing prevents challengers from doing so. Thus, although public financing may increase the competitiveness of races, it tends to advantage incumbents by preventing challengers from substantially outspending them. This has proven true in North Carolina, as no justice seeking reelection has been defeated since the adoption of public financing. Thus Chris Bonneau and Melinda Gann Hall have concluded that the shifts to nonpartisan election and to public financing "appear to have strengthened the incumbency advantage rather than promote electoral competition."[64]

One should hesitate in generalizing from the North Carolina experience, both because that experience may be idiosyncratic and because it is difficult to distinguish the effects of public financing from those attributable to the shift to nonpartisan election. Nonetheless, it seems likely that North Carolina's system of public financing, which has been proposed as the model for other states, has reduced judicial accountability. In the wake of the switch to public financing, the level of per-candidate campaign expenditures (and thus the extent of candidates' communication with voters) declined. So too did the level of voter participation in judicial elections and the frequency of electoral challenges to incumbents. Finally, no justices who sought reelection were defeated. Public financing of judicial elections raises the tone of such contests and reduces concerns about the appearance or reality of judicial bias, though there is scant evidence of this. But these results may be achieved at the cost of judicial accountability.

A Single Nonrenewable Term

If one wishes a system of state judicial selection and tenure that promotes both independence and accountability, one should consider the systems of selection and tenure instituted by European countries.[65] The key element of these systems is that members of those countries' constitutional courts are chosen by a different mode of selection and serve for a different tenure than do judges of their ordinary courts.[66] Thus, in Germany all federal courts are exclusively courts of appeals: the Federal Court of Justice, the Federal Administrative Court, the Federal Finance Court, the Federal Labor Court, and the Federal Social Court serve as supreme courts of ordinary, administrative, financial, labor, and social jurisdiction respectively.[67] For each, the judges are chosen jointly by the appropriate federal minister and a committee for the selection of judges consisting of the appropriate *land* ministers and an equal number of members elected by the Bundestag (the lower house of the Parliament).[68] The members of these courts serve until a mandatory retirement age, and they "may be involuntarily dismissed, permanently or temporarily suspended, transferred, or retired before the expiration of their term of office only by virtue of judicial decision and only for the reasons and in the manner specified by the laws."[69] In contrast, judges of the Federal Constitutional Court are elected, half by the Bundestag and half by the Bundesrat (the upper house of the Parliament). They serve twelve-year terms and are not eligible for reelection.[70] In Italy, "appointment to the [ordinary] judiciary is based on competitive examinations," and judges "may not be dismissed, suspended, or moved to other jurisdictions or functions except either by decision of the superior council of the judiciary for reasons and with opportunity of defense as defined by the organizational law, or by their own consent."[71] However, the fifteen members of the Constitutional Court are appointed—one-third by the president, one-third by parliament in joint session, and one-third by ordinary and administrative supreme courts—and they serve a single nonrenewable nine-year term.[72]

France too differentiates among its courts. Judges who serve on ordinary courts attend the Ecole Nationale de la Magistrature and are assigned to a civil or criminal court upon graduation, and Title VIII, Article 64, section 4 of the Constitution mandates that "judges may not be removed from office."[73] In contrast, members of the Constitutional Council (Conseil Constitutional) serve a nonrenewable term of nine years, with one-third appointed by the president of the Republic, one-third by the president of the National Assembly, and one-third by the president of the Senate.[74] Spain, Italy, Portugal, and other European countries likewise have established distinctive, political modes of selection and limited tenure for their constitutional courts.

These differences in selection and tenure for judges on ordinary courts and judges on constitutional courts reflect an understanding that constitutional courts play a distinctive political role. A constitutional court exercises the power of judicial review, whereas ordinary courts do not, and passing on the constitutionality of governmental enactments is different from the ordinary interpretation of the law. In ordinary litigation, the concern is impartiality between the two parties at trial, but in constitutional litigation, as Kate Malleson has put it, "judges are often called upon to decide between the competing ideologies, values, or policies which underlie the law [and] the notion of impartiality is more problematic."[75] Because judicial review inevitably involves political as well as legal judgment, or at least a legal judgment quite different from that expected in ordinary litigation, it follows that those exercising such judgment should be chosen through a political selection process.

Obviously, there are differences between these constitutional courts and American state supreme courts. Whereas judicial review in civil law systems is usually centralized in a single tribunal, all courts in the United States exercise the power of judicial review. Conversely, whereas constitutional courts in Europe decide only constitutional questions, state supreme courts decide a wide range of nonconstitutional cases—indeed, constitutional questions represent a small percentage of state supreme court caseloads.[76] Whereas constitutional courts in Europe have the final judicial say on constitutional questions, at least within their borders (ignoring possible review by supranational courts), the rulings of state supreme courts may be subject to review by the US Supreme Court if a federal question is involved. Whereas state supreme courts generally can rule on the constitutionality of legislation only in the context of deciding a case or controversy, most constitutional courts in Europe exercise abstract review, that is, they rule on the constitutionality of proposed legislation prior to its adoption. This last distinction is only partially accurate: ten state supreme courts exercise a form of abstract review through their power (or responsibility) to issue advisory opinions, and some constitutional courts—for example, Germany's—exercise both concrete and abstract review, as well as responding to constitutional complaints brought by individuals or entities vested with rights under the constitution.[77]

However, these differences should not be overstated. Although judicial review is not centralized in state supreme courts, some state constitutions do mandate that the supreme court hear appeals in cases in which a federal or state law has been declared unconstitutional; even in the absence of such requirements, state supreme courts use their discretionary jurisdiction to hear such cases, so in practice something like centralized review prevails in that a single court makes the determinative ruling on constitutional issues. In addition, although state supreme courts hear nonconstitutional cases, this does not mean that they are not "political courts," as they may exercise an important political role even in some of those cases—for example, in developing common law. Indeed, the creation of intermediate courts of appeals in most states was designed to allow the justices to select the issues they wish to address, and "almost surely this has affected the self-perception of the judges of the high courts, who tend to view themselves primarily as policymakers."[78] Although in some cases the US Supreme Court can review state supreme court rulings, this is true only when the rulings do not rest on "independent and adequate state grounds."[79]

Moreover, even when the power does exist, it rarely is exercised—for example, in its 2008 term, the US Supreme Court decided with full opinion only fifteen cases on appeal from state courts.[80] In sum, state supreme courts—like constitutional courts in Europe—play a distinctive policy role, ruling on controversial policy issues and overseeing the development of state law—that differentiates them from other courts in the states. Indeed, Bashers' complaints about state "judicial activism" focus almost exclusively on state supreme courts precisely because they play this distinctive role. Given this distinctive role, the arrangements for selection and tenure pioneered in Europe for constitutional courts—that is, political selection to serve a single nonrenewable term—may be appropriate in the American states as well.

In view of the prolonged debate over modes of state judicial selection, it is important to note that under a single-term plan the mode of initial selection is not crucial. Justices could be either elected or appointed, although the single-term idea is likely to be more acceptable to voters if they are not required to give up altogether their say as to who should serve on state supreme courts, and I shall therefore proceed in this discussion as if the initial selection is by contested election. Nor, within limits, is the exact length of the judicial term crucial. That might vary from state to state, as it does now. One would certainly not wish the term of office to be unduly short: justices need time to master their responsibilities, and too short a term might render service on the court unattractive. However, most state supreme court justices currently serve terms of eight years or longer, and that would seem sufficient, as it is comparable to the terms of office for the judges on most European constitutional courts.[81]

What is crucial is that state supreme court justices serve only a single term and not be eligible to stand for reelection. Such a system enhances judicial independence by freeing justices to decide cases according to their best understanding of the law, without fear of retribution or hope of support in future elections. Defenders insist that a major disadvantage of state systems of judicial selection is that sitting judges can be targeted for defeat because of one or a few controversial decisions.[82] The requirement of seeking reelection makes courageous judges vulnerable when they adhere to the law in defiance of powerful interests or prevailing community sentiment, and it tempts less courageous judges to tailor their rulings to accommodate powerful interests or community sentiment in order to avoid retribution at the polls. In neither case are justice and judicial independence served.

The findings in a recent study by Joanna Shepherd suggest that the single nonrenewable term may alleviate these concerns, at least to some extent. Analyzing state supreme court decisions from 1995–98, Shepherd found that justices who were seeking reelection in Republican jurisdictions tended to decide cases conservatively, whereas judges in Democratic jurisdictions tended to decide cases more liberally. Although correlation does not indicate causation, this is consistent with what one would expect if judges took reelection prospects into account in their decision making. But what was striking in her study was that this did not operate across the board. Judges with permanent tenure or serving their final term of office—that is, judges not facing reelection—did not exhibit the same voting pattern.[83]

Defenders also are concerned about public perceptions that justice is for sale, that some litigants receive favored treatment because of their contributions to judicial campaigns. The single nonrenewable term likewise addresses that concern, at least in part. For whatever the contributions a group makes to a justice's election, the justice knows that she does not need to satisfy that group because she does not need to keep its support for a future election. This may discourage blatant attempts to "buy" votes on state supreme courts. In addition, groups will not be able to take revenge at the polls if a justice rules against their interests when adherence to the law requires it. Under the single-term proposal, thus, the situation of the justice on a state supreme court is similar to that of a federal judge. Whatever the political support drawn upon to secure appointment, federal judges retain their decisional independence because they will never have to draw upon that support again. As presidents have learned to their regret in at least some instances, once appointed, justices on the Supreme Court can go their own way.

Yet the reference to federal judges raises a question. If tenure during good behavior has the effect of insulating judges from undue pressures, why not opt for that on the state level instead of a single nonrenewable term? In part the response is a practical one: few states currently award tenure during good behavior, and there is no reason to expect other states would support a radical extension of judicial terms of office. In part, however, the response is that providing an opportunity for periodic public input about the *general direction* of law and policy emanating from the state's highest court is important for judicial accountability. Once one acknowledges that state supreme court justices are involved in more than merely technical application of the law and make decisions with broad societal consequences, the case for popular input into public law becomes compelling. The key is to promote judicial accountability without compromising judicial independence, and a single nonrenewable term does precisely that. Decisional independence requires that the individual judge be free to decide cases impartially, without fear or favor, based on his or her best understanding of the law. The single nonrenewable term promotes that by removing the ability of political officials, interest groups, or voters to extend the judge's tenure because individual justices are not obliged (or permitted) to seek reappointment or public approval of their performance in office. Judicial accountability requires that the public or their representatives have the opportunity to assess judicial rulings and ensure that they reflect the values and perspectives of the public. Accountability therefore focuses not on the votes of individual justices but on the general direction of the court. The single nonrenewable term facilitates accountability at the level of the court as a whole by a periodic turnover of its membership. If the public or its representatives are satisfied with the overall legal or policy direction of the state supreme court, they can ensure that new justices share the prevailing perspective on the court. But if they are dissatisfied with the court's rulings, they can place on the court justices with a different legal or political perspective. Such considerations currently are important in the selection of justices of the US Supreme Court. What the single nonrenewable term does is to regularize turnover, rather than have it determined by the health of the justices or their efforts to ensure that their successors share their legal or political orientation.[84]

One can imagine a number of concerns about a single nonrenewable term, and responding to them may help to flesh out this proposal. One concern might be that a single nonrenewable term would undermine the quality of state supreme courts because it would be difficult to attract distinguished attorneys to serve on state supreme courts if they were limited to a single term of office. However, the experience of constitutional courts in Europe tends to refute this. The single nonrenewable term has not impeded the recruitment of highly qualified judges for those courts. Moreover, if as Defenders allege, the necessity of fund-raising and campaigning deters distinguished attorneys from seeking to serve, the single nonrenewable term reduces the problem because prospective judges will have to seek office only once.

Yet if changing the tenure of justices does not interfere with the recruitment of highly qualified jurists, it may alter the career paths of those who aspire to serve on the state high court. Currently, attorneys in their forties and fifties may seek elevation to the state supreme court with the expectation that this will be their final professional position because they can serve multiple terms. However, when this prospect is eliminated, prospective judges can be expected to alter their behavior accordingly. With a single nonrenewable term, service on the state supreme court might come to be seen as a career-capping move, with attorneys in private practice putting themselves forth only at a late stage in their careers. Or judges who have served on lower courts may become candidates for the state supreme court at the conclusion of their careers.

Yet even if justices were elected at the same age they are now, a single non-renewable term would not necessarily jeopardize their career prospects. The current behavior of attorneys and of federal and state judges offers some support for this. Attorneys regularly accept political appointments in midcareer, sometimes serving for periods as long as the proposed term for state supreme court justices, and they are then able to return to private practice without significant disruption. Certainly there is no evidence that federal judges and state supreme court justices who voluntarily leave the bench have difficulty finding employment with major law firms, universities, or other organizations. The same holds true for those who leave involuntarily. For example, after their defeat in retention elections, Penny White became the Elvin E. Overton Distinguished Professor of Law and Director of the Center for Advocacy at the University of Tennessee College of Law, and David Lanphier joined the Broom, Johnson law firm in Omaha. One suspects that justices who leave the bench following completion of their term will likewise have attractive opportunities available to them.

Another concern might be that an eight-year or ten-year term would be too short for judges to become expert in their responsibilities. Yet the proposed term of office is no shorter than the term most justices currently serve; the only difference is that justices will not serve additional terms. In addition, one should not assume that those elevated to state high courts will have to learn the job of a judge from scratch, that they will have no prior judicial experience. More than two-thirds of state supreme court justices had prior judicial experience, and this may well continue even with the switch to a single nonrenewable term.[85]

A further concern is that the elimination of reeligibility would deprive states of distinguished justices whom one might wish to retain on the bench. This is true, and it is undoubtedly a cost. But the real question is whether the costs of non-reeligibility, of which this is one, outweigh the benefits of a single term. The cost of possibly losing an effective incumbent is one that states have been willing to bear in other contexts. For example, many states have term limits for legislators and for governors. Some have also mandated a retirement age of seventy for judges, even though this might unseat distinguished jurists who could continue to serve effectively. The question is not whether there are costs associated with a single-term requirement—there are—but whether the benefits outweigh the costs.

If justices are elected, allowing state supreme court justices to serve only a single term means that all judicial elections will be open-seat elections. This is likely to increase electoral competition because open seats attract candidates. In states with nonpartisan elections, this will have a major effect because races with incumbents are particularly likely to be uncontested or noncompetitive.[86] The effect will be felt as well in states with partisan elections, as open seats promote competitive elections. If party competition is strong, the competition will be along partisan lines. If it is not, competition will likely take place in the primary election, as candidates vie for the dominant party's endorsement, as occurred in Alabama after the state—and the state bench— turned heavily Republican. Thus, limiting justices to a single term will encourage greater competition, greater spending to attract voters, and hence the possibility of more informed voter choice. All of this promotes greater accountability without undermining judicial independence.

One may speculate on how these more contested elections would play out. The single nonrenewable term offers an opportunity for voters to register their approval or disapproval of the direction that a supreme court is going. It may also give candidates an incentive to frame their campaigns in terms of a referendum on recent rulings of the court. *Republican Party of Minnesota v. White*, by permitting judicial candidates greater freedom to express their legal and political views, may encourage candidates to voice their approval or disapproval of those rulings. Insofar as candidates frame their campaigns in this fashion, it would facilitate voters using judicial elections as a form of referendum on the state supreme court. But even in the absence of such a strategy, a single nonrenewable term has the potential to enforce judicial accountability.

Shifting the Debate

For many Bashers, I suspect, the proposal for a single, nonrenewable term will seem inadequate because it does not directly confront "judicial activism." Judges who are perceived as making rather than interpreting the law are not threatened with the loss of their positions, so the single nonrenewable term eliminates the incentive for appropriate judicial behavior posed by the threat of electoral defeat. In addition, the form of accountability that it provides is long-delayed and hardly foolproof. There is no guarantee that the justice who succeeds an allegedly activist judge will, once on the court, exhibit any greater fidelity to the law. These are serious concerns, and they point to the difficulty of controlling judicial behavior while respecting judicial independence.

Leading scholars have suggested that judicial independence and judicial accountability "are complementary concepts that can and should be regarded as allies."[87] But our analysis suggests that the two concepts are opposed or at least in tension, and choices must be made. Therefore, a broader perspective might be appropriate, one that focuses on the substance of the law rather than solely on the independence or accountability of its interpreters. Whereas Defenders insist ordinary citizens lack the expertise to determine whether judges have followed the law, they certainly can determine what they want the law to be. This is not to say, of course, that everyone will agree on what the law should be, what results are desirable in constitutional or other policy-relevant cases. It merely acknowledges that in a system of self-government the people should determine, either directly or through their elected representatives, the substance of the law. Judges may say what the law is, but the people say what it should be.

Curtailing Judicial Discretion

Defenders and Bashers may find themselves in unaccustomed agreement as to the desirability of shifting political discourse from denunciations of judges to discussion of what sorts of legal outcomes are desirable. But how does one do so? The pertinent model might be found in how state constitution-makers dealt with perceived legislative transgressions during the nineteenth century. When legislators failed to follow the wishes of their constituents, responding to special interests or substituting their own views for those of their constituents, state constitution-makers limited their discretion. They expressly prohibited certain types of legislation—for example, the enactment of special laws when general laws were possible —and they inserted into state constitutions specific policy provisions, essentially transferring policy-making from the people's representatives to the people themselves. In so doing, they operated on the assumption that the more detailed and precise the constitutional proscriptions and prescriptions, the less legislative discretion, and hence the less opportunity for legislators to betray the public trust.[88]

A similar approach might be used in dealing with perceived "judicial activism," crafting statutes and constitutional provisions to limit and channel judicial discretion. Indeed, to some extent this has already occurred. Criminal justice offers one example. State trial judges exercise only limited discretion, but one area in which they have done so is in sentencing those convicted of crime.[89] When the public in several states concluded judges had done a poor job in sentencing criminals, their representatives enacted sentencing guide-lines that limited judicial discretion.[90] And when the public believed judges were too lenient in their sentencing, their representatives established "manda-tory minimum" sentences for certain offenses and prescribed long and man-datory terms of imprisonment for repeat offenders.[91] One may well debate the wisdom of these policies—indeed, there is a vast literature that does precisely that—and experience has led some states to reintroduce judicial discretion in sentencing. But the point here is that the sentencing guidelines and manda-tory minimums that were adopted did curtail judicial choice, and they did so without invading judicial independence. Some judges have complained about the laws, but despite this judicial unhappiness, it is undoubtedly the respon-sibility of the legislature to define offenses and prescribe punishments, so the fact that in the past it authorized judges to exercise discretion in sentencing does not mean that it was acting inappropriately when it limited or withdrew that authority.

The Common Law

Similar efforts to constrain judicial choice have occurred in dealing with the common law. During the decades after World War II, state supreme courts revolutionized the field of tort law, transforming standards for determin-ing liability, abolishing long-standing immunities, eliminating common law limitations on causes of action, and generally making it easier for plaintiffs to pursue their claims. Given the possibility of changing the law through judi-cial decisions, trial attorneys on the one hand and business and insurance groups on the other have contributed heavily to judicial campaigns and have sponsored their own television ads in the hope of influencing the composi-tion of state supreme courts and the direction of legal change. However, those unhappy with the direction of court-imposed change have also looked to state legislatures for redress, seeking to alter the law rather than change the justices. Beginning in the 1980s, state legislatures attempted to rein in court-initiated changes in tort law by enacting "tort-reform" statutes that restricted recovery and shifted the law in ways favorable to defendants in tort cases.[92] The plain-tiffs' bar responded by challenging some of these statutes as unconstitutional. For example, they argued that statutory limits on punitive or noneconomic damages violated state constitutional guarantees of jury trial because they limited the discretion of jurors in awarding damages. They also contended that statutes of limitations and statutes of repose violated the "open courts" provisions of state constitutions, which guarantee that the courts be available for the redress of injuries.[93] These arguments enjoyed some success: during the 1980s and 1990s, supreme courts in twenty-six states struck down more than ninety tort-reform statutes.[94] Nonetheless, despite these rulings, state legislatures have reversed various judicial initiatives and introduced substantial changes in tort law.

Thus, as with the criminal law, the people's representatives had the option of changing the substance of the common law rather than its interpreters, and many states availed themselves of that option. Debate continues as to whether these judicial innovations promoted a better balance between plaintiff and defendant or merely encouraged excessive litigation and a proliferation of dubious claims. There is continuing debate as well as to whether various tort reforms have restored a balance in tort law or have advantaged businesses, insurance companies, physicians, and others at the expense of those injured by their malfeasance. But these debates focus on the substance of tort law and the distribution of risk, rather than on the character of the judges elaborating tort law, and thus do not threaten judicial independence.

Statutory Interpretation

This same shift of focus from judges to the substance of law can be seen in the statutory realm as well. Judges have the responsibility of interpreting statutes, but if legislators disagree with judicial interpretations, they can overturn these interpretations by clarifying—or changing—their meaning in subsequent legislation. Although overturning judicial interpretations is a drain on legislative resources, scholars have documented numerous instances of congressional overriding of statutory interpretations by the US Supreme Court.[95] There have unfortunately been no comparable studies of state legislatures overriding state courts, but it stands to reason that such overriding occurs at the state level as well.[96]

State legislatures have not limited themselves to overriding judicial interpretations of particular statutes. They have in recent years sought to direct judicial interpretation of their handiwork by prescribing rules to govern judicial interpretation of statutes.[97] Thus in 2001 the Oregon Legislature enacted a law seeking to elevate the role of legislative history in statutory interpretation, responding to a 1993 Oregon Supreme Court ruling that had prescribed a textualist approach for statutory interpretation in Oregon courts.[98] Texas too enacted a set of interpretive rules, codified in the state "Code Construction

Act," that rejected the textualist approach to statutory interpretation dominant on the Texas Court of Criminal Appeals and mandated that courts "liberally constru[e]" all statutes "to achieve their purpose and to promote justice."[99] In Connecticut the General Assembly passed legislation reaffirming the "plain-meaning rule" in response to a supreme court ruling abandoning it in favor of a more eclectic approach to statutory interpretation.[100] These are hardly isolated occurrences: according to Abbe Gluck, "every state legislature in the Nation has enacted a number of canons of construction" to guide the interpretation of its enactments.[101]

State courts have sometimes rebelled against these prescriptions, either ignoring the legislated interpretive rules or insisting that they infringe on judicial authority.[102] Whether this latter claim is valid is complicated by the diversity of institutional arrangements among the states, as well as by the fact that the division of authority among the branches of state government need not parallel the division within the federal government.[103] Certainly the ubiquity of legislative efforts to prescribe interpretive methodology testifies to a perception that legislatures can limit judicial approaches to statutory interpretation before the fact, even if they cannot prescribe the outcomes in specific cases.

Constitutional Interpretation

During the last four decades, state supreme courts have inaugurated a new judicial federalism, relying on state declarations of rights to provide greater protections for rights than are available under current interpretations of the federal Bill of Rights.[104] Looking to state constitutional text and history, they have also elaborated a distinctive state constitutional law dealing with the separation of powers and other issues.[105] Many of these rulings have proved controversial. This is not because there is anything intrinsically wrong with reliance on state constitutions to decide cases. The discovery or rediscovery of the distinctiveness of state rights guarantees and state institutional arrangements is a healthy development. But judicial interpretations of state constitutions may be mistaken or, even if they are not, they may not coincide with popular understandings of what the state constitution should mean. In such circumstances, voters have the opportunity to amend the constitution in order to ensure that their constitutional understanding prevails. For example, voters in California, Massachusetts, and New Jersey have overridden state supreme court rulings dealing with capital punishment.[106] Voters in California and Hawaii have overridden rulings relating to same-sex marriage.[107] Whatever one thinks of the wisdom of these popular interventions, their legitimacy is undeniable.

State voters have also sometimes sought to head off disfavored judicial interpretations by inserting in the state constitution highly specific language. This has occurred particularly when rulings by courts in other states have sparked a concern that the courts in one's own state might issue similar rulings or when broad constitutional language might seem to invite interpretations with which voters would disagree. Thus, in the wake of state supreme court rulings in Massachusetts and other states recognizing a right to same-sex marriage, voters in thirty states adopted amendments restricting marriage to male-female couples, thereby precluding their state supreme courts from recognizing a state constitutional right to same-sex marriage.[108]

Finally, in addition to preempting particular decisions, state voters have adopted amendments that restrict in broad terms the interpretation of preexisting provisions. For example, Californians adopted a "lockstep" amendment that requires state courts to conform their interpretations of state provisions dealing with the rights of defendants to the interpretation of analogous federal provisions by the US Supreme Court, and Floridians did the same with regard to its guarantee against unreasonable search and seizure.[109] These amendments thus attempted to dictate how state constitutional provisions would be interpreted, just as state legislatures have attempted to dictate how state courts interpret state statutes. There is a crucial difference, however. Whereas state courts may object that legislative efforts to mandate interpretive methodologies violate the separation of powers and invade judicial authority, no such claim can be made when voters adopt constitutional amendments. For voters are not prescribing how judges shall discover constitutional meaning; rather, they are themselves establishing the meaning of the constitution. And when judges thereafter fail to adhere to these clear, current expressions of the popular will, they are acting inappropriately and can be held accountable.[110]

For the populace to play such an active role in establishing constitutional meaning and policing the interpretation of the state constitution, there must be mechanisms for translating the popular will into constitutional command. At the federal level, the cumbersome process of constitutional amendment, as well as the lack of direct popular involvement in the proposal and ratification of amendments, precludes this sort of popular constitutionalism.[111] But at the state level, there are more and easier mechanisms for introducing constitutional change, including changes designed to overturn or foreclose state constitutional rulings. Legislative proposal of amendments tends to be easier: nine states allow amendments to be proposed by simple majorities of those elected to both legislative chambers, and twelve permit proposal by simple majorities in successive legislative sessions.[112] In addition, sixteen states allow amendments by constitutional initiative, and those states have been the most active in seeking to overturn or preempt judicial rulings.[113] Constitutional conventions can also be called, with sixteen states authorizing the legislature by simple majority to put the question of a convention before the people, fourteen states requiring that the people be asked periodically whether they wish to call a convention, and Florida and South Dakota authorizing the calling of a convention by constitutional initiative. The popular role in constitutional change extends to ratification as well: forty-nine states (Delaware is the outlier) provide for ratification by popular vote, in many states by a simple majority of those voting on a measure.

The idea of a popular vote on judicial rulings recalls Theodore Roosevelt's proposal for popular recall of judicial decisions, and the fact that the amending power has been used relatively infrequently to influence or supplant judicial rulings offers some support for Roosevelt's claim that voters would not abuse their power to recall judicial decisions. However, the current use of the constitutional initiative improves on Roosevelt's proposal.[114] Those who attacked the popular recall of judicial decisions argued that voters lacked the legal expertise necessary to assess whether judges had interpreted the constitution correctly. Whatever the merits of this argument, it does not apply to the constitutional initiative because the people are changing the constitution, not rendering a verdict on whether judges had properly interpreted it. In addition, whereas popular recall of judicial decisions only allowed voters to respond to decisions that they deemed mistaken, the constitutional initiative allows voters to be proactive, to prevent disfavored judicial decisions by amending the text the judges will interpret.

These observations bring us full circle, as the debate over judicial independence and judicial accountability intersects with the debate over the judicial role, which figured so prominently in the early decades of the American Republic. If the judiciary dominates the elaboration of constitutional meaning, then it must be expected that efforts will be made to hold judges accountable for how well they perform this task. Attacks on the judiciary are an almost inevitable consequence of expanding judicial authority. But if a more popular constitutionalism operates in the states, with judicial determinations of legal meaning subject to ready reversal by the legislature (in the case of the common law or statutory law) or by the citizenry (in the case of constitutional law), then political energies are more likely to be devoted to the substance of the law. Defenders are seldom in the forefront of movements to facilitate popularly initiated legal change, but perhaps they should be. In the twenty-first century, there may well be a trade-off between judicial power and judicial independence.

In this regard, it is instructive to compare the aftermath of two rulings striking down restrictions on same-sex marriage—the Iowa Supreme Court's ruling in *Varnum v. Brien* (2010) and the California Supreme Court's ruling in *In re Marriage Cases* (2008). Opponents of the Iowa ruling first sought to overturn it by amending the state constitution, but state legislators declined to propose such an amendment. Because Iowa had no means by which opponents could directly put such an amendment on the ballot, their only recourse for changing the ruling was to change the composition of the Supreme Court. They did this first by organizing opposition to three justices who were up for retention in 2010. This effort succeeded as all three justices were defeated. Some legislators introduced impeachment resolutions against the four remaining justices who had struck down the Iowa prohibition on same-sex marriage, but this effort failed. Nevertheless, many commentators expressed concern that the nonretention of some justices, plus the shot across the bow of impeachment resolutions, might damage the decisional independence of Iowa judges.

Like Iowa, California conducts retention elections for the members of its supreme court, and in 1986 three justices were removed because of their rulings. However, none of the California justices was up for election immediately after the ruling in *In re Marriage Cases* (2008), so even if there was the political will to unseat the California justices—itself a dubious proposition—there was no opportunity to do so. This is far more common than the situation in Iowa, where a controversial ruling was handed down only months before a retention election. For opponents of the Iowa ruling, the fact that it was announced so close to retention elections was a matter of pure luck.

What is significant in California was that opposition to the court's ruling focused on overturning the ruling rather than on punishing the judges who rendered it. There was no serious effort to impeach the California justices. Rather the availability of the constitutional initiative provided a more focused, yet effective, mechanism for countering a disfavored decision. After voters in California approved Proposition 8, a constitutional amendment that limited civil marriage to opposite-sex couples, the same justices who had decided *In re Marriage Cases* upheld the amendments against state constitutional challenge in *Strauss v. Horton*. In sum, the California system seems far superior to the Iowa system in terms of judicial independence because the populace can on its own overturn by amendments good-faith rulings with which it disagrees without imperiling the judges who issued the rulings. There is a lesson here for other states as well.

Notes

Introduction

1. Caustic criticism of judges is not limited to those on the political Right. After the Supreme Court's ruling in *Bush v. Gore*, 531 U.S. 98 (2000), Vincent Bugliosi branded the Supreme Court majority the "felonious five," "transparent shills for the right wing of the Republican Party," and "judicial sociopaths" who "belong behind bars" for their "treasonous behavior" (Bugliosi, "None Dare Call It Treason," pp. 11, 14, and 15).

2. Thus, one antitax activist in Montana characterized the Montana Supreme Court as "seven black-robed terrorists" (quoted in Manweller, *People Versus the Courts*, p. 203).

3. Quoted in Champagne, "Politics of Criticizing Judges."

4. DeMuniz, "Politicizing State Judicial Elections," p. 764.

5. Illustrative is the critical response of federal judges to the Feeney Amendment, which required the federal judiciary to report to Congress instances in which judges departed downward from sentencing guidelines. See "What Do Judges Think About the Feeney Amendment?"

6. See, for example, Geyh, "Why Judicial Elections Stink."

7. Grodin, *In Pursuit of Justice*, p. 163.

8. See Shepard, "Judicial Independence," p. 9. Prominent groups in the Defender camp include the American Bar Association, which has created a Standing Committee on Judicial Independence; the American Judicature Society, which has established a Task Force on Judicial Independence and Accountability; and NGO's and advocacy groups such as Justice at Stake, the Brennan Center for Justice, and Citizens for Independent Courts.

10. This is captured well in Justice Hugo Black's characterization of courts as "havens of refuge for those who might otherwise suffer because they are helpless,

weak, and outnumbered, or because they are non-conforming victims of prejudice and public excitement." *Chambers v. Florida*, 309 U.S. 227, 241 (1940). Similar sentiments were voiced by a longtime director of the American Judicature Society, extolling "the critical role of the judiciary as the final rampart for personal freedom and public welfare." See Winters and Allard, "Judicial Selection and Tenure," p. 147.

11. See Ross, *Muted Fury*; and—more generally—Geyh, *When Courts and Congress Collide*. Geyh emphasizes that although the players and the tactics may have changed in recent years, "bouts of court-directed animus have come and gone at generational intervals since the founding of the nation" (p. 2). William Lasser has argued that these episodic conflicts reflect dissatisfaction with particular decisions rather than with the courts as a whole (see Lasser, *Limits of Judicial Power*, pp. 256–57).

12. When I worked on the State Court Assessment Project of the American Bar Association's Standing Committee on Judicial Independence, state judges would often express interest in the project but insist it not be framed in terms of "judicial independence," as the term was unacceptable politically in their states. On the similar suspicion of "judicial accountability," see Geyh, "Rescuing Judicial Accountability," p. 913.

13. Burbank, "What Do We Mean by 'Judicial Independence'?", p. 323.

14. This oft-quoted language is drawn from Goldberg, *New Politics of Judicial Elections 2000*, p. 8.

Chapter 1

1. The diversity among the states requires a caveat. Some historians analyze particular episodes or states in great detail; others sacrifice detail for a more comprehensive or comparative account. Our analysis belongs to that latter category, offering a broad-brush picture, illuminated by examples, rather than an exhaustive state-by-state analysis. For a state-by-state survey of judicial independence in the American colonies and during the founding, see Gerber, *Distinct Judicial Power*.

2. In proprietary states, the proprietor exercised this function.

3. Blackstone, *Commentaries*, p. 132.

4. How much service at the pleasure of the executive interfered with judicial independence is hard to determine. For example, in Massachusetts no judges were removed from office from 1760–74. Also, judicial salaries were under the control of the legislature, and when the Crown undertook to pay such salaries, the legislature threatened to impeach judges who accepted payments from the executive. W. Nelson, *Americanization of the Common Law*, pp. 32–33.

5. Massachusetts Declaration of Rights, Art. 29; and Maryland Declaration of Rights, Art. 30.

6. J. Reid, *Legislating the Courts*, p. 8. Reid contends that his story of judicial dependence in New Hampshire is "representative of what was occurring in all American jurisdictions, except the federal" (p. 7).

7. Wood, *Creation of the American*, p. 161.

8. To a very limited extent, popular election of judges did occur during the eighteenth century. Under the Vermont Constitution of 1777 (Ch. II, sec. 27), "freemen in every county" had "the liberty of choosing the judges of inferior courts of common pleas, sheriff, justices of the peace, and judges of probates." See also Georgia Constitution of 1798, Art. 3, sec. 1.

9. Wood, *Creation of the American Republic,* p. 143. Wood suggests that for state constitution-makers "emasculation of their governors lay at the heart of their constitutional reforms in 1776" (p. 149).

10. Ibid., p. 161. See also Lutz, *Popular Consent,* pp. 95–97.

11. J. Reid, *Legislating the Courts,* chap. 3. See also Hamburger, *Law and Judicial Duty,* pp. 526–35.

12. Volcansek and Lafon, *Judicial Selection,* pp. 24–25. The case is *Trevett v. Weeden,* one of the earliest examples of judicial review. For discussion of judicial review in the states before 1787, see Snowiss, *Judicial Review,* chap. 2. *Bayard v. Singleton* (1786), a North Carolina case, provides an example of legislative intervention in ongoing litigation by calling judges to account. See L. Kramer, *People Themselves,* p. 67.

13. The controversy involved the interpretation of the tenure clause of the Ohio Constitution (Art. III, sec. 2), which provided that judges "shall hold their offices for the term of seven years, if so long they behave well." For judges appointed midterm, the question was whether their appointment was for the remainder of the unexpired term or for a new full term. The controversy was resolved with repeal of the resolution depriving the judges of office, with those judges newly appointed to take their place likewise retaining their seats. Melhorn, *Lest We Be Marshall'd.*

14. J. Reid, *Legislating the Courts,* p. 13.

15. Galie, *Ordered Liberty,* p. 83.

16. The controversy in Kentucky led temporarily to the simultaneous operation of two supreme courts. See Ruger, "'A Question Which Convulses a Nation,'" pp. 826–97.

17. As John Phillip Reid has observed, "For political theorists who interpreted the doctrine of consent broadly, all officers of the state, including the judiciary, were answerable to the people, and in constitutional theory "the people" did not refer to those citizens possessed of the right to vote but to the representatives whom they elected to the legislature" (J. Reid, *Legislating the Courts,* p. 4).

18. "Return of the Town of Sutton on the Massachusetts Constitution of 1778," in Handlin and Handlin, *Popular Sources,* p. 237.

19. In contrast, Maryland did not authorize the legislature to impeach judges, permitting removal "only for misbehaviour, on conviction in a Court of Law." Maryland Constitution, Art. 40.

20. New York Constitution, Art. 33; South Carolina Constitution, Art. 23; and New Hampshire Constitution, Art. 38.

21. Although in theory, the governor had discretion as to whether to remove a judge on address by the legislature, in practice legislative address was usually a mandate rather than a request. But see J. Reid, *Legislating the Courts,* p. 12.

22. Hoffer and Hull, *Impeachment in America,* p. 64.

23. Kentucky Constitution, Art. 4, sec. 3 (1799).

24. These are the grounds for impeachment in both the Kentucky Constitution of 1792 (Art. 4, sec. 4) and the Pennsylvania Constitution of 1790 (Art. 4, sec. 3).

25. Kentucky Constitution, Art. 4, sec. 3. See also the Pennsylvania Constitution of 1790, Art. 5, sec. 2. This latter provision is particularly striking because it appears in the "more conservative" successor to Pennsylvania's radical 1776 constitution, after complaints had been raised in the 1780s about excessive legislative interference with the judiciary.

26. Berger, *Impeachment*, p. 2.

27. On the debate over removal by address in the Constitutional Convention, see Geyh, *When Courts and Congress Collide*, pp. 29–30.

28. Ellis, *Jeffersonian Crisis*, pp. 71–72. Jefferson is quoted in Zuckert, "Founder of the Natural Rights Republic," p. 44.

29. Hoffer and Hull, *Impeachment in America*, pp. 79–80, 126–30, 169, 172–73; 193–96; Ellis, *Jeffersonian Crisis*, chaps. 10–11; and Carpenter, *Judicial Tenure*, pp. 126–31.

30. Hoffer and Hull, *Impeachment in America*, p. 182.

31. Ellis, *Jeffersonian Crisis*, pp. 69–75, 164–65.

32. Ibid., chaps. 7 and 11–12; and Rowe, *Embattled Bench*, chap. 14.

33. Ellis, *Jeffersonian Crisis*, chaps. 7 and 11–12.

34. Although Jeffersonians agreed on this point, they divided on how aggressively to seek the removal of Federalists and their replacement by Republicans. See Ellis, *Jeffersonian Crisis*, chap. 15 and passim. Lawrence Friedman has characterized the result as "a kind of social compromise," under which "there would be no more impeachments, but also no more judges like Chase. What carried the day, in a sense, was the John Marshall solution. The judges would take refuge in professional decorum" (Friedman, *History of American Law*, p. 85).

35. Quoted in Carpenter, *Judicial Tenure*, p. 165.

36. For the federal discussion, see Geyh, *When Courts and Congress Collide*, chap. 3.

37. On the implications of the Chase impeachment, see Whittington, *Constitutional Construction*, chap. 2.

38. See Rakove, "Origins of Judicial Review," p. 1035. Not everyone shares Rakove's view. Charles Geyh and Emily Field Van Tassel argue that "events leading up to the Constitutional Convention created a perceived need for judges to be independent individually as decision makers, and collectively as a separate branch of government." See Geyh and Van Tassel, "Independence," p. 38.

39. Adams, *First American Constitutions*, p. 269.

40. Brutus, "No. 15, March 20, 1788," in Kurland and Lerner, *Founders' Constitution*, 4:141.

41. On the judicial duty to render judgment unaffected by human will, see Hamburger, *Law and Judicial Duty*, chap. 5. Yet what is striking is how state constitution-makers relied on institutional mechanisms to enforce this duty.

42. See Vile, *Constitutionalism*, p. 134; and, more generally, Tarr, "Interpreting the Separation of Powers," pp. 329–40. Even the ban on dual office-holding did not apply

universally. Members of the legislative and privy councils under the Delaware Constitution of 1776 (Art. 12) were also made "'justices of the peace for the whole state," and
in Virginia justices of the county courts were eligible to run for either house of the
state legislature. See Adams, *First American Constitutions*, p. 265.

43. On the importance of memorials and instructions from the people, see Fritz,
American Sovereigns, especially pp. 125–27.

44. Tarr, *Understanding State Constitutions*, pp. 118–21.

45. C. Nelson, "Re-Evaluation of Scholarly Explanations"; and K. Hall, "Judiciary
on Trial."

46. Thus Andrew Hanssen has attributed the legislative power over judges during
the initial decades of the Republic to, among other things, "the lack of a clearly distinct judicial role." Hanssen, "Learning About Judicial Independence," p. 443.

47. This focus on judicial review is unfortunate for two reasons. First, as Larry
Kramer has noted, "Our intensive focus on the question [of judicial review] is an artifact of what judicial review subsequently became and of our natural curiosity, as a
result, to understand its origins. In trying to get a sense of the historical context, however, it is important not to exaggerate the significance of what was, in fact, insignifi-
cant to the vast majority of Americans" (L. Kramer, *People Themselves*, p. 71). Second,
the meaning of judicial review itself changed over time. To ask whether the founders
intended to establish judicial review is anachronistic, because "no one meant to establish what eventually became judicial review; it could scarcely have been imagined.
Like most developments in history, judicial review was unplanned and unintended"
(see Wood, "Origins," p. 1295).

48. Locke, *Second Treatise*, chap. 12. According to Donald Lutz, "Both Whig theory
and English practice made [the judiciary] part of the executive power—a practice
dating back to the time when the king traveled from place to place in his realm, adjudicating differences among his subjects" (Lutz, *Popular Consent*, p. 95).

49. See Stoner, "Constitutionalism," pp. 208–9. Stoner argues that *The Federalist
Papers* themselves at times seem to reflect this understanding of the judiciary as sub-
servient to the executive.

50. Thus Article I of the New Jersey Constitution of 1776 indicated that "the government of this Province shall be vested in a Governor, Legislative Council, and General Assembly." The Virginia Constitution of 1776 was the first to define the judiciary
as a distinct branch of government. See Adams, *First American Constitutions*, p. 265.

51. See L. Scalia, *America's Jeffersonian Experiment*, pp. 130–31.

52. See Desan, "Constitutional Commitment," pp. 1381–446.

53. Even public bills may resemble judicial decisions. As James Madison noted in
Federalist No. 10: "Yet what are many of the most important acts of legislation but so
many judicial determinations, not indeed concerning the rights of single persons, but
concerning the rights of large bodies of citizens" (Hamilton et al., *Federalist Papers*,
p. 47). On the legislative output of colonial and early state legislatures, showing that
creation of new law was the exception rather than the rule, see W. Nelson, *Americanization of the Common Law*, p. 14.

54. For a ban on bills of attainder, see Massachusetts Constitution, Part I, Art. 12, and for a ban on retrospective laws, see New Hampshire Constitution of 1792, Art. 23.

55. John Reid suggests that "the most important function of special legislative adjudication was to serve as a substitute for an equity jurisdiction" (J. Reid, *Legislating the Courts*, p. 67).

56. Jefferson, *Notes on the State of Virginia*, Query 13.

57. See Friedman, *History of American Law*, pp. 143–44. Chap. III, Art. 2 of the Massachusetts Constitution anticipated this transformation: "All cases of marriage, divorce, and alimony, and all appeals from the judges of probate, shall be heard and determined by the governor and council *until the legislature shall, by law, make other provisions*" (emphasis added).

58. Georgia Constitution, Art. 3, sec. 9.

59. See Desan, "Rights and Remedies."

60. New Jersey Constitution, Art. 9; Vermont Constitution, Art. 11; and Delaware Constitution, Art. 17. Although Georgia did not create a nonjudicial body to exercise ultimate appellate authority, neither did it create a judicial body for that purpose, managing without a supreme court until 1845. Hill, *Georgia State Constitution*, p. 5.

61. Rakove, "Origins of Judicial Review," p. 1064.

62. New Jersey Constitution, Art. 22.

63. De Tocqueville, *Democracy in America*, p. 273.

64. Quoted in Stimson, *American Revolution in the Law*, p. 56.

65. Our account of the American jury during the eighteenth and nineteenth centuries relies on Stimson, *American Revolution in the Law*; and on W. Nelson, *Americanization of the Common Law*.

66. Pennsylvania Constitution, Declaration of Rights, Art. 9; Massachusetts Constitution, Declaration of Rights, Art. 15; and Georgia Constitution, Art. 41.

67. W. Nelson, *Americanization of the Common Law*, p. 97.

68. Friedman, *History of American Law*, pp. 108–9.

69. W. Nelson, *Americanization of the Common Law*, p. 166.

70. Quoted in Stimson, *American Revolution in the Law*, p. 49. Not all scholars view the judge's role as so limited; see Lerner, "Transformation of the American Civil Trial," p. 197: "Much has been made of the independence of juries in America's early history. But it is not so well understood that this formal independence coexisted with a large amount of informal influence by the judge on the jury."

71. Quoted in Stimson, *American Revolution in the Law*, p. 87.

72. Quoted in ibid., p. 57. Adams's view was hardly eccentric. See Bloomfield, *American Lawyers in a Changing Society*, pp. 47–49.

73. See Harrington, "Law-Finding Function," pp. 377–440.

74. See Lerner, "Transformation of the American Civil Trial," p. 197.

75. F. Miller, *Juries and Judges Versus the Law*, pp. 27–28.

76. Stimson, *American Revolution in the Law*, p. 84.

77. W. Nelson, *Marbury v. Madison*, p. 13.

78. Skowronek, *Building a New American State*. Courts, Skowronek argued, "filled a governmental vacuum left by abortive experiments in the administrative promotion of economic development" (p. 27).

79. De Tocqueville, *Democracy in America*, pp. 67 and 69.

80. This reliance on justices of the peace, usually local notables without legal training, was controversial in republican circles because it seemed to empower long-standing local elites and frustrate popular control. See Roeber, *Faithful Magistrates and Republican Lawyers*.

81. Georgia Constitution, Art. 1, sec. 25; and Wood, *Creation of the American Republic*, p. 154. Even juries undertook administrative tasks, being employed in North Carolina to lay out roads and to ascertain any damage to private property that occurred in the process. See Stimson, *American Revolution in the Law*, p. 61; and Landsman, "Civil Jury in America," pp. 579–619.

82. New York Constitution, Art. 3.

83. Galie, *Ordered Liberty*, pp. 43–47.

84. See, for example, Massachusetts Constitution, Chap. III, Art. 1. Of the ten states that now provide for advisory opinions, six were among the original thirteen states. See Topf, *Doubtful and Perilous Experiment*.

85. For a discussion of the monarchial use of advisory opinions to pressure judges, see Hamburger, *Law and Judicial Duty*, pp. 151–54; for the use of advisory opinions in the United States to address structural issues, which forced judges to disappoint one or another contending party in the state legislature, see ibid., pp. 371–77.

86. Our account of the Virginia conflict and of judicial resolutions more generally relies on Hamburger, *Law and Judicial Duty*, pp. 554–74. However, whereas Hamburger criticizes the judges for "stray[ing] beyond their office," the judges were merely emulating early seventeenth-century English judges, suggesting that the contours of the judicial office were not yet clearly demarcated.

87. Wood, *Creation of the American Republic*, p. 154.

88. Even when New Jersey replaced its initial constitution in 1844, it continued to vest ultimate appellate authority in a body only partially composed of judges. The successor to the Court of Appeals was the Courts of Errors and Appeals, comprised of the chancellor of the Chancery Court (the state's intermediate appellate court for chancery cases), the chief justice and eight associate justices of the Supreme Court (the intermediate appellate court for law cases), and six "lay" members, usually lawyers. See Tarr and Porter, *State Supreme Courts*, pp. 188–89.

89. In *Law and Judicial Duty*, Philip Hamburger offers an alternative interpretation. Highlighting "the common law ideals of law and judicial duty," he argues that "these two ideals, taken together, required judges to hold unconstitutional acts unlawful" (17). From this perspective, judicial review was not an invention of judges or an innovation. Constitutional review of the actions of subordinate officials, although not of acts of Parliament, had occurred in England since at least the sixteenth century, and colonial judges regularly reviewed the actions of colonial officials and legislatures. However, if other institutions or the general populace had shared

the judicial view of judicial duty and of the scope of judicial authority, the early exercise of judicial review in the states would not have been so controversial. Hamburger claims that judges exercising judicial review "typically encountered problems only in the lower houses of state legislatures," and he insists that "outside these populist venues, there was considerable recognition that freedom depended on the law of the land and the dedication of the judges in doing what their office required of them" (407). Yet with annual elections and the instruction of representatives, these "populist venues" usually reflected popular views, so there was hardly a societal consensus in favor of judicial review, though one did develop before the end of the eighteenth century. Even so, agreement about the importance of the rule of law and even about the legitimacy of judicial review did not necessarily mean that judicial understandings of that law should be authoritative.

90. Snowiss, *Judicial Review*, p. 181. Our analysis relies on Snowiss's account.

91. In "Judicial Review Before *Marbury*," pp. 455–561, William Michael Treanor challenges the standard account of the development of judicial review elaborated here, claiming that judicial review was more common in the decades following independence than was previously understood and that courts were willing to strike down laws even when they were not clearly unconstitutional. Yet for present purposes, what is important is not the number of instances of judicial review but the fact that it was common and accepted prior to *Marbury*. On this there is no disagreement between the prevailing historical consensus and Treanor. See, *inter alia*, Hobson, *Great Chief Justice*, pp. 58–64; W. Nelson, *Marbury v. Madison*; and Graber, "Problematic Establishment of Judicial Review."

Treanor further argues that state courts invalidated laws that "affected coordinate constitutional departments that were not part of the political process that had produced the legislation." The "coordinate constitutional departments" he identifies are juries and courts, so his argument can be restated as: courts used the power of judicial review in order to protect the judicial branch against the usurpations of other branches. This is not a significant departure from the position taken by Snowiss and other scholars who see judicial review initially as part of a system of checks and balances rather than reflecting a claimed monopoly over authoritative interpretation of the law.

What is distinctive is Treanor's contention that state courts invalidated laws even when "there was no obvious inconsistency between the legislation and the constitutional text." Yet the view of Snowiss and other scholars is that courts from the outset were invalidating laws on the basis of clear constitutional principles, whether written or unwritten, so the reference to the "constitutional text" is irrelevant. See Sherry, "Founders' Unwritten Constitution," pp. 1127–77. Indeed, reliance on unwritten principles is perfectly consistent with Snowiss's argument that judges were not engaged in the task of interpreting a legal text. As to whether the inconsistency between constitutional principles and the acts that state courts invalidated was "obvious" or not is, of course, a matter on which reasonable people might disagree.

92. The relation between early judicial review, particularly Chief Justice Marshall's opinion in *Marbury v. Madison*, and judicial supremacy in constitutional

interpretation is hotly debated. See, for example, "The Constitutional Journey of *Marbury v. Madison,*" in White, *History and the Constitution*; L. Kramer, *People Themselves*; and Van Alstyne, "Critical Guide to *Marbury v. Madison,*" pp. 1–17.

93. Pennsylvania Constitution of 1776, sec. 47; Vermont Constitution of 1793, Chap. 2, sec. 43; and New York Constitution of 1777, Art. 3. In assessing the wisdom of proposed laws, the Council of Revision actually inhibited the development of judicial review in New York because approval by the council seemed to indicate an absence of both political and constitutional objections. Under the New York's 1777 Constitution, only three laws were declared unconstitutional. However, once the Council of Revision was abolished, judicial review increased dramatically. From 1821–47, the New York Supreme Court struck down fourteen laws, and from 1848–67, sixty-six. See Galie, *Ordered Liberty*, p. 80.

94. Snowiss, *Judicial Review*, pp. 36–37.

95. Quoted in ibid., p. 20. See also Hamburger, *Law and Judicial Duty*, pp. 346–57.

96. Geyh and Van Tassel, "Independence of the Judicial Branch," p. 37.

97. Snowiss, *Judicial Review*, p. 59. See also Hamburger, *Law and Judicial Duty*, pp. 435–49.

98. W. Nelson, "Changing Conceptions of Judicial Review," pp. 1169–70; and W. Nelson, *Marbury v. Madison*, p. 86.

99. R. Clinton, Marbury v. Madison *and Judicial Review*, pp. 102–3; and L. Kramer, *People Themselves*, chap. 4.

100. Melhorn, *Lest We Be Marshall'd*, p. 182; and Rowe, *Embattled Bench*, p. 233.

101. The sole judicial challenge to judicial review was Judge Gibson's famous dissent in *Eakin v. Raub*, 12 Sergeant & Rawl 330 (1825). Yet this was a solitary dissent, and indicative of the widespread acceptance of judicial review was Judge Gibson's later recantation in *Norris v. Clymer*, 2 Pa. 277, 281 (1845). The Georgia Legislature in 1815 did adopt a resolution rejecting the claim of judicial authority to invalidate statutes, noting that it "can not refrain from an expression of their entire disapprobation of the power assumed by them [the judiciary] of determining upon the constitutionality of laws regularly passed by the General Assembly" (quoted in J. Reid, *Legislating the Courts*, p. 16).

102. Fehrenbacher, *Constitutions and Constitutionalism*, p. 20.

103. W. Nelson, "Changing Conceptions of Judicial Review," p. 1173.

104. Ibid., p. 1181.

105. M. Nelson, *Study of Judicial Review in Virginia*, p. 54; and W. Nelson, Marbury v. Madison, p. 84. William Nelson detects some change after 1830 in the character of cases coming before state courts and in their willingness to strike down statutes in controversial cases, whereas Lawrence Friedman dates the change from the latter half of the nineteenth century. See W. Nelson, "Changing Conceptions of Judicial Review," pp. 1178–81; and Friedman, *History of American Law*, pp. 266–72.

106. *McCormick v. Alexander* (1825), discussed in Melhorn, *Lest We Be Marshall'd*, p. 187.

107. Ibid.

108. Snowiss, *Judicial Review*, pp. 121–22. See also Sherry, "Intellectual Background of *Marbury v. Madison*," pp. 50–53; and Griffin, *American Constitutionalism*, pp. 11–19.

109. This account of the events in Kentucky relies on Ruger, "'Question Which Convulses a Nation.'"

110. Ibid., p. 853.

111. Quoted in ibid., pp. 860–61, 865.

112. Friedman, *History of American Law*, p. 66.

113. Zainaldin, *Law in Antebellum Society*, p. 10; and K. Hall, *Magic Mirror*, p. 79.

114. Bloomfield, *American Lawyers*, p. 80.

115. For a definitive discussion with implications that extend beyond New Hampshire, see J. Reid, *Controlling the Law*.

116. Shankman, "Malcontents and Tertium Quids," p. 56.

117. New York Constitution of 1777, Art. 35.

118. Nelson, *Americanization of the Common Law*, chap. 5.

119. Quoted in Zainaldin, *Law in Antebellum Society*, p. 11.

120. J. Reid, *Controlling the Law*, p. 36.

121. Horwitz, *Transformation of American Law*, p. 1.

122. Zainaldin, *Law in Antebellum Society*, pp. 54–55.

123. See Cook, *American Codification Movement*.

124. Horwitz, *Transformation of American Law*, p. 18.

125. Stimson, *American Revolution in the Law*, p. 57.

126. W. Nelson, *Americanization of the Common Law*, p. 170.

127. Ibid., pp. 2, 165.

128. Horwitz, *Transformation of American Law*, p. 28.

129. W. Nelson, *Americanization of the Common Law*, pp. 170–71.

130. Horwitz, *Transformation of American Law*, p. 1.

131. Wood, *Creation of the American Republic*, p. 161.

132. On the legalization of the Constitution, see Griffin, *American Constitutionalism*, pp. 11–19.

133. Rakove, "Origins of Judicial Review," pp. 1034–35.

134. For the importance of this theme in Jacksonian thought, see Meyers, *Jacksonian Persuasion*. However, this was hardly a novel theme—see Hutson, "American Revolutionaries," pp. 1079–105.

135. Hanssen, "Learning about Judicial Independence," p. 436.

136. See the data reported in Shugerman, "Economic Crisis," p. 1147, appendix B; and in Friedman, *History of American Law*, pp. 266–72.

137. K. Hall, "Constitutional Machinery and Judicial Professionalism," p. 36.

Chapter 2

1. See Thach, *Creation of the Presidency*; and Adams, *First American Constitutions*, chap. 12.

2. Haynes, *Selection and Tenure of Judges*, pp. 101–35.

3. Shugerman, *People's Courts*, p. 117.

4. Haynes, *Selection and Tenure of Judges*, pp. 101–35.

5. Keyssar, *Right to Vote*, pp. 40–41.

6. Quoted in Carpenter, *Judicial Tenure in the United States*, p. 176.

7. Balkin and Levinson, "Understanding the Constitutional Revolution," p. 1066.

8. Carpenter, *Judicial Tenure in the United States*, pp. 173–74. There was political support for limited terms in Alabama from 1819 onward, and amendments to limit tenure were introduced in virtually every legislative session, albeit without success until 1828. See McMillan, *Constitutional Development in Alabama*, pp. 47–51.

9. Carpenter, *Judicial Tenure in the United States*, p. 174.

10. For discussion of conflicts between the Ohio legislature and judiciary, see Melhorn, *"Lest We Be Marshall'd."*

11. On horizontal federalism and constitutional emulation, see Tarr, *Understanding State Constitutions*, pp. 98–99.

12. Shugerman, "Economic Crisis," pp. 1070–76 and 1097–107.

13. The shift to judicial elections in the mid-nineteenth century has been extensively studied. See K. Hall, "Judiciary on Trial," pp. 337–54; C. Nelson, "Re-evaluation of Scholarly Explanations"; Hanssen, "Learning about Judicial Independence," pp. 431–73; Shugerman, "Economic Crisis"; and Shugerman, *People's Courts*.

14. Haynes, *Selection and Tenure of Judges*, p. 100.

15. For an overview of these changes, see Hanssen, "Learning about Judicial Independence," pp. 437–53. Even states that adopted merit selection during the twentieth century embraced elections, although they substituted noncontested retention elections for contested elections.

16. K. Hall, "Judiciary on Trial," p. 337.

17. Ibid., p. 342. Haynes notes that "it was charged in several states that judicial appointments were made in caucus by the legislators of the dominant party." Haynes, *Selection and Tenure of Judges*, p. 97.

18. *Debates and Proceedings of the Minnesota Constitutional Convention*, p. 495.

19. Wilentz, *Rise of American Democracy*, pp. 189–98.

20. Bryce, *Modern Democracies*, p. 92.

21. Shugerman, *People's Courts*, chap. 3.

22. B. Miller, *Louisiana Judiciary*, pp. 23–24.

23. In *Chisholm v. Georgia*, 2 U.S. 419 (1793), the US Supreme Court ruled that a state could be sued without its consent by a citizen of another state, a decision overturned by the Eleventh Amendment. In *Fletcher v. Peck*, 10 U.S. 87 (1810), the court struck down a Georgia enactment that attempted to rescind land grants previously made to land companies that had bribed members of the Georgia Legislature.

24. Saye, *Constitutional History of Georgia*, p. 167.

25. Shugerman, "Economic Crisis," p. 1072.

26. On Mississippi's shift to judicial elections, see Shugerman, *People's Courts*, chap. 3.

27. *Worcester v. Georgia*, 31 U.S. 515 (1832), restricted the power of state governments over Indian tribes, a serious concern in frontier states like Mississippi.

28. Under the 1832 Constitution, judges on the Court of Errors and Appeals and on the Chancery Courts served six-year terms, while judges on the Circuit Court served four-year terms. See Mississippi Constitution of 1832, Article 4, sections. 2, 11, and 16.

29. See Norton, "Michigan's First Supreme Court Elections, 1850–51," pp. 507–24; and more generally, McLeod, "Excess of Participation."

30. Shugerman, *People's Courts*, p. 121.

31. Scholars have debated how influential New York actually was. Kermit Hall dismissed the notion that "other states simply copied the work of the New York delegates" as a "persistent myth," insisting that "as frequently, delegates cited the Mississippi constitution as a model" (K. Hall, "Judiciary on Trial," p. 340n13). Caleb Nelson argued that "while there is no doubt that New York helped legitimate the elective system, its change did not carry overwhelming weight" (C. Nelson, "Re-evaluation of Scholarly Explanations," p. 193). However, Jed Shugerman has shown that New York's adoption settled the concerns of moderates who wanted political cover and sought evidence that judicial elections could work in a more industrial, commercial state. He further demonstrates the influence of the New York example in the conventions in Wisconsin, Illinois, and California, particularly among delegates who were originally natives of that state. Shugerman, *People's Courts*, chap. 5; and Shugerman, "Economic Crisis," pp. 1092–93.

32. Carpenter, *Judicial Tenure*, p. 181.

33. South Carolina's refusal to abandon legislative election of judges fit in with its general approach to politics: the "omnipotent legislature . . . in 1860 still chose nearly all state and local officials, including presidential electors." See Fehrenbacher, *Constitutions and Constitutionalism*, p. 11.

34. W. Nelson, "Re-evaluation of Scholarly Explanations," p. 213.

35. McMillan, *Constitutional Development in Alabama*, pp. 175, 200. On Louisiana, see B. Miller, *Louisiana Judiciary*, pp. 38–43.

36. Eight states by constitutional amendment adopted judicial elections or extended them to courts whose members had not previously been chosen via popular election.

37. This analysis draws on Tarr, *Understanding State Constitutions*, pp. 109–12. Key sources detailing the states' involvement in economic boosterism include: Hovenkamp, *Enterprise and American Law*; Hartz, *Economic Policy and Democratic Thought*; Handlin and Handlin, *Commonwealth*; and J. Larson, *Internal Improvement*.

38. Wallis, "Constitutions, Corporations, and Corruption," p. 216.

39. Tarr, *Understanding State Constitutions*, p. 112.

40. State constitution-makers "imposed procedural restrictions designed to prevent duplicity and promote greater openness and deliberation, assuming that greater transparency in the legislative process would deter legislative abuses or at least increase accountability for them. Thus, state constitutions mandated that all bills be referred to committee, that they be read three times prior to enactment, that their

titles accurately describe their contents, that they embrace a single subject, that they not be altered during passage so as to change their original purpose, and so on" (Tarr, *Understanding State Constitutions*, p. 119).

41. Wallis, "Constitutions, Corporations, and Corruption," p. 248.

42. State constitution-makers also reduced the power of state legislatures by making elective some local offices that had previously been appointive.

43. W. Nelson, "Re-evaluation of Scholarly Explanations," p. 191. Similar sentiments were voiced in the New York constitutional convention of 1847—see Bergan, *History of the New York Court of Appeals*, p. 21.

44. Carrington and Long, "Independence and Democratic Accountability," p. 456.

45. *Debates and Proceedings of the Maryland Reform Convention, to Revise the State Constitution, Commenced at Annapolis, November 4, 1850*, I:490.

46. *Report of the Debates and Proceedings of the Convention for the Revision of the Constitution of the State of Ohio, 1850–51*, I:66.

47. *Report of the Debates and Proceedings of the Convention for the Revision of the Constitution of the State of New York*, p. 104, quoted in W. Nelson, "Re-evaluation of Scholarly Explanations," p. 195.

48. *Massachusetts Debates*, p. 706, quoted in W. Nelson, "Re-evaluation of Scholarly Explanations," p. 194.

49. *The Kentucky Yeoman* (Frankfort), 5 July 1849, quoted in K. Hall, "Judiciary on Trial," p. 347.

50. *Official Report of the Debates and Proceedings in the State Convention, Assembled May 4th, 1853, to Revise and Amend the Constitution of the Commonwealth of Massachusetts*, I:788, quoted in W. Nelson, "Re-evaluation of Scholarly Explanations," p. 196. Delegates in other states made similar arguments. For example, a delegate to the Ohio constitutional convention of 1851 noted, "We have reason to hope that the people will make wiser and far better selections [than the legislature]. Indeed, the whole people can have but one motive; and if they fail in the selection of good men, it will be by mistake and not design. Intrigue, combination, and faction, which oftentimes prove so potent with small bodies of men, are powerless with the whole mass of voters" (quoted in Bemar, *Election vs. Appointment of Judges*, p. 163).

51. [Illinois] *Constitutional Debates of 1847*, p. 462.

52. Ibid., p. 466.

53. K. Hall, "Progressive Reform and the Decline of Democratic Accountability," p. 348n13.

54. *Report of the Debates and Proceedings of the Convention for the Revision of the Constitution of the State of Indiana*, II:1808–9, quoted in W. Nelson, "Re-evaluation of Scholarly Explanations," pp. 205–6.

55. *Massachusetts Debates*, p. 370, quoted in K. Hall, "Judiciary on Trial," p. 350. As a delegate to the Louisiana constitutional convention of 1864 observed, "Which is more ennobling to the intellectual man, to be placed in the judicial chair by the voice and suffrage of the people, or beg, fawn, smile, or crouch to the executive and ask of him to give them what the people gave unto him—a position?" (*Debates in the*

Convention for the Revision and Amendment of the Constitution of the State of Louisiana, p. 282).

56. *New York Debates*, pp. 670–71; quoted in K. Hall, "Judiciary on Trial," pp. 350–51. This idea of expanding the power of state government while at the same time curtailing and channeling legislative power is a continuing theme in state constitutional development. See Bridges, "Managing the Periphery," pp. 32–58.

57. *Debates and Proceedings of the Constitutional Convention of the State of Illinois*, II:1002. A delegate to the Kentucky constitutional convention of 1890 concurred: "Are Judges intended to reflect the will of the people? Are they intended to represent any party or any measure? Certainly not. In so far as a Judge represents any party or measure, to that extent is he unfit for the office" (*Official Report of the Proceedings and Debates in the Convention Assembled at Frankfort, on the Eighth Day of September, 1890, to Adopt, Amend, or Change the Constitution of the State of Kentucky*, II:3043).

58. Ibid.

59. *Debates and Proceedings of the Constitutional Convention of the State of Illinois*, p. 1002.

60. Ibid., at 1005.

61. See Shugerman, *People's Courts*, chap. 5.

62. Michigan Constitution of 1850, Art. VI, sec. 20.

63. K. Hall, "Judiciary on Trial," p. 354.

64. K. Hall, "Progressive Reform and the Decline of Democratic Accountability," pp. 352–53.

65. During the period from 1830–80 the professions in America were under "withering attack." Haber, *Quest for Authority and Honor*, p. xii. This is reflected in a lowering of the states' entry barriers for the practice of law. Whereas in 1800 three-quarters of the states had educational requirements for the practice of law, by 1860 only one-quarter had such requirements. See Haber, *Quest for Authority*, p. 115; and Johnson, *American Legal Culture*, p. 21. Indeed, the Indiana Constitution of 1851 mandated that "every person of good moral character, being a voter, shall be entitled to admission to practice law in all courts of justice" (Indiana Constitution, Art. VII, sec. 2). The New Hampshire legislature too authorized any citizen, aged twenty-one and of good moral character, to petition for an examination by the supreme court upon the recommendation of any attorney in the state. This followed the abolition of a required period of preparation for the practice of law in Georgia, Tennessee, South Carolina, Louisiana, Mississippi, and Arkansas. See Gawalt, *Promise of Power*, p. 188.

The constitutionalization of more demanding professional qualifications for judges is directly contrary to this trend and was not universally applauded. As a delegate to the Minnesota constitutional convention of 1857 observed, "If you are going to give the election of judges to the people, I do not see why you should trammel the people by specifying what sort of men they are to elect as judges" (*Debates and Proceedings of the Minnesota Constitutional Convention*, p. 513). Other scholars argue that "the antiprofessional movement . . . was simply overwhelmed by a professional countermovement" of the bench and bar between the 1750s and 1850s, see W. Nelson,

Americanization of the Common Law, p. 70; and, more generally, Kimball, *"True Professional Model" in America.*

66. M. Nelson, *Study of Judicial Review in Virginia,* pp. 35, 54, 80.

67. Keller, *Affairs of State,* p. 362; and Shugerman, "Economic Crisis," pp. 1147–48, appendix B.

68. Corwin, "Extension of Judicial Review in New York," pp. 283–85; and Keller, *Affairs of State,* p. 362.

69. Shugerman, "Economic Crisis," part IV. Richard Drew reported similar results in his study of judicial review in Alabama, Indiana, Massachusetts, New Hampshire, New York, Ohio, Pennsylvania, and Virginia. He found that the supreme courts in those states struck down twenty-five laws from 1790–1839, but from 1840–59 they struck down state laws in one hundred twenty-two cases. See Drew, "Surge and Consolidation," p. 5.

70. Shugerman, "Economic Crisis," p. 1150, appendix D.

71. State provisions expressly authorizing judicial review include: Virginia Constitution of 1850, Art. I, sec. 2; and Georgia Constitution of 1877, Art. I, sec. 4, para. 2. The Missouri Constitution of 1870 specifically called on state judges to resolve conflicts over whether the legislature had passed a special law when a general law was possible, and an amendment to the Kansas Constitution did the same. See Missouri Constitution, Art. 4, sec. 53; and Kansas Constitution, 1906 amendment to Art. 2, sec. 17.

72. K. Hall, "Constitutional Machinery and Judicial Professionalism," p. 33. Hall notes that "partisan ballots and popular elections fostered a distinctive career path for would-be state appellate judges that encouraged prior judicial and public legal service" (ibid., p. 34).

73. Bryce, *American Commonwealth,* I:457. Kermit Hall concurs, noting that "in their quality and social diversity, elected state appellate judges resembled lower federal judges" (K. Hall, "Constitutional Machinery," p. 42).

74. K. Hall, "Progressive Reform and the Decline of Democratic Accountability," p. 355, tab. 1. This level of competitiveness did not translate into politicized campaigns for judicial office; rather, judicial candidates mounted low-key campaigns that emphasized party loyalty and local pride. Nancarrow, "Vox Populi," p. 90.

75. K. Hall, "Progressive Reform and the Decline of Democratic Accountability," p. 355, tab. 1. Voter roll-off in judicial elections was also very low—see ibid., pp. 360–62.

76. W. Nelson, "Re-evaluation of Scholarly Explanations," p. 199.

77. K. Hall, "Progressive Reform and the Decline of Democratic Accountability," pp. 362–65.

78. K. Hall, "Constitutional Machinery," p. 38. Limited tenure "became in practice tenure during good behavior, due to the strength of the popular feeling that satisfactory sitting judges should be returned to office" (see Hurst, *Growth of American Law,* p. 138).

79. *Debates of the Convention to Amend the Constitution of Pennsylvania,* III:742.

80. *Debates of the Convention to Amend the Constitution of Pennsylvania,* III:751–61 and 772–79, quoted in Branning, *Pennsylvania Constitutional Development,* p. 83.

81. Carpenter, *Judicial Tenure*, pp. 182–83.

82. K. Hall, "Constitutional Machinery," p. 36.

83. Opponents of extended tenure disagreed that a longer-term enhanced performance in office. As a delegate to the Ohio Constitutional Convention of 1873 noted in defending a five–year term for judges, "That is long enough for a bad judge to occupy the position, and if he be a good one, it is easy for us to reelect him" (*Official Report of the Proceedings and Debates of the Third Constitutional Convention of Ohio*, II:698).

84. This distrust may be rooted in what has been described in a study of American political culture in the early nineteenth century as a lack of "powerful norms of respect for hierarchies of authority" and the lack of a "level of routinization of obedience to lawfully constituted authority" (see L. Goldstein, *Constituting Federal Sovereignty*, p. 50).

85. On the legal profession's role in promoting popular election of judges, see K. Hall, "Judiciary on Trial."

86. Hanssen, "Learning About Judicial Independence," p. 349. This was important because, as Magali Larson has observed, "the American legal profession . . . decisively moved toward professionalization in the Progressive Era" (M. Larson, *Rise of Professionalism*, p. 169).

87. See Dinan, "Foreword," pp. 983–1039.

88. Hurst, *Lawmakers*, p. 137. On the development of the understanding that impeachment was not to be used to discipline federal judges because of their rulings, see Geyh, *When Courts and Congress Collide*, chap. 3. Geyh's volume documents how shared understandings of "customary independence" have supplemented the federal Constitution's protections of judicial independence. These shared understandings developed more slowly at the state level and are less firmly entrenched.

89. Hurst, *Lawmakers*, p. 139.

90. Quoted in Nancarrow, *Vox Populi*, p. 192.

91. For an overview of these attacks, see Ross, *Muted Fury.* Some scholarly commentators have supported the claims voiced by critics of the courts. See, for example, Paul, *Conservative Crisis and the Rule of Law*; and Forbath, *Law and the Shaping of the American Labor Movement.* Other scholars have denied that state judges excessively restricted state legislatures. See Semonche, *Charting the Future*; and Urofsky, "State Courts and Protective Legislation," pp. 63–92. Some recent scholars have portrayed judges as motivated by a concern to safeguard against legislation offering advantages to special interests, a continuation of the Jacksonian distinction between the people and special interests. See Gillman, *Constitution Besieged.*

92. Roe, *Our Judicial Oligarchy*, 107. Roe further noted (p. 225) that "the judiciary is undoubtedly looked upon as the last and final bulwark of Special Privilege."

93. Dodd, "Recall and Political Responsibility," pp. 85–86.

94. Quoted in Forbath, *Law and the Shaping of the American Labor Movement*, p. 47.

95. Quoted in Roe, *Our Judicial Oligarchy*, p. 14.

96. Pound, "Causes of Popular Dissatisfaction," p. 178, quoted in Berkson and Caufield, *Judicial Selection in the United States.*

97. Taft, "Selection and Tenure of Judges," p. 418, quoted in Berkson and Caufield, *Judicial Selection in the United States.*

98. Quoted in Mowry, *Theodore Roosevelt,* p. 171.

99. The analysis in this paragraph relies on Ross, *Muted Fury,* pp. 10–13. For further elaboration of the differences between the populists and progressives, see Goodwyn, *Democratic Promise*; and Hofstadter, *Progressive Movement.*

100. In *Lochner v. New York,* 198 U.S. 45 (1905), the US Supreme Court by a 5–4 vote struck down a New York statute that limited hours of labor in bakeries to ten hours a day or sixty hours a week. The law had been uniformly upheld by New York courts, and critics accused the Court of reading its own social and political predilections into the law. For background and an overview, see Kens, *Judicial Power and Reform Politics.* In *Standard Oil Co. of New Jersey v. United States,* 221 U.S. 1 (1911), the Supreme Court blunted the effect of the federal Sherman Antitrust Act by holding that its prohibition against restraint of trade extended only to "undue restraints" and was to be interpreted in accordance with "the standard of reason" (see Ross, *Muted Fury,* pp. 44–45).

101. For data on the recall, see Zimmerman, *Recall.* For the debate during the progressive era, see Ross, *Muted Fury,* chap. 5; and Beard and Shultz, *Documents on the State-Wide Initiative, Referendum, and Recall.*

102. Botein, "'What We Shall Meet Afterwards in Heaven,'" p. 55.

103. For discussion of the events in Arizona, see Ross, *Muted Fury,* pp. 111–15; and Leshy, *Arizona State Constitution,* pp. 17–18.

104. The quotations are from New York attorney William Hornblower and Massachusetts representative Samuel McCall, quoted in Ross, *Muted Fury,* pp. 116–17; and from Butler, *Why Should We Change our Form of Government?,* p. 40.

105. Quoted in Beard and Shultz, *Documents on the State-Wide Initiative, Referendum, and Recall,* p. 59.

106. Quoted in ibid., p. 57.

107. Butler, *Why Should We Change our Form of Government?,* p. 43.

108. Wilcox, *Government by All the People,* p. 217.

109. Roe, *Our Judicial Oligarchy,* p. 217.

110. Ibid., p. 216.

111. Goff, *Records of the Arizona Constitutional Convention of 1910,* pp. 159–60.

112. Quoted in Beard and Shultz, *Documents on the State-Wide Initiative, Referendum, and Recall,* p. 62.

113. Quoted in Stagner, "Recall of Judicial Decisions and the Due Process Debate," p. 258. Roosevelt initially limited his proposal to the recall of state rulings, though he expected that ultimately it would result in an amendment to authorize the recall of US Supreme Court rulings as well. See Ross, *Muted Fury,* p. 144.

114. During this period popular majorities in the states did continue to use their amendment power to overturn state judicial rulings with which they disagreed or to preempt such rulings. For example, rulings invalidating state laws restricting maximum hours laws led to constitutional amendments in California, Michigan, and Nebraska. Amendments authorizing laws limiting hours for workers in hazardous

occupations were adopted in Colorado, Idaho, Montana, and Oklahoma, and amendments authorizing enactment of minimum wage laws in California, Nebraska, Ohio, and Utah. See Dinan, "Court-Constraining Amendments," pp. 992–94. However, when state courts based their rulings on the due process clause of the Fourteenth Amendment, they thereby insulated their decisions from being overturned by state constitutional amendments.

115. Lewis, "New Method of Constitutional Amendment," p. 319.

116. Ballantine, "Labor Legislation and the Judicial Veto," p. 227.

117. Ross, *Muted Fury*, p. 142. Under Colorado's version of the recall of decisions, for example, supporters would have to gain the signatures on a petition of at least 5 percent of the state's qualified electors within sixty days of the decision. If they succeeded, the question of whether to recall the decision would be placed on the ballot for popular approval, in a fashion similar to that for a constitutional amendment. See Haines, *American Doctrine of Judicial Supremacy*, pp. 484–85.

118. Frederick, "Significance of the Recall," p. 48, quoted in Ross, *Muted Fury*, p. 146.

119. Although a majority of the bar was critical of Roosevelt's proposal, some attorneys supported the recall of judicial decisions. See Stagner, "Recall of Judicial Decisions."

120. "All Taft Wants Is a Square Deal," p. 4, quoted in Ross, *Muted Fury*, p. 138.

121. "Taft Shows Peril in Roosevelt Policy," p. 1, quoted in Ross, *Muted Fury*, p. 147.

122. Roe, *Our Judicial Oligarchy*, p. 219.

123. *People v. Western Union*, 198 P.2d 146 (Colo. 1921).

124. *People v. Max*, 198 P.2d 150 (Colo. 1921).

125. See Carrington, "Judicial Independence and Democratic Accountability," pp. 94–95. The pertinent constitutional provisions include: Nebraska Constitution, Art. V, sec. 2; North Dakota Constitution, Art. VI, sec. 4; and Ohio Constitution, Art. IV, sec. 2.

126. The 1912 Ohio convention proposed forty-two amendments, of which thirty-four were adopted, including seven amendments that directly negated supreme court rulings. See Walker, "Ohio Constitution," p. 457. Roosevelt himself addressed the Ohio convention, urging the recall of judicial decisions. See Steinglass and Scarselli, *Ohio State Constitution*, p. 49.

127. Nebraska Constitution, Art. V, sec. 2; and North Dakota Constitution, Art. VI, sec. 4. North Dakota also requires that the supreme court give in writing the reasons for its rulings, thereby facilitating public scrutiny. North Dakota Constitution, Art. VI, sec. 5.

128. Miewald and Longo, *Nebraska State Constitution*, p. 100. See also Leahy, *North Dakota State Constitution*, p. 103.

129. Quoted in Haynes, *Selection and Tenure of Judges*, p. 214.

130. After the initial wave of adoptions of nonpartisan elections, a smattering of states shifted in succeeding years. From 1921–40, three states; from 1941–60, four states; from 1961–80, two states; and since 1981, three states. All the states that adopted nonpartisan elections previously had partisan judicial elections. For a listing, see Hanssen, "Learning about Judicial Independence," p. 459, tab. 2.

131. This was not true in all states. For example, Michigan in 1939 amended its state constitution to make all state judicial elections nonpartisan and to have a candidate's status as an incumbent on the ballot.

132. Nancarrow, "Vox Populi," p. 344.

133. Winters, "Judicial Selection and Tenure," p. 24.

134. Hanssen, "Learning About Judicial Independence," p. 468.

135. Kales, "Methods of Selecting Judges," pp. 425–29. Kales developed his plan at the urging of Roscoe Pound. On the development of merit selection and its endorsement by reform groups, see Winters, "Merit Plan," in *Judicial Selection and Tenure*, pp. 29–37.

136. Kales, *Unpopular Government*, p. 227.

137. Unsurprisingly, Kales's solution for judicial bias or misconduct likewise relied on professional expertise: "The best protection against arbitrary and disagreeable actions by judges is a duly constituted body of fellow judges who hold a position of superior power and authority and to whom complaints as to the conduct of judges may be brought and who may investigate those complaints and exercise a corrective influence" (see ibid., pp. 247–48).

138. Actually, the first victory for merit selection was in 1934, when California instituted merit selection for appellate judges and allowed counties to adopt the plan by local option for selection of trial judges of general jurisdiction. See Winters and Allard, "Judicial Selection and Tenure in the United States," p. 151. Merit selection was supported by the California Chamber of Commerce and the Republican Party but opposed by labor unions and the Democratic Party. See Grodin, *In Pursuit of Justice*, p. 166. On the adoption of merit selection in Missouri, see Dunne, *Missouri Supreme Court*, pp. 122–26; and Watson and Downing, *Politics of the Bench and Bar*, pp. 1–14.

139. Winters, *Judicial Selection and Tenure*, p. 41.

140. These data are drawn from the "Summary of Initial Selection Methods" compiled by the American Judicature Society, available at www.judicialselection.us.

141. Ross, *Muted Fury*, pp. 20–21.

142. Carrington, "Judicial Independence and Democratic Accountability," p. 106.

Chapter 3

1. See Holmes and Emrey, "Court Diversification," p. 6, tab. 1.

2. Information on states' modes of selection and reforms is found at http://www.judicialselection.us/judicial_selection/reform_efforts/formal_changes_since_inception.cfm?state= .

3. M. Hall, "State Supreme Courts in American Democracy," p. 324. See also Bonneau and Hall, "Predicting Challengers," pp. 337–49; and Bonneau, "Patterns of Campaign Spending," pp. 21–38. An earlier study by Philip Dubois found that in state supreme court contests outside the South from 1948–74, only 49 percent of nonpartisan elections were contested. Dubois, *From Ballot to Bench*, p. 50, tab. 3.

4. Glick, "Promise and Performance," p. 519.

5. As one candidate described it: "Forty-four years ago, I participated in a judicial campaign in Dallas. We put up a few billboards, pasted fliers on telephone poles, and passed out small handbills. Our successful campaign cost a few thousand dollars" (quoted in Thomas, Boyer, and Hrebenar, "Interest Groups and State Court Elections," p. 137).

6. Champagne, "Interest Groups and Judicial Elections," p. 1393.

7. See Briffault, "Judicial Campaign Codes," pp. 181–238.

8. Bayne, "Lynchard's Candidacy," quoted in Schotland, "Financing Judicial Elections," p. 213.

9. This paragraph is based on information collected at http://www.judicial selection.us/judicial_selection/reform_efforts/formal_changes_since_inception. cfm?state=. See also Streb and Frederick, "Judicial Reform and the Future of Judicial Elections."

10. In 2009 both houses of the Indiana Legislature passed a bill that would have replaced merit selection of superior court judges in St. Joseph County with nonpartisan election, but it was vetoed by the governor. In 2011 the Kansas House passed a bill that would have shifted from merit selection to gubernatorial appointment with Senate confirmation for the Court of Appeals, but the bill failed to pass the Senate. For more detail, see http://www.judicialselection.us/judicial_selection/reform_efforts /failed_reform_efforts.cfm?state=.

11. See Tarr, "Do Retention Elections Work?", pp. 615–16; and Tarr, "Politicizing the Process," pp. 68–69.

12. These changes have occurred primarily at the state supreme court level, but some observers have detected a politicization of races for state intermediate courts of appeals as well. See Goldberg et al., *New Politics of Judicial Elections 2006*, pp. 24–28.

13. These figures were calculated from data in Bonneau and Hall, *In Defense of Judicial Elections*, p. 80, tab. 4.2.

14. Goldberg et al., *New Politics of Judicial Elections 2000*, p. 2.

15. Thus, Stephen Bright has concluded that "retention elections have the same potential for intimidation and a chilling effect on judicial decisionmaking as direct elections" (Bright, "Can Judicial Independence Be Attained in the South," p. 859). In fact, "retention elections, with their simple yes or no choice, more directly but crudely hold judges politically accountable on a single popular issue, usually but not always crime, and therefore are a greater challenge to judicial independence and courage" (Linde, "Elective Judges," p. 2004).

16. Burbank and Friedman, "Reconsidering Judicial Independence," p. 37.

17. Seven states that employ merit selection do not use retention elections, either awarding tenure during good behavior or to a retirement age or providing for reappointment rather than election for continuation in office. For information about selection in various states, see http://www.judicialselection.us/judicial_selection /reform_efforts/formal_changes_since_inception.cfm?state=.

18. These figures are derived from data at http://www.judicialselection.us /uploads/documents/Judicial_Selection_Charts_1196376173077.pdf.

19. See Schotland, "New Challenges to States' Judicial Selection," p. 1105.

20. Sample et al., *New Politics of Judicial Elections 2000–2009*, p. 8. Unless otherwise noted, data reported in this and succeeding paragraphs are drawn from that study.

21. As Linda King has noted, "Millions of dollars spent by special interests each year to influence state elections go essentially unreported to the public. [Independent expenditures] form the single-largest loophole in the laws and administrative procedures implementing transparency in state electoral politics" (see King, *Indecent Disclosure*).

22. Sample, *New Politics of Judicial Elections 2000–2009*, chap. 2.

23. Bonneau, "Patterns of Campaign Spending and Electoral Competition."

24. Michigan and Ohio are classified as partisan-election states, even though party affiliations do not appear on the general-election ballot. Judicial candidates in both states are nominated in partisan primary elections and endorsed by political parties.

25. Bonneau and Hall, *In Defense of Judicial Elections*, p. 66.

26. *Caperton v. A. T. Massey Coal Co.*, 129 S.Ct. 2252 (2009).

27. Sample et al., *New Politics of Judicial Elections 2000–2009*, pp. 5 and 28.

28. Ibid., p. 18.

29. See, "Essay on Judicial Selection," pp. 111–12n114.

30. Schotland, "To the Endangered Species List," p. 1407n40.

31. Thus, Bonneau and Hall found that "incumbent spending on average significantly outpaced challenger spending from 1990 through 2004. In every election cycle during that period, incumbents on average outspent challengers by sizable sums" (Bonneau and Hall, *In Defense of Judicial Elections*, p. 99).

32. Sample et al., *New Politics of Judicial Elections 2000–2009*, p. 19.

33. Bonneau, "Effects of Campaign Spending," pp. 489–99. Bonneau calculates that "if the losing candidate increased spending by 1 percent, the winner's percentage of the vote would be reduced by 0.01 percent" (Bonneau, "Vacancies on the Bench," p. 153).

34. Justice Paul Pfeifer of the Ohio Supreme Court, quoted in Sample et al., *New Politics of Judicial Elections 2000–2009*, p. 27.

35. Carrington, "Judicial Independence and Democratic Accountability," p. 112.

36. For a collection and analysis of poll data, see Pozen, "Irony of Judicial Elections," pp. 304–6. For an experimental analysis, Gibson, "Challenges to the Impartiality of State Supreme Courts," pp. 59–75.

37. Bonneau and Hall, *In Defense of Judicial Elections*, p. 38.

38. Ibid., p. 131. As Lawrence Baum and David Klein observe, "The more that voters know about the candidates, the less likely they are to skip over that contest in the election booth" (Baum and Klein, "Voter Responses to High-Visibility Judicial Campaigns," p. 142).

39. Manweller, *People Versus the Courts*, p. 210.

40. Peters, "Campaigning for State Supreme Court 2006," p. 182.

41. Sample et al., *New Politics of Judicial Elections 2000–2009*, pp. 25 and 29.

42. Ibid., p. 29.

43. Ibid., p. 21.

44. Peters, "Campaigning for State Supreme Court," p. 183.

45. Sample et al., *New Politics of Judicial Elections 2000–2009*, p. 32. Ads by candidates for judicial office usually are positive in character and moderate in tone, but not always. For example, in 1996 an incumbent supreme court justice in Alabama ran an ad in which a picture of a skunk faded into a picture of the challenger in the race, with the voice-over: "Some things you can smell a mile away." See http://www.judicial selection.us/judicial_selection/index.cfm?state=AL.

46. Sample et al., *New Politics of Judicial Elections 2000–2009*, p. 26. The examples in this paragraph are drawn from that source.

47. DeMuniz, "Eroding the Public's Confidence in Judicial Impartiality," p. 764; Carrington, "Judicial Independence and Democratic Accountability," p. 111; and Thomas, Boyer, and Hrebenar, "Interest Groups and State Court Elections," p. 138.

48. Champagne, "Television Ads," pp. 688–89.

49. Zemans, "Accountable Judge," p. 640.

50. Sample et al., *New Politics of Judicial Elections 2000–2009*, p. 17.

51. Although the conventional wisdom has been that negative ads reduce turnout, more recent studies dispute this. See Kaufmann, Petrocik, and Shaw, *Unconventional Wisdom*, pp. 168–69, tab. 8.1.

52. Pozen, "Irony of Judicial Elections," p. 307.

53. See Black and Black, *Rise of the Southern Republicans*; and Lublin, *Republican South*.

54. Eisenstein, "Financing Pennsylvania's Supreme Court Candidates," p. 12.

55. Sample et al., *New Politics of Judicial Elections 2000–2009*, p. 20.

56. On the partisan transformation in Texas, see Champagne and Cheek, "Cycle of Judicial Elections," p. 929. The greater competitiveness led to an escalation of the costs of general-election campaigns. See Champagne and Cheek, "Money in Texas Supreme Court Elections," pp. 20–25. Heavy expenditures continued, even as Republicans came to dominate the Texas bench. See Sample et al., *New Politics of Judicial Selection*, p. 20, fig. 11.

57. Cheek and Champagne, "Money in Texas Supreme Court Elections," p. 22.

58. For more recent election results, see www.justiceatstake.org/contentViewer .asp>breadcrumb=4,126,111,462.

59. See Tarr and Porter, *State Supreme Courts*, chap. 3. See also Equal Justice Initiative, "Criminal Justice Reform in Alabama."

60. Salokar and Shaw, "Impact of National Politics," pp. 59–60.

61. Quoted in Watson and Downing, *Politics of the Bench and the Bar*, p. 58.

62. See Brewer, "Rise of Partisanship and the Expansion of Partisan Conflict," pp. 219–29.

63. See McCarty, Poole, and Rosenthal, "Hunt for Party Discipline in Congress," pp. 673–87; and Snyder and Groseclose, "Estimating Party Influence," pp. 193–211.

64. Jacobson, "Party Polarization in National Politics," p. 25.

65. Our analysis relies on Kagan et al., "Business of State Supreme Courts," pp. 121–56; and Kagan et al., "Evolution of State Supreme Courts," pp. 961–1005.

66. Groot, "Effects of an Intermediate Appellate Court," pp. 548–72; and Flango and Blair, "Creating an Intermediate Appellate Court," pp. 74–84.

67. Kagan et al., "Business of State Supreme Courts," p. 155.

68. As Justice Antonin Scalia wrote for the Court in *Republican Party of Minnesota v. White*: "Not only do state-court judges possess the power to 'make' common law, but they have the immense power to shape the States' constitutions as well. Which is precisely why the election of state judges became popular" (536 U.S. 765, 784 [2002]).

69. Carrington, Meador, and Rosenberg, *Justice on Appeal*, p. 150.

70. Keeton, *Venturing to Do Justice*, p. 3.

71. Peck, "In Defense of Fundamental Principles," pp. 672–82.

72. For a listing of cases, see Schwartz and Lorber, "Judicial Nullification of Civil Justice Reform Violates," pp. 939–51.

73. Bonneau and Hall, *In Defense of Judicial Elections*, p. 66. Joanna Shepherd has noted that "in most states, the majority of the contributions to state judicial campaigns comes from groups hoping to shape tort law" (Shepherd, "Money, Politics, and Impartial Justice," p. 644).

74. Tarr, *Understanding State Constitutions*, pp. 161–70; and R. Williams, *Law of American State Constitutions*, chap. 5.

75. Herschkoff, "State Courts and the 'Passive Virtues,'" p. 1890.

76. On school finance litigation, see Reed, *On Equal Terms*; and Bauries, "State Constitutions and Individual Rights," pp. 301–66.

77. See California Constitution, Art. 1, sec. 27, overruling *People v. Anderson*, 493 P.2d 880 (Calif. 1973), and Massachusetts Constitution, Declaration of Rights, Art. 26, amendment 1116, overruling *District Attorney v. Watson*, 411 N.E.2d 1274 (Mass. 1980).

78. Quoted in Preston, "Iowa Holds a Major Judicial Election."

79. Quoted in Thomas, Boyer, and Hrebenar, "Interest Groups and State Court Elections," p. 135.

80. Sample et al., *New Politics of Judicial Elections 2000–2009*, p. 49; and the website of Democracy Rising Pennsylvania, at http://www.democracyrisingpa.com/index.cfm?organization_id=66&section_id=1060&page_id=4303.

81. Sample et al., *New Politics of Judicial Elections 2000–2009*, p. 15.

82. Ware, "Money, Politics, and Judicial Decisions," p. 656.

83. Quoted in Sample et al., *New Politics of Judicial Elections 2000–2009*, p. 40.

84. Ibid., p. 13.

85. "Kilbridge and Madigan." This is hardly an isolated occurrence. On the use of crime-control ads by the US Chamber of Commerce, see Champagne, "Television Ads in Judicial Campaigns," pp. 688–89. Nor is it confined to groups interested in tort law. As an Oregon activist supporting a property-rights initiative stated, "If they strike down Measure 7, it's war . . . . We're going to go after the judge with everything we've

got. We found out he let a child molester go on a technicality. We're going to use that against him [in the next election]" (quoted in Manweller, *People Versus the Courts*, p. 199).

86. Quoted in "Alabama Supreme Court Elections."

87. Linde, "Judge as Political Candidate," p. 7.

88. *Republican Party of Minnesota v. White*, 536 U.S. 765 (2002).

89. American Bar Association Commission on the 21st Century Judiciary, p. 29. The rules on appearance at party events differ in states with partisan judicial elections.

90. Pozen, "Irony of Judicial Elections," p. 299.

91. *Republican Party of Minnesota v. White*, at 781.

92. Pozen, "Irony of Judicial Elections," p. 299. The Minnesota provision at issue in *White* was based on Canon 78 of the Code of Judicial Conduct adopted by the American Bar Association in 1972; and the ABA itself was sufficiently concerned about the provision's constitutionality that it deleted it from its revised Model Code in 1990. See Briffault, "Judicial Campaign Codes," pp. 202–3. When *White* was decided, only nine states had retained the "announce clause," again because of doubts about its constitutionality. See Geyh, "Preserving the Delicate Balance," p. 359.

93. Goldberg, Sample, and Pozen, "Best Defense," p. 506.

94. See *Weaver v. Bonner*, 309 F.3d 1312 (11th Cir. 2002); *Spargo v. New York State Commission on Judicial Conduct*, 244 F. Supp. 2d 72 (N.D.N.Y. 2003); *Republican Party of Minnesota v. White (White* II), 416 F.3d 738 (8th Cir. 2005) (*en banc*); and *North Dakota Family Alliance v. Bader*, 361 F.Supp.2d 1021 (D.N.D. 2005). For an overview of developments, see Caufield, "In the Wake of *White*," pp. 625–47.

95. "Developments in the Law," p. 1143.

96. Peters, "Campaigning for State Supreme Court," p. 177, tab. 6.

97. Quoted in Caufield, "Foreboding National Trends in Judicial Elections."

98. P. White, "Relinquished Responsibilities," pp. 120–21.

99. Bonneau and Hall, "In Defense of Judicial Elections," p. 134.

100. Gibson, "Challenges to the Impartiality," p. 72.

101. Pozen, "Irony of Judicial Elections," p. 317.

102. *Citizens United v. Federal Election Commission*, 130 S.Ct. 876 (2010).

103. Ibid., at 904.

104. Ibid., at 909, reiterating its position in *Caperton v. A. T. Massey Coal Co.*, 129 S.Ct. 2252, 2252 (2009).

105. Ibid., at 968.

106. Samuels, "Hanging a 'For Sale' Sign Over the Judiciary," p. A22; and Skaggs, "Buying Justice."

107. *Minnesota Citizens Concerned for Life v. Swanson*, application 10A422 (2010).

108. This is true for both constitutional and statutory interpretation. See Gerhardt, *Constitutional Theory*; Eskridge, *Dynamics of Statutory Interpretation*; and Scalia, *Matter of Interpretation*.

109. W. Marshall, "Constitutional Law as Political Spoils," p. 205.

110. Ibid., pp. 194 and 209.

111. W. Marshall, "Judicial Accountability," p. 943. As Patrick Brennan aptly observed, "The bell announcing Legal Realism cannot be unrung" (Brennan, "Locating Authority in Law," p. 169).

112. See Campbell Public Affairs Institute.

113. See Greenberg Quinlan Rosner Research, Inc., Justice at Stake Campaign, Justice at Stake National Survey Results. These results are discussed in McLeod, "If at First You Don't Succeed," pp. 499–522.

114. Annenberg Judicial Independence Survey (2006). Similar results were reported in a 2005 survey by the American Bar Association: 56 percent of respondents believed that judicial activism was a contemporary "crisis," while 46 percent agreed that judges were "arrogant, out-of-control, and unaccountable." See Lindquist and Cross, *Measuring Judicial Activism*, p. 10.

115. Bybee, *All Judges Are Political*, chap. 1.

116. Quoted in Freund, "Appointment of Justices," p. 1146.

117. Goldberg et al., *New Politics of Judicial Elections 2000*, p. 8.

Chapter 4

1. Ferejohn and Kramer, "Independent Judges, Dependent Judiciary," p. 970. They further note, "Most people assume, reasonably enough, that political actors face pressures to abandon or subvert legal rules for legally inappropriate reasons. So we create a forum for adjudication removed from politics, presided over by actors immune from overt political compulsion or inducement" (Ferejohn and Kramer, "Independent Judges, Dependent Judiciary," p. 968). See also Burbank, "Judicial Accountability," p. 48.

2. Martin Shapiro's account of the rule of law underscores its connection to judicial independence: "Although the sovereign is the sole source of law, even the sovereign is bound by the law once it is enacted and until it is modified or repealed. Thus, while the sovereign could intervene at any time to change the general law that the courts were applying, he ought not to interfere in particular cases to compel results contrary to the existing law" (Shapiro, *Courts*, p. 67).

3. See Geyh, "Why Judicial Elections Stink," pp. 48–49.

4. See Fogelsong, "Dynamics of Judicial (In)dependence in Russia"; and Dodson and Jackson, "Judicial Independence and Instability in Central America."

5. Several studies confirm this. See Aspin and Hall, "Retention Elections and Judicial Behavior," p. 32, tab. 4; Brace and Hall, "Studying Courts Comparatively," pp. 13–24; Traut and Emmert, "Expanding the Integrated Model," p. 1177; Huber and Gordon, "Accountability and Coercion," pp. 247–63; and Bright, "Can Judicial Independence Be Attained in the South," pp. 817–60.

6. The three-fold division of judicial accountability corresponds with that used by Geyh, "Rescuing Judicial Accountability," pp. 917–24. According to Ruth Gavison, accountability includes "anything from specific responses of the system concerning individual judges, with the aim of disciplining them or removing them from office,

through official responses directed generally at the judicature and their working conditions, to critical responses by society or social groups which may affect, in a diffuse way, the status of the judicature, their decisions, and their conduct generally" (see Gavison, "Implications of Jurisprudential Theories," pp. 1619–20).

7. Grant and Keohane, "Accountability and Abuses in World Politics," p. 29.

8. As an Idaho anticourt activist put it, "These guys need to know we can get them. They sit down there in Boise thinking they're above the law. . . . We only need to pick off one. The rest will get the message" (quoted in Manweller, *People Versus the Courts*, p. 84).

9. Frohnmayer, "Election of State Appellate Judges," p. 1255.

10. Tarr, "Judicial Branch," pp. 86–87. Ferejohn and Kramer have argued that in the United States institutional accountability is more effective than individual accountability because the weapons for enforcing accountability are better and the willingness to use them greater (see Ferejohn and Kramer, "Independent Judges, Dependent Judiciary").

11. Judicial Councils Reform and Judicial Conduct and Disability Act of 1980, 28 U.S.C. sec 1 (1988). For an overview, see Lubet, "Judicial Discipline and Judicial Independence," pp. 59–74.

12. This was proposed in 2005 by Representative James Sensenbrenner of Wisconsin. See Sensenbrenner, "Zola Lecture in Public Policy."

13. Geyh, "Informal Methods of Judicial Discipline," p. 280.

14. Ibid., p. 311.

15. Toma, "Congressional Influence and the Supreme Court," pp. 131–46.

16. *Claremont School District v. Governor*, 703 A.2d 1353 (1997).

17. Defenders of the New Hampshire justices accused the legislature of targeting them because of their school-finance ruling, thereby minimizing the serious misconduct that had occurred. Those favoring impeachment insisted their only aim was to address the misconduct. See Demary, "Legislative-Judicial Relations on Contested Issues," p. 205.

18. See Hartley and Douglas, "Politics of Court Budgeting in the States," pp. 441–54; and Douglas and Hartley, "State Court Budgeting and Judicial Independence," pp. 54–78.

19. Thus one commentator wrote of *Planned Parenthood of Southeastern Pennsylvania v. Casey*, 505 U.S. 833 (1992): "The Court's opinion presupposes a people who, as the Court says, are dedicated to the rule of law, and who, as the Court also says, understand the rule of law in terms of deference to the judiciary." See Eisgruber, "Judicial Supremacy and Constitutional Distortion," pp. 84–85.

20. The California Supreme Court invalidated limiting marriage to opposite-sex couples in *In re Marriage Cases*, 183 P.3d 384 (2008). California voters in 2008 adopted a constitutional amendment via the initiative process to overturn the Court's ruling. The California Supreme Court subsequently upheld the constitutionality of the initiative amendment in *Strauss v. Horton*, 46 Cal. 4th 364 (2009).

21. We use the term "law-makers" because those changing the law may include the public, through constitutional amendment or the initiative, as well as legislators.

22. Geyh, *When Courts and Congress Collide*, chap. 2.

23. Lubet, "Judicial Discipline and Judicial Independence," p. 62.

24. On the development of these norms at the federal level, see Geyh, *When Courts and Congress Collide*, chap. 3.

25. Task Forces of Citizens for Independent Courts, *Uncertain Justice*, p. 149.

26. Hoffer and Hull, *Impeachment in America*, p. 64.

27. The statement about federal judges holds true only for Article III judges. Magistrate judges (created by Congress in 1968) and bankruptcy judges (created in 1984) serve for fixed and renewable terms of eight and fourteen years respectively.

28. U.S. Constitution, Art. III, sec. 2, para. 2.

29. Dowdle, "Public Accountability," p. 4.

30. Schotland, "New Challenges in States' Judicial Selection," p. 1105. Yet in states with judicial elections many judges are initially appointed to office to fill unexpired terms, and some never encounter electoral challenges to their remaining in office, thus transforming a nominally elective selection process into an essentially appointive one. See Tarr, ""Designing an Appointive System," pp. 291–92.

31. Voters may vote for or against a judicial incumbent for reasons other than enforcing accountability—based on party affiliation, ethnicity, name familiarity, or other factors.

32. See Stephenson, *Campaigns and the Court*.

33. Zimmerman, *Recall*, pp. 46–49.

34. Quotation in *Michael Moncur's (Cynical) Quotations*.

35. For presentation of this viewpoint, see Farber and Sherry, *Judgment Calls*.

36. As an early contributor to the debate observed, "While the judges are bound to act in accordance with the established law and to interpret and apply that law to specific controversies, they ought to be just as responsible to the people and the legislature are for the performance of their respective functions" (see Wilcox, *Government by All the People*, p. 217). Historically, "accountability to the electorate was thought both an inducement to responsible performance of public duty and an assurance that the courts would interpret legal texts to reflect the values of the people, not their own eccentric preferences or those of a professional class" (see Carrington, *Stewards of Democracy*, p. 20). As Ruth Gavison has noted, when the law is unclear, accountability serves to ensure judges are responsive to "preexisting and not idiosyncratic social or political norms" (Gavison, "Implications of Jurisprudential Theories," p. 1657).

37. *United States v. Butler*, 297 U.S. 62 (1936).

38. On Legal Realism, see Duxbury, *Patterns of American Jurisprudence*; and Rumble, *American Legal Realism*. On the connection between judicial attitudes and judicial votes, see Segal and Spaeth, *Supreme Court and the Attitudinal Model*; and Peretti, "Does Judicial Independence Exist?" On the indeterminacy of law and the necessity of choice, see, *inter alia*, Feldman, *American Legal Thought*; and W. Marshall, "Judicial Accountability," pp. 937–45.

39. Accountability to the law implies that the law determines case outcomes. Yet judges with the same understanding of the law can come to different resolutions of a case because they disagree on the facts of the case, and judges applying the same legal

standards may arrive at different conclusions. This may be particularly true in contemporary constitutional law, which often involves the use of balancing tests.

40. See Behn, *Rethinking Democratic Accountability*, p. 42.

41. Gavison, "Implications of Jurisprudential Theories," p. 1634.

42. On the desirability of judges' conforming statutes to changing conditions, see Calabresi, *Common Law*.

43. See Feeley and Rubin, *Judicial Policy Making and the Modern State*, especially pp. 21–22. Those concerned with limiting judicial discretion tend to favor rules rather than standards for just this reason. See Scalia, "Rule of Law as a Law of Rules," pp. 1173–88.

44. Ferejohn and Kramer, "Independent Judges, Dependent Judiciary," p. 997.

45. Justice Hansen, in *State ex rel. Warren v. Nusbaum*, 198 N.W.2d 630, 653 (Wisc. 1972).

46. Geyh, "Rescuing Judicial Accountability," p. 927.

47. See Cover, "Uses of Jurisdictional Redundancy," pp. 639–81; and Shapiro, "Toward a Theory of *Stare Decisis*," pp. 125–34. Appellate review involves not just accountability but also collective judgment, and a collective judgment that is unanimous or nearly unanimous gives greater weight to a ruling.

48. For the US Supreme Court, see "Statistics," p. 389. During its 2008 term, the Court decided with full opinion only fifteen cases from state courts. For data on courts of appeals, see http://www.uscourts.gov/Statistics/FederalJudicialCaseload Statistics/FederalJudicialCaseloadStatistics2009.aspx.

49. For data on state court caseloads, see http://www.ncsconline.org/D_Research /csp/2004 http://www.ncsconline.org/d_research/csp/CSP_Main_Page.html.

50. Cass, *Rule of Law*, p. 50.

51. Phillips, "Comment," p. 129.

52. For an early elaboration of this point, see *Herb v. Pitcairn*, 324 U.S. 117, 126 (1945).

53. As Charles Geyh notes, "Retention elections are designed to minimize the risk of non-retention, by stripping elections of features that might inspire voters to become interested enough to oust incumbents. Thus, there is no choice to make between competing candidates or viewpoints, no race to follow, no opportunity to pick a new winner, and no political party to support" (see Geyh, "Why Judicial Elections Stink," p. 55).

54. *Justice in Jeopardy*, p. v.

55. Chief Justice Thomas Phillips of the Texas Supreme Court has warned that "if we do nothing, [about judicial elections], we risk not just an erosion, but indeed a meltdown in respect for the courts and the rule of law" (Phillips, "Electoral Accountability and Judicial Independence," p. 142).

56. Indeed, Richard Garnett has suggested that whereas charges of judicial activism usually do little more than denote disagreement with a decision, invocations of judicial independence often "seem to signal little more than impatience with those who persist in registering such disapproval" (see Garnett, "Virtue of Humility").

57. See, for example, Bright, "Political Attacks on the Judiciary," pp. 308–30.

58. Burbank, "Is It Time for a National Commission," pp. 177–78.

59. De Tocqueville, *Democracy in America*, I:142.

60. *Bush v. Gore*, 531 U.S. 98 (2000). See Mate and Wright, "2000 Presidential Election Controversy." Data about public support for the court are available from the Harris Poll and the Pew Research Center and are collected at http://poll.orspub.com/search.php?action=addall.

61. In 2006 the Annenberg Poll found that 64 percent of respondents agreed or strongly agreed that the courts in their state "can usually be trusted to make rulings that are right for the state as a whole" and the same percentage trusted the Supreme Court "to operate in the best interests of the American people." However, Christine Kelleher and Jennifer Wolak found less diffuse confidence in state judiciaries than in the federal judiciary and lower confidence in state courts than state executives. Kelleher and Wolak, "Explaining Public Confidence," pp. 707–21.

62. Linde, "Judge as Political Candidate," p. 14.

63. Abrahamson, "Ballot and the Bench," pp. 973–1004.

64. Chief Judge Judith Kaye of the New York Court of Appeals has argued that the legal profession has an obligation to defend the courts against irresponsible criticism (see Kaye, "Safeguarding a Crown Jewel," pp. 703–27).

65. Geyh, "Why Judicial Elections Stink," p. 9.

66. M. Freedman, "Threat to Judicial Independence," p. 737.

67. "Drawing the Line on Inappropriate Criticism," at www.justiceatstake.org/contentViewer.asp?breadrumb=3,551,866. Suffice it to say that "demagoguery" is in the eye of the beholder.

68. *New York Times v. Sullivan*, 376 U.S. 254, 270 (1964).

69. Ibid., at 273.

70. Quoted in Manweiler, *People Versus the Courts*, p. 203.

71. As one Defender colorfully put it, "A judge has no constituency except the unenfranchised lady with the blindfold and scales, no platform except equal and impartial justice under law" (Rosenberg, "Qualities of Justice," p. 1069).

72. As Ruth Gavison writes, "Independence requires some freedom to make mistakes or to arrive at controversial decisions, since the essence of independence is the willingness to make up one's own mind without seeking to please interest groups or power holders" (Gavison, "Implications of Jurisprudential Theories," p. 1621).

73. See Geyh, "Rescuing Judicial Accountability," pp. 928–33.

74. Levin, *Men in Black*, pp. 12, 13.

75. Ibid., p. 91 (italics added).

76. Ibid., p. 12.

77. Ibid., p. 74.

78. However, chapter 2 of Levin's volume is entitled "Judicial Review: The Counter-Revolution of 1803."

79. Levin, *Men in Black*, pp. 70, 195, 210.

80. Ibid., p. 145.

81. For Scalia's elaboration of this position, see *A Matter of Interpretation*.

82. Wold and Culver, "Rose Bird and the Politics of Judicial Accountability in California," pp. 81–89; and Wold and Culver, "Defeat of the California Justices," pp. 348–55.

83. Sniderman, Brody, and Tetlock, *Reasoning and Choice*, p. 19.

84. Burbank and Friedman, "Reconsidering Judicial Independence," in *Judicial Independence at the Crossroads*, p. 37.

85. Streb, "Judicial Elections," p. 185.

86. Barber and Fleming, *Constitutional Interpretation*, pp. 4–5.

87. On the distinction between strong and weak indeterminacy, see Solum, "Indeterminacy and Equity," p. 46.

88. The quotation is drawn from Brennan, "Locating Authority in Law," p. 169.

89. Ferejohn and Kramer note with considerable understatement that "the standards for measuring judgments as rightly or wrongly decided are more uncertain" than in the past (Ferejohn and Kramer, "Independent Judges, Dependent Judiciary," p. 971).

90. Gavison, "Implications of Jurisprudential Theories," p. 1648. This is hardly a new position. As James Madison noted in Federalist No. 37, "all new laws, though penned with the greatest technical skill, and passed on the fullest and most mature deliberation, are considered as more or less obscure and equivocal, until their meaning be liquidated and ascertained by a series of particular discussions and adjudications."

91. M. Kramer, *Objectivity and the Rule of Law*, pp. 45–46.

92. Ibid., p. 14. Richard Posner has observed, "Legalism does exist, and so not everything is permitted. But its kingdom has shrunk and greyed to the point where today it is largely limited to routine cases, and so a great deal is permitted to judges" (Posner, *How Judges Think*, p. 1).

93. Gavison, "Implications of Jurisprudential Theories," p. 1627.

94. Farber and Sherry, *Judgment Calls*, p. 36.

95. M. Kramer, *Objectivity and the Rule of Law*, p. 17.

96. Ibid., p. 18.

97. Lindquist and Cross, *Measuring Judicial Activism*, p. 39. Liberals and conservatives each have lists of cases in which they claim that judges were activist (for example, ruled on the basis of their own predilections rather than on the basis of law), but they seldom overlap (pp. 19–20).

98. Farber and Sherry, *Judgment Calls*, p. 29.

99. Ibid., pp. 78–80.

100. Perry, *Constitution in the Courts*, p. 103.

101. Ferejohn and Kramer, "Independent Judges, Dependent Judiciary," p. 972.

102. Ibid.

103. Geyh, "Rescuing Judicial Accountability," p. 927.

104. W. Marshall, "Judicial Accountability," p. 938.

105. This may be what happened when Justice Penny White of Tennessee and Justice David Lanphier of Nebraska were removed in retention elections. See T. Reid, "Politicization of Judicial Retention Elections."

106. W. Marshall, "Judicial Accountability," p. 943.

107. This telling phrase is from Barber and Fleming, *Constitutional Interpretation*, p. 187.

108. Eisgruber, "Judicial Supremacy and Constitutional Distortion," p. 73.

Chapter 5

1. Schotland, "Comment," p. 150. More than a decade earlier, Philip Dubois offered a similar assessment: "It is fairly certain that no single subject has consumed as many pages in law reviews and law-related publications over the past 50 years as the subject of judicial selection" (Dubois, "Accountability, Independence," p. 31).

2. Connecticut switched to merit selection from gubernatorial appointment in 1986, New Mexico adopted a hybrid system with elements of merit selection in 1988, and Rhode Island switched from legislative election to merit selection in 1994.

3. Pertinent poll data are summarized in Tarr, "Do Retention Elections Work?", pp. 616–18; and in Bybee, *All Judges Are Political*, pp. 8–10.

4. See Goldberg, *New Politics of Judicial Elections*; American Bar Association Commission on the 21st Century Judiciary, *Justice in Jeopardy*, pp. 13–50; and Tarr, "Politicizing the Process." As David Pozen has noted, "With remarkable speed, the distinctive rules, norms, and politics of judicial elections have begun to disappear" (Pozen, "Irony of Judicial Elections," p. 268).

5. Leading political science critiques include Bonneau and Hall, *In Defense of Judicial Elections*; and Dubois, *From Ballot to Bench*. Legal scholars have also contributed to the rethinking of merit selection. See Dimino, "Futile Quest for a System of Judicial 'Merit' Selection," pp. 803–19; Dimino, "Worst Way of Selecting Judges," pp. 267–304; Fitzpatrick, "Politics of Merit Selection," pp. 675–710; and Ware, "Missouri Plan in National Perspective," pp. 751–76. The quotation about judicial elections going normal rather than going wild is drawn from Pozen, "Irony of Judicial Elections," p. 269.

6. Throughout this chapter, we refer to positions taken by "Defenders" without specific citations in order to avoid a proliferation of repetitive endnotes. Key sources elaborating the Defenders' perspective include: American Bar Association Commission on the 21st Century Judiciary, *Justice in Jeopardy*; American Judicature Society, *Merit Selection*; Geyh, "Why Judicial Elections Stink," pp. 43–79; Justice at Stake, *Justice at Stake & Judicial Issues*; Sandra Day O'Connor Project on the State of the Judiciary; and Sample et al., *New Politics of Judicial Elections*.

7. Even some proponents of judicial elections worry that voters may be "unwilling and incapable of holding its judiciary accountable through elections" (see Dubois, *From Ballot to Bench*, p. 36).

8. Geyh, "Why Judicial Elections Stink," p. 52.

9. This argument was crucial for Albert M. Kales, the architect of merit selection; see his *Unpopular Government in the United States*, pp. 226–29.

10. Bonneau and Hall, *In Defense of Judicial Elections*, p. 23. It should be noted that trial court elections are considerably less competitive than elections for state supreme

court seats. A recent study found that "over 75 percent of contestable judicial elections used to fill seats on general jurisdiction trial courts are uncontested" (M. Nelson, "Uncontested and Unaccountable?", p. 209).

11. Bonneau and Hall, *In Defense of Judicial Elections*, p. 23 and p. 27, tab. 2.2.

12. Dubois, *From Ballot to Bench*, p. 50, tab. 3.

13. Bonneau and Hall, *In Defense of Judicial Elections*, p. 80, tab. 4.2.

14. Kritzer, "Competitiveness in State Supreme Court Elections," pp. 237–59.

15. Bonneau and Hall, *In Defense of Judicial Elections*, p. 80, tab. 4.2.

16. Carbon, "Judicial Retention Elections," p. 221.

17. M. Hall, "Competition as Accountability," p. 177, tab. 9.4.

18. Aspin and Hall, "Judicial Retention Election Trends," p. 210.

19. Ibid.

20. Ibid., p. 209, tab. 1.

21. Bonneau and Hall, *In Defense of Judicial Elections*, p. 82, tab. 4.3.

22. Ibid., p. 84, tab. 4.4.

23. Ibid., p. 86, tab. 4.5. A recent commentator has questioned whether contested state supreme court elections have become more competitive outside the South (see Kritzer, "Competitiveness in State Supreme Court Elections," pp. 253–54, figs. 8 and 9).

24. Garwood, "Democracy and the Popular Election of Judges," p. 229. Even if this characterization of how judges decide is simplistic, the myth has considerable resonance. See Geyh, "Can the Rule of Law Survive Judicial Politics?"; and Gibson, "Judging the Politics of Judging."

25. Grodin, *In Pursuit of Justice*, pp. 163, 175. As Charles Geyh put it, "It is one thing to expect voters with no training in the law to decide whether the policies favored by senators and governors (who may not be lawyers either) coincide with their own positions, and quite another to expect them to decide whether the rulings of judges coincide with the law" (Geyh, "Why Judicial Elections Stink," p. 59).

26. Kales, *Unpopular Government*, pp. 248–50.

27. For analysis of differences in the composition of nominating commissions, see Ware, "Missouri Plan in National Perspective," pp. 751–75.

28. Carrington, "Judicial Independence and Democratic Accountability," p. 98.

29. In a 2001 national public opinion poll, "29 percent of Americans who do not vote regularly or at all in state judicial elections give as their reason that they do not know enough about the candidates running for office" (Schaffner and Diascro, "Judicial Elections in the News," p. 115). Similarly, in a 1995 poll, two-thirds of voters in Washington said that they "seldom had enough information to cast an informed vote in judicial elections," which are nonpartisan (ibid., p. 116). In several studies members of the public have reported having little information of any kind about the candidates or the major issues in judicial campaign. See Griffin and Horan, "Patterns of Voter Behavior," p. 72; Dubois, *From Ballot to Bench*, p. 64; Klots, "Selection of Judges"; and Sheldon and Lovrich, "Voter Knowledge, Behavior, and Attitudes," p. 216.

30. For a review of pertinent poll data, see Bybee, "Introduction," in *Bench Press*, pp. 3–5. Not everyone subscribes to the notion of a woefully uninformed public. For

an impressive counterargument criticizing reliance on the recall of particular factual information, see Gibson and Caldeira, *Citizens, Courts, and Confirmations*, chap. 2. However, our position does not depend on acceptance of the Gibson-Caldeira argument.

31. Freedman, Franz, and Goldstein, "Campaign Advertising and Democratic Citizenship," p. 723.

32. Of course, information levels vary among voters, who range from politically committed and aware to uncommitted and unaware, and these differences in attention and information affect how they choose among judicial candidates.

33. "In a low-information contest, the ballot itself is the primary source of information about the candidates" (Baum, "Judicial Elections and Judicial Independence," p. 21).

34. Lupia and McCubbins, *Democratic Dilemma*, pp. 36–37. Eric Smith has noted that "the public's lack of information was so well established that scholars lost interest in studying the subject" (Smith, *Unchanging American Voter*, p. 159). Yet most scholars have also concluded that "voters are far more competent than an assessment of their factual knowledge would suggest" (see Popkin and Dimock, "Political Knowledge and Civic Competence," p. 117). Moreover, when one changes the level of analysis from the individual voter to the electorate as a whole, concerns about voter irrationality and lack of knowledge tend to disappear. Although "most Americans care little about politics and possess a level of knowledge of the details of public life that is consistent with not caring, . . . [a]ll these facts, insofar as they lead us to believe that the electorate acts without purpose, lead us astray." On "the extraordinary sophistication of the collective electorate," see Erickson, Mackuen, and. Stimson, *Macro Polity*, p. 7.

35. Gerber and Lupia, "Voter Competence in Direct Legislation Elections," p. 149.

36. Sniderman, Brody, and Tetlock, *Reasoning and Choice*, p. 119.

37. Popkin, *Reasoning Voter*, p. 236.

38. This horrified reaction to the politicization of judicial elections pervades publications of leading Defender organizations; see, for example, Sample et al. *New Politics of Judicial Elections 2000–2009*. It also can be seen in the guidelines urged by leading Defender opponents of judicial elections: see, for example, the website of the Sandra Day O'Connor Project on the State of the Judiciary, at http://www.law.george town.edu/judiciary/.

39. Blackmar, "Missouri's Nonpartisan Court Plan," p. 216. For documentation of the increasing use of televised attack ads and condemnation of their effects, see Sample et al., *New Politics of Judicial Elections*, chap. 2.

40. See Bierman, "Comment on Paper by Cheek and Champagne," pp. 1387–91.

41. Carrington, "Judicial Independence and Democratic Accountability," p. 111.

42. Such appeals often occur in cases involving capital punishment, so it is no surprise that the justices defeated in retention elections have most often been targeted based on their rulings in death penalty cases. See T. Reid, "Politicization of Judicial Retention Elections." More generally, see Bright and Keenan, "Judges and the Politics

of Death," pp. 759–835. The 2010 defeat of three Iowa justices based on their votes in a same-sex-marriage case is a recent counterexample.

43. Lau et al., "Effects of Negative Political Advertisements," p. 856.

44. Goldstein and Freedman, "Campaign Advertising and Voter Turnout," p. 733. For an overview of recent studies, see Kaufmann, Petrocik, and Shaw, *Unconventional Wisdom*, p. 198.

45. Clinton and Lapinski, "'Targeted' Advertising and Voter Turnout," pp. 69–96; and Lau and Pomper, "Effectiveness of Negative Campaigning in U.S. Senate Elections," pp. 47–66.

46. This argument relies on Richardson, *Pulp Politics*, chap. 3; and on Freedman, Franz, and Goldstein, "Campaign Advertising and Democratic Citizenship," pp. 723–41. In fairness, the Defenders' concern may be precisely that judicial elections are becoming more like other elections.

47. *New York Times v. Sullivan*, 376 U.S. 254, 270 (1964).

48. Linde, "Judge as Political Candidate," p. 7.

49. Richardson, *Pulp Politics*, p. 6. Steven Croley has criticized judicial elections for reflecting "the will of 'the impassioned majority' rather than 'the enlightened majority'" (Croley, "Majoritarian Difficulty," p. 726).

50. Jamieson, *Dirty Politics*, p. 103.

51. Phillips, "Comment," p. 135.

52. Baum, "Judicial Elections," p. 38.

53. One should be wary of overestimating the effect of television ads on a largely inattentive public. See Baum, "Judicial Election and Appointment at the State Level," pp. 645–70; and Klein and Baum, "Ballot Information and Voting Decisions in Judicial Elections," pp. 709–28.

54. Flanigan and Zingale, *Political Behavior*, pp. 233–34.

55. Dubois, *From Ballot to Bench*, p. 74. Lawrence Baum has reported similarly strong correlations between votes for governor and votes for supreme court justices in more recent elections (Baum, "Judicial Elections," p. 26).

56. Quoted in Rosenman, "Better Way to Select Judges," p. 88.

57. Nardulli, *Popular Efficacy*, p. 129.

58. Schaffner, Streb, and Wright, "Teams Without Uniforms," p. 26. The consensus among political scientists is that nonpartisan elections are "a classic example of an institutional reform that hinders reasoned choice" (Lupia and McCubbins, *Democratic Dilemma*, pp. 36–37).

59. Lupia and McCubbins, *Democratic Dilemma*, p. 245.

60. For examples of the influence of extraneous factors, such as ethnicity and name familiarity, on voter choice, see Wiseman, "So You Want to Stay a Judge," p. 643.

61. *Justice in Jeopardy*, pp. v–vi.

62. These criteria for retention are drawn from the Standards on State Judicial Selection approved by the American Bar Association in 2000, available at http://www2.americanbar.org/committees_migrated/judind/PublicDocuments/reformat.pdf.

63. Ibid.

64. It has been suggested that voter scrutiny of political events more closely approximates that of a firefighter rather than of a police officer. Instead of a constant surveillance, voters react only when an alarm indicates that something has gone wrong. See Nardulli, *Popular Efficacy*, pp. 6–10. Thus Michael Dimino, a leading proponent of judicial elections, writes that "merit selection hopes to limit the pressure on incumbents to rule in particular ways by ensuring that there will be no candidate opposing the incumbent, and therefore less chance that the public will be alerted to those instances where the judge has flouted the popular will" (Dimino, "Futile Quest for a System," p. 805). Charles Geyh, a leading opponent of electing judges, concurs: "Retention elections are designed to minimize the risk of non-retention, by stripping elections of features that might inspire voters to become interested enough to oust incumbents. Thus, there is no choice to make between competing candidates or viewpoints, no race to follow, no opportunity to pick a new winner, and no political party to support" (Geyh, "Why Judicial Elections Stink," p. 55).

65. Schaffner and Diascro, "Judicial Elections in the News," pp. 131–32. Schaffner and Diascro found that partisan races drew more coverage than nonpartisan ones and contested races than uncontested ones.

66. Aspin, "Judicial Retention Election Trends," p. 210.

67. For arguments in favor of voter guides and performance evaluations, see P. White, "Using Judicial Performance Evaluations," pp. 635–66; Caufield, "Reconciling the Judicial Ideal," pp. 573–604; and Brody, "Use of Judicial Performance Evaluation," pp. 115–56.

68. See Kourles and Singer, "Using Judicial Performance Evaluations," pp. 200–207.

69. Ibid., p. 207.

70. For information on particular states, see www.judicialselection.us/judicial_selection/campaigns_and_elections/voter_guides.cfm?state= ; and www.judicialselection.us/judicial_selection/methods/judicial_performance_evaluations.cfm?state=.

71. Kourles and Singer, "Using Judicial Performance Evaluations," p. 212. David Brody reports that "over 90 percent of judges evaluated across the country receive positive recommendations from their JPE commissions" (Brody, "Use of Judicial Performance Evaluation," p. 134).

72. Finley, "Judicial Selection in Alaska," p. 61. Earlier studies confirmed that most voters were unaware of bar polls. See Reddick, "Merit Selection," p. 736.

73. Sample et al., *New Politics of Judicial Elections, 2000–2009*, p. 25. For data over time, see ibid., chap. 2.

74. Franklin, "Behavioral Factors Affecting Judicial Independence," p. 152.

75. Ibid., p. 154.

76. Other Defenders echo this sentiment. David Brody describes judicial performance evaluations as providing "a missing ingredient for judicial elections to *appropriately* and effectively facilitate judicial accountability" and "by providing information voters can use in judicial elections that is not issue-based but rather on whether a judges does his or her job as one would expect from a judge" (Brody, "Use of Judicial Performance Evaluation," pp. 129, 131).

77. Geyh, "Why Judicial Elections Stink," p. 62.

78. Posner, *How Judges Think*, p. 1.

79. For a treatment of the popular role in constitutional interpretation, see L. Kramer, *People Themselves*.

80. Even if one accepts the premise of this more radical argument, there are complications. Voters may remove judges based on their votes in cases in which the law was clear and was followed by the judges. This, it is argued, was the case for Justices Penny White and David Lanphier. See T. Reid, "Politicization of Judicial Retention Elections," pp. 45–72. Thus, one is left to balance the disadvantages of such mistakes against the advantages of popular input.

81. Hall and Aspin, "What Twenty Years of Judicial Retention Elections Have Told Us," pp. 340–47.

82. Dubois, *From Ballot to Bench*.

83. Rosenberg, "Qualities of Justice," p. 1069.

84. James Gibson has found that although campaign contributions may diminish institutional legitimacy, they "have nearly identical consequences for judicial and legislative legitimacy." While this finding casts doubt on the distinctiveness of judicial elections, it hardly puts to rest concerns about how fund-raising affects the image of the courts. See Gibson, "Challenges to the Impartiality," p. 69.

85. Geyh, "Preserving Public Confidence," p. 35.

86. *New York State Bd. of Elections v. Lopez Torres*, 552 U.S. 196, 212 (2008).

87. *Republican Party of Minnesota v. White*, 536 U.S. 765 (2002).

88. Pozen, "Irony of Judicial Elections," p. 299.

89. *Republican Party v. White*, 416 F.3d 738 (8th Cir., 2005); *Weaver v. Bonner*, 309 F.3d 1312 (11th Cir. 2002; *Carey v. Wolnitzek*, No. 3:06–36–KKc (E.D. Ky. Oct. 10, 2006); and *Kansas Judicial Watch v. Stout*, 440 F.Supp. 2d 1209 (D. Kan. 2006). For discussion of these cases, see Bopp and Neeley, "How Not to Reform Judicial Elections," pp. 201–5.

90. See, for example, *Citizens United v. Federal Election Commission*, 130 S.Ct. 876 (2009). As Justice John Paul Stevens observed in his dissenting opinion: "The consequences of today's holding will not be limited to the legislative or executive context. The majority of the States select their judges through popular elections. At a time when concerns about the conduct of judicial elections have reached a fever pitch . . . the Court today unleashes the floodgates of corporate and union general treasury spending in these races" (130 S.Ct. 876, 968).

91. Bonneau and Hall, *In Defense of Judicial Elections*, p. 134.

92. Gibson, "Challenges to the Impartiality of State Supreme Courts," p. 70.

93. American Bar Association, Standing Committee on Judicial Independence, *Public Financing of Judicial Campaigns*, p. 61.

94. See Devins and Mansker, "Public Opinion and State Supreme Courts," pp. 455–96. State supreme court justices "have a tendency to vote in accordance with perceived constituency preferences on visible issues, simply because the failure to do so is politically dangerous" (see M. Hall, "Justices as Representatives," pp. 489–90).

95. Uelman, "Crocodiles in the Bathtub," p. 1133. David Pozen concurs, arguing that "an elective regime might influence jurisprudence at a sub-conscious level, such that its judges, without fully theorizing or even processing what they are doing, will be more prone to conflate electorally popular outcomes with legally sound ones" (Pozen, "Irony of Judicial Elections," p. 277).

96. Bonneau and Hall, *In Defense of Judicial Elections*, chap. 3.

97. Neely, *How Courts Govern America*, p. 35.

98. The ABA poll results are available at www.abanet.org/media/aug02/apnews confrevised8–8.html. The Justice at Stake results are found at http://faircourts. org/files/JASNationalSurveyResults.pdf. These data are reported and discussed in McLeod, "If at First You Don't Succeed," p. 509. The Maxwell School poll results are found at www.maxwell.syracuse.edu/campbell/Poll/CitizenshipPoll.htm.

99. For additional poll data, see White and Reddick, "Response to Professor Fitzpatrick," p. 542; and Brown, "Political Judges and Popular Justice," pp. 1560–61.

100. *Caperton v. A. T. Massey Co.*, 129 S.Ct. 2252 (2009).

101. Ware, "Money, Politics, and Judicial Decisions," pp. 645–86.

102. McCall, "Buying Justice in Texas," pp. 349–73; McCall, "Politics of Judicial Elections," pp. 314–43; and Waltenberg and Lopeman, "Tort Decisions and Campaign Dollars," pp. 241–63. For incisive comment on the causation issue, see Epstein, "Shedding (Empirical) Light on Judicial Selection," pp. 565–67.

103. Cann, "Justice for Sale?", pp. 281–99; McLeod, "Bidding for Justice," pp. 385–405; and Shepherd, "Money, Politics, and Impartial Justice," p. 625.

104. Williams and Ditslear, "Bidding for Justice," p. 152.

105. See Stratmann, "Can Special Interests Buy Congressional Votes?", p. 351.

106. A comprehensive analysis of studies on the relation between campaign contributions and legislative voting behavior largely supports this conclusion. Stratman, "Some Talk," pp. 135–46.

107. M. Marshall, "Promise of Neutrality," p. 3.

108. Aspin and Hall, "Retention Elections and Judicial Behavior," p. 312, tab. 4. Other studies have produced similarly troubling findings. See Brace and Hall, "Studying Courts Comparatively," pp. 13–24; Traut and Emmert, "Expanding the Integrated Model," pp. 1166–80; and Huber and Gordon, "Accountability and Coercion," pp. 247–63. For consideration of the implications of these findings, see Shane, "Interbranch Accountability," pp. 21–54.

109. Aspin and Hall, "Retention Elections and Judicial Behavior," p. 312.

110. Huber and Gordon, "Accountability and Coercion," p. 261.

111. Shepherd, "Money, Politics, and Impartial Justice," pp. 623–85.

112. *Bridges v. California*, 314 U.S. 252 (1941).

113. Ibid., at 273.

114. Thus Joanna Shepherd reports that "most interest group contributions have no systematic relationship with the voting of retiring judges" (see Shepherd, "Money, Politics, and Impartial Justice," p. 673).

115. Cann and Yates, "Homegrown Institutional Legitimacy," p. 313. They do note, however, that "the use of nonpartisan elections or merit selection does not significantly affect state court legitimacy" (ibid., p. 313).

116. For description and discussion of these poll results, see Geyh, "Can the Rule of Law Survive Judicial Politics?", pp. 191–264.

117. Compare Princeton Survey Research Associates, "Separate Branches, Shared Responsibilities: A National Survey of Public Expectations on Solving Justice Issues," April 2009; with Princeton Survey Research Associates International, "2006 Annenberg Judicial Independence Survey," August 2006.

118. Maxwell Survey, October 2005, at www.maxwell.syracuse.edu/campbell/Poll /CitizenshipPoll.htm. For an enlightening analysis of these and other poll data on popular attitudes toward the judiciary, see Bybee, *All Judges Are Political*.

119. National Survey for Justice at Stake, September 2005, cited in note 41, above.

120. Annenberg Judicial Independence Survey (2006), available at www.annenberg publicpolicycenter.org/NewsDetails.aspx?myId=218.

121. Maxwell Survey, October 2005, at www.maxwell.syracuse.edu/campbell/Poll /CitizenshipPoll.htm.

122. Information on state-by-state consideration of changes in judicial selection is found at www.ajs.org/selection/sel_stateselect.asp.

123. Consider on this point the impassioned plea of one participant in state judicial races: "The media and the legal establishment think you the voters are too ignorant to make such decisions. Yet when the issues of a judicial campaign get a full airing before the public, so that voters can be educated about the candidates, the media and legal experts complain about how all the debate and controversy are ruining the reputation of the judiciary. But what about covering up the problems in the judiciary? Does that somehow enhance the judiciary's reputation?" Jordan, *Courting Votes in Alabama*, p. 258.

124. W. Marshall, "Constitutional Law as Political Spoils," p. 536. One need not claim innovative rulings are always wrong to recognize that they feed public skepticism about whether judicial pronouncements are rooted in law.

125. For the claim that these concerns are influential, see Alexander, "Let Them Do Their Jobs," pp. 669–721. But this is dubious at best. See Bopp and Neeley, "How Not to Reform Judicial Elections," p. 196.

126. Gallagher, "Disarming the Confirmation Process," pp. 516–17.

127. McLeod, "Party on the Bench." McLeod notes that there are more cross-party appointments in merit systems than in nonmerit appointive systems.

128. Blackmar, "Missouri's Nonpartisan Court Plan from 1942 to 2005," p. 206.

129. For examples of state judges being denied reappointment because of their decisions, see Baum, "Judicial Elections and Judicial Independence," p. 15.

130. American Bar Association, Standards of State Judicial Selection (2000).

131. American Judicature Society, "Judges Relieved of Political Stress," p. 41.

132. Watson and Downing, *Politics of the Bench and Bar*, pp. 348–50.

133. See Henschen, Moog, and Davis, "Judicial Nominating Commissioners," pp. 331–32; and Salokar and Shaw, "Impact of National Politics on State Courts," pp. 62–63.

134. 531 U.S. 98 (2000); see also Salokar and Shaw, "Impact of National Politics," pp. 57–58.

135. Salokar, Berggren, and DePalo, "Merit Selection Redefined," p. 126.

136. For citations to the relevant literature and a summary of its findings, see Reddick, "Merit Selection," pp. 729–45.

137. Caufield, "What Makes Merit Selection Different?" p. 782.

138. Redick, *Judging the Quality of Judicial Selection Methods*.

139. Gardner, "New York's Inbred Judiciary," pp. 15–28. The Court of Appeals is New York's supreme court.

140. Ibid., p. 18.

141. Ibid., pp. 22–23.

142. Ibid., p. 20, citing Choi, Gulati, and Posner, "Which States Have the Best (and Worst) High Courts?" For a ranking of state supreme courts based on citation rates, see Dear and Nessen, "'Followed Rates' and Leading State Court Cases," pp. 683–711. Dear and Nessen place New York thirteenth (p. 696, graph 3), but their data do not differentiate between eras, making it difficult to know whether their study supports Gardner's analysis.

143. See Watson and Downing, *Politics of the Bench and Bar*, pp. 324–26; O'Callaghan, "Another Test for the Merit Plan," p. 482; and Romero, Romero, and Ford, "Influence of Selection Method," p. 27. Our analysis in this paragraph relies on Caufield, "What Makes Merit Selection Different," pp. 784–85.

144. See Gryski, Main, and Dixon, "Models of State High Court Decision Making in Sex Discrimination Cases," pp. 143–55; Brace and Hall, "Studying Courts Comparatively," pp. 5–29; and Pinello, *Impact of Judicial-Selection Method*, pp. 73–104.

145. Frost and Lindquist, "Countering the Majoritarian Difficulty," pp. 758–60.

146. Choi, Gulati, and Posner, "Professionals or Politicians," pp. 290–336.

147. Ibid., p. 328.

148. McLeod, *Excess of Participation*, p. 1.

149. Resnick, "Judicial Selection and Democratic Theory," p. 594.

Chapter 6

1. See, for example, American Bar Association, *Draft Report of the Judicial Disqualification Project* (September 2008), pp. 34–42. In his concurring opinion in *Republican Party of Minnesota v. White*, 536 U.S. 765, 794 (2002), Justice Anthony Kennedy endorsed the use of disqualification and recusal as a solution to adverse effects from the politicization of judicial elections, noting that states "may adopt recusal standards more rigorous than due process requires, and censure judges who violate these standards." More generally, see Shaman et al., *Judicial Conduct and Ethics*, chap. 4.

2. Sample, "*Caperton*," pp. 293–304. See also Williams and Ditslear, "Bidding for Justice," pp. 135–56.

3. Lochner, "Judicial Recusal and the Search for the Bright Line," pp. 231–37.

4. Sample, Pozen, and Young, *Fair Courts*, p. 17.

5. The Illinois case is *Avery v. State Farm Mutual Insurance Company*, 835 N.E.2d 801 (Ill. 2005). Not all commentators agree that Justice Benjamin acted improperly in failing to recuse himself. See Frey and Berger, "Solution in Search of a Problem," pp. 279–92.

6. McKeown, "Don't Shoot the Canons," p. 45. See also Goldberg, Sample, and Pozen, "Best Defense," pp. 503–34.

7. As Steven Lubet has noted, "There is no good justification for such a procedure—and if anyone has provided a rigorous defense of it, I have not seen it" (Lubet, "It Takes a Court," p. 226).

8. White, "Relinquishing Responsibilities," p. 136.

9. American Bar Association, *Draft Report of the Judicial Disqualification Project*, p. 14.

10. See Shaman and Goldschmidt, *Judicial Disqualification*.

11. Sample and Young, "Invigorating Judicial Disqualification," pp. 27–28.

12. Pozen and Young, *Fair Courts*, pp. 29–30.

13. Lubet, "It Takes a Court," p. 221.

14. See Schotland, "Plea for Reality," pp. 520–21.

15. Pozen and Young, *Fair Courts*, pp. 31–32.

16. See American Bar Association, *Draft Report of the Judicial Disqualification Project*, pp. 74–84; Schotland, "Plea for Reality"; and Pozen and Young, *Fair Courts*.

17. See, for example, Sample, Cozen, and Young, *Fair Courts*, p. 8.

18. See Geyh and Lee, "Taking Disqualification Seriously," pp. 12–17.

19. Prior to the recent increase in contested supreme court races, only about half of incumbent justices were challenged when they sought reelection, and from 1967–2007 no incumbent justice was defeated. Bonneau and Hall, *In Defense of Judicial Elections*, p. 125.

20. In New Mexico, judges who are appointed to fill vacancies initially run in partisan elections and, if returned to office, subsequently run in retention elections. There is no public funding for retention elections.

21. Our account of public financing of judicial elections draws on: American Bar Association, *Public Financing of Judicial Campaigns: Report of the Commission on Public Financing of Judicial Campaigns*; Democracy North Carolina, "Profile of the Judicial Public Financing Program, 2004–06";and Center for Governmental Studies, "Public Campaign Financing: North Carolina Judiciary."

22. Haussameh, "Judicial Candidate Appeals Public Finance Ruling."

23. *Arizona Free Enterprise Club's Freedom Club PAC v. Bennett*, 131 S.Ct. 2806 (2011).

24. Wallison and Gora. *Better Parties, Better Government*, p. 73. See also Malbin and Gais, *Day After Reform*, pp. 52–53, which identifies twenty-two states as having public financing, differentiating between party-only and candidate programs.

25. The public's opposition to public financing of political campaigns is not limited to judicial races. "From 1990 to 2000, polling organizations asked seven

straightforward questions about public opposition to or support for public financing of congressional or political campaigns. Five of the surveys indicated that more than 65 percent of the public opposed it. None of the seven showed more people favoring than opposing public financing" (Samples, *Fallacy of Campaign Finance Reform*, p. 183).

26. Kenzevich, "Public Finance Campaign Supporters Worried about Pilot Program"; and Korbitz, "Legislature Sends State Budget Bill to Gov. Walker."

27. See American Bar Association, *Justice in Jeopardy*, p. 81, reaffirming a position taken by the ABA's Commission on Public Financing of Judicial Campaigns in 2001. This is a fall-back position "for states that do not abandon contested elections at the point of initial selection or reselection," as the ABA continues to favor the elimination of judicial elections altogether. See *Justice in Jeopardy*, pp. 70–73. Most state judges have likewise endorsed public financing. See Justice at Stake, "2001 Poll of State Judges."

28. *Citizens United v. Federal Election Commission*, 558 U.S. 50 (2010).

29. Brandenburg, "Citizens United."

30. *Citizens United v. Federal Election Commission*, 130 S.Ct. 876, 968 (2010). Similarly, in *Republican Party of Minnesota v. White*, Justice Antonin Scalia wrote, " So if . . . it violates due process for a judge to sit in a case in which ruling one way rather than another increases his prospects for reelection, then —quite simply — the practice of electing judges is itself a violation of due process" (536 U.S. 762, 782). These words were included in the court's opinion not to endorse but to mock the idea that judicial elections violate due process, but Defenders have insisted that Scalia's barb contains an essential truth. See P. White, "Relinquished Responsibilities," p. 120.

31. See, for example, Samuels, "Hanging a 'For Sale' Sign over the Judiciary."

32. See Zemans, "Accountable Judge," p. 640.

33. Justice at Stake, "2004 National Opinion Poll."

34. Gibson, "Challenges to the Impartiality of State Supreme Courts," p. 69.

35. Gibson, "Effects of Electoral Campaigns on the Legitimacy of Courts," p. 407.

36. See, for example, Schotland, "Comment," pp. 152–53.

37. White, "Relinquished Responsibilities," pp. 120–25; and Schotland, "Plea for Reality," pp. 517–18.

38. The only supreme court races in New Mexico since the adoption of public funding in 2007 were the retention elections in 2008 for Justices Charles Daniels and Patricio Serna. No public funds were available for these races, and expenditures were modest: Justice Daniels raised slightly more than $51,000, and Justice Serna reported raising no money. See the website of National Institute on Money in State Politics, "High Court Candidates."

39. This lack of popular participation in check-off schemes is not limited to Wisconsin or to public financing of judicial races. Popular participation in check-off schemes nationwide declined from 20% in 1975 to 11% in 1994. Samples, *Fallacy of Campaign Finance Reform*, p. 185.

40. Williams and Ditslear, "Bidding for Justice," p. 141.

41. Data are available on the website of the National Institute for Money in State Politics.

42. For accounts of the Wisconsin race, see Tarr, *Judicial Process and Judicial Policymaking*, p. 58; and Rutledge, *New Politics of Judicial Elections*, pp. 27–29.

43. Hardin, "More News on Wisconsin Public Financing."

44. Our account of the 2011 election relies primarily on Brennan Center for Justice, "Judicial Public Financing in Wisconsin—2011"; on Justice at Stake Campaign, "Nasty Campaign Deepens 'Crisis' for Wisconsin High Court"; and Grow, "Tuesday's Wisconsin Supreme Court Election Morphs."

45. Center for Governmental Studies, *Public Campaign Funding*, pp. 11–14.

46. Center for Governmental Studies, *Public Campaign Funding*, p. 1.

47. Ibid., p. 11.

48. Ibid., pp. 22.

49. Justice at Stake, *New Politics of Judicial Elections*, p. 38; and Center for Governmental Studies, *Public Campaign Funding*, pp. 27–28.

50. Schultz, "Introduction," in *Money, Politics, and Campaign Finance Reform Law*, p. 22.

51. Justice Anthony Kennedy referred to independent expenditures as "contributions" in his opinion for the Court in *Caperton*, thereby underscoring both the interchangeability of contributions and independent expenditures and the assistance that such expenditures provide to candidates.

52. Carrington, "Judicial Independence and Democratic Accountability," p. 111; and Thomas, Boyer, and Hrebenar, "Interest Groups and State Court Elections," p. 138.

53. Critics of public financing dispute the claim that public funds come without strings, noting that recipients of those funds typically cannot raise private money and must limit their expenditures. In the words of John Samples, "most come with strings attached, and many come with ropes" (Samples, *Fallacy of Campaign Spending Reform*, p. 63).

54. Detailed data are found in Bonneau and Hall, *In Defense of Judicial Elections*, pp. 110–11.

55. Crosson, "Impact of the 2004 North Carolina Judicial Voter Guide," pp. 28–29.

56. Bonneau and Hall, *In Defense of Judicial Elections*, p. 113, tab. 5.2. The authors define ballot roll-off as "the percentage of the electorate casting votes for the major office on the ballot who do *not* vote in each supreme court race" (ibid., p. 23).

57. M. Hall, "Voting in State Supreme Court Elections," pp. 1147–59.

58. Bonneau and Hall, *In Defense of Judicial Elections*, pp. 113–14. In Wisconsin, the only other state with public financing from 1980–2000, roll-off was 59.22 percent when judicial elections were held simultaneous with election for other offices. However, supreme court elections in Wisconsin are usually scheduled at times other than November (see Hall, "Voting in State Supreme Court Elections," pp. 149–50).

59. Wallison and Gora, *Better Parties, Better Government*, p. 6.

60. Geyh, "Publicly Financed Judicial Elections," p. 1480.

61. Bonneau and Hall, *In Defense of Judicial Elections*, p. 111, tab. 5.1.

62. Bonneau, "Patterns of Campaign Spending," pp. 30–35. This holds true for other elections as well: a study of congressional races during 1990s concluded that "the campaign spending variable was far and away the most important variable in determining the congressional vote." Campbell and Jurek, "Decline of Competition and Change in Congressional Elections," p. 17. A study of state elections more generally has concluded, "Low contribution limits, public financing, and spending limits all fail to do much to equalize political power among private interests, reduce the total amount of money spent on elections, or produce equal contests between challengers and incumbents." In fact, public financing does little to affect competition, defined as number or percentage of candidates in close races (Malbin and Gais, *Day After Reform*, pp. 162, 166).

63. Bonneau, "Vacancies on the Bench," p. 144.

64. Bonneau and Hall, *In Defense of Judicial Elections*, p. 111.

65. Others have endorsed limited terms without reeligibility. For justices of the US Supreme Court, see Cramton and Carrington, *Reforming the Court*. For state supreme court justices, Dimino, "Accountability Before the Fact," pp. 451–72 .

66. For a summary of the mode of selection and tenure of members of European constitutional courts, see Stone, *Governing with Judges*, pp. 46–49.

67. Basic Law, Federal Republic of Germany, Art. 95, sec. 1.

68. Basic Law, Federal Republic of Germany, Art. 95, sec. 2.

69. Basic Law, Federal Republic of Germany, Art. 97, sec. 2.

70. Basic Law, Federal Republic of Germany, Art. 94, sec. 1.

71. Constitution of Italy, Arts. 106–7.

72. Constitution of Italy, Art. 135, secs. 1, 3, and 4.

73. On judicial selection in France, see Provine and Garapon, "Selection of Judges in France."

74. In addition to these nine members, former presidents of the republic serve as ex-officio life members of the Constitutional Council, as long as they do not engage in politics. See Constitution of France, Title VII, Art. 56, sec. 2.

75. Malleson, "Introduction," in Malleson and Russell, *Appointing Judges*, p. 6.

76. This has been true historically as well. See Kagan et al., "Business of State Supreme Courts," pp. 121–56.

77. See Note, "State Advisory Opinion in Perspective," pp. 81–113. More generally, see Guarnieri and Pederzoli, *Power of Judges*, pp. 134–47.

78. Carrington, Meador, and Rosenberg, *Justice on Appeal*, p. 150. For historical confirmation, see Kagan et al., "Evolution of State Supreme Courts," pp. 961–1001.

79. On the doctrine of "adequate and independent state grounds," see R. Williams, *State Constitutional Law Cases and Materials*, pp. 269–82.

80. "Statistics," p. 391, tab. III.

81. On the terms of office of judges on European constitutional courts, see Guarnieri and Pederzoli, *Power of Judges*, pp. 137–49.

82. See, for example, Lubet, "Judicial Discipline and Judicial Independence," pp. 59–74; and Geyh, "Why Judicial Elections Stink," pp. 43–80.

83. See Shepherd, "Influence of Retention Politics on Judges' Voting," pp. 169–203. Earlier studies that found judges changing their behavior in the face of pending elections include M. Hall, "Constituent Influence in State Supreme Courts," pp. 1117–24; and M. Hall, "Electoral Politics and Strategic Voting in State Supreme Courts," pp. 427–46.

84. On the efforts of US Supreme Court justices to time their retirements in order to influence the future direction of the court, see Atkinson, *Leaving the Bench.*

85. Wefing, "State Supreme Court Justices—Who Are They?", pp. 89–95.

86. Bonneau and Hall, *In Defense of Judicial Elections,* chap. 4.

87. Burbank and Friedman, "Reconsidering Judicial Independence," p. 10.

88. See Tarr, *Understanding State Constitutions,* pp. 119–21 and 125–26.

89. See Allen, *Decline of the Rehabilitative Ideal.*

90. This of course occurred at the federal level as well.

91. See Shane-DuBow, Brown, and Olsen, *Sentencing Reform in the United States*; and Zimring, *Punishment and Democracy.*

92. For a survey of tort-reform efforts, see Burke, *Lawyers, Lawsuits, and Legal Rights.*

93. Peck, "In Defense of Fundamental Principles," pp. 672–82.

94. For a listing of these cases, see Schwartz and Lorber, "Judicial Nullification of Civil Justice Reform Violates the Fundamental Federal Constitutional Principle of Separation of Powers," pp. 939–76.

95. Eskridge, "Overriding Supreme Court Statutory Interpretation Decisions," pp. 331–417; and more generally O'Brien, *Storm Center,* pp. 359–63.

96. Kaye, "State Courts at the Dawn of a New Century," p. 3. More generally, see the Court Statistics Project of the National Center for State Courts.

97. This analysis relies primarily on Gluck, "States as Laboratories of Statutory Interpretation," pp. 1750–862.

98. The Oregon statute (Oregon Revised Statutes sec. 174–020 [2007]) was enacted in 2001 in response to *Portland General Electric Co. v. Bureau of Labor and Industries,* 850 P.2d 1143 (Or. 1993), in which the Oregon Supreme Court unanimously announced a three-step methodology to govern all future statutory interpretations. For detailed discussion of the conflict in Oregon, see Gluck, "States as Laboratories," pp. 1775–85.

99. Texas Gov't. Code Annotated, sec. 312.005 (Vernon 2005). The Court of Criminal Appeals is court of last resort in criminal matters, whereas the Texas Supreme Court is the court of last resort in civil matters. For detailed discussion of the conflict between the judiciary and the legislature in Texas, see Gluck, "States as Laboratories," pp. 1787–91.

100. The Connecticut statute (Connecticut General Statutes sec. 1–2Z [2003]) sought to overrule *State v. Courchesne,* 816 A.2d 562 (Conn. 2003) and reinstate the "plain meaning rule," which the Connecticut Supreme Court had abandoned in that case. For discussion of the dispute in Connecticut, see Gluck, "States as Laboratories," pp. 1791–97.

101. Gluck, "States as Laboratories," p. 1771. She writes, "Every state legislature in the nation has enacted certain rules of interpretation, which some state courts are, in an unexpected twist, flouting" (ibid., p. 1754).

102. Thus Oregon Supreme Court for more than eight years ignored the Legislature's attempt to alter its approach to statutory interpretation, and the Texas Court of Criminal Appeals in *Boykin v. State*, 818 S.W.2d 782, 786 (Tex. Crim. App. 1991) held that legislative rules for statutory interpretation infringe on judicial authority and violate the separation of powers. Abbe Gluck sees this reaction against legislatively imposed rules of interpretation as a general trend, rather than something limited to Oregon and Texas (see Gluck, "States as Laboratories," pp. 1783, 1788, and 1824–25). This extends as well to legislative mandates expressly abrogating the long-standing principle that statutes in derogation of the common law be strictly construed (see Einer Elhauge, "Preference-Eliciting Statutory Default Rules," p. 2268).

103. As Justice Oliver Wendell Holmes observed in *Prentis v. Atlantic Coast Line Co.*, 211 U.S. 210 (1908), the federal Constitution imposes no separation-of-powers restrictions on state governments. Similarly, in *Bush v. Gore*, 531 U.S. 98 (2000), Chief Justice Rehnquist noted that "in ordinary cases, the distribution of powers among the branches of a State's government raises no questions of federal constitutional law" (at 112). More generally, see Tarr, "Interpreting the Separation of Powers in State Constitutions," pp. 329–40.

104. For an overview of the new judicial federalism, see R. Williams, *Law of American State Constitutions*, chap. 5.

105. Tarr, "Interpreting the Separation of Powers in State Constitutions"; and Williams, *Law of American State Constitutions*, chaps. 8–11.

106. California Constitution, Art. I, sec. 27, overruling *People v. Anderson*, 439 P.2d 880 (1972); Massachusetts Constitution, Declaration of Rights, Art. 26, overruling *District Attorney v. Watson*, 411 N.E.2d 1274 (1980); and New Jersey Constitution, Art. I, sec. 12, overruling *State v. Gerald*, 549 A.2d 792 (1988). This last provision has been in effect superseded by the New Jersey Legislature's outlawing of the death penalty.

107. California Constitution, Art. I, sec. 7.5, overruling *In re Marriage Cases*, 183 P.3d 384 (2008); and Hawaii Constitution, Art. I, responding to *Baehr v. Lewin*, 852 P.2d 44 (1993).

108. As of 2012, state constitutional amendments banning same-sex marriage had been adopted in Alaska, Arizona, California, Colorado, Mississippi, Missouri, Montana, Nevada, Oregon, and Tennessee. State constitutional amendments banning both same-sex marriage and civil unions had been adopted in Alabama, Arkansas, Florida, Georgia, Idaho, Kansas, Kentucky, Louisiana, Michigan, Nebraska, North Dakota, Ohio, Oklahoma, South Carolina, South Dakota, Utah, Virginia, and Wisconsin. Hawaii adopted an amendment authorizing the state legislature to limit marriage to opposite-sex couples.

109. California Constitution, Art. I, sec. 24, para. 2; Florida Constitution, Art. I, sec. 12.

110. This occurred most notoriously in California where, after voters adopted a constitutional amendment reinstating the capital punishment, Chief Justice Rose Bird voted in every case against the imposition of the death penalty. This refusal to adhere to the constitutional will of the people led to her overwhelming defeat in a retention election in 1986. See Latzer, "California's Constitutional Revolution."

111. Donald Lutz has documented that the United States Constitution is among the most difficult constitutions to amend in the entire world (se Lutz, "Toward a Theory of Constitutional Amendment," pp. 355–70).

112. Benjamin, "Constitutional Amendment and Revision," pp. 181–82. For the implications of these constitutional changeability, see Cain and Noll, "Malleable Constitutions," pp. 1517–44.

113. Massachusetts and Mississippi use the indirect initiative to propose amendments, thereby giving the legislature input into the process. See Benjamin, "Constitutional Amendment and Revision," p. 186.

114. We use "constitutional initiative" here to stand for the popular use of constitutional amendment to deal with the threat or actuality of disfavored state constitutional rulings. It is possible that other modes of constitutional amendment might likewise serve this purpose—indeed, most of the constitutional amendments prohibiting same-sex marriage and/or civil unions originated in state legislatures.

Bibliography

Books and Articles

Abrahamson, Shirley S. "The Ballot and the Bench." *New York University Law Review* 76 (October 2001): 973–1004.

Adams, Willie Paul. *The First American Constitutions: Republican Ideology and the Making of the State Constitutions of the Revolutionary Era.* Rev. ed. Lanham, MD: Rowman & Littlefield, 2001.

"Alabama Supreme Court Elections," at http://judgepedia.org/index.php/Alabama_ Supreme_Court_elections#cite_note-11.

Alexander, Mark C. "Let Them Do Their Jobs: The Compelling Government Interest in Protecting the Time of Candidates and Elected Officials." *Loyola University of Chicago Law Review* 37 (summer 2006): 669–721.

"All Taft Wants Is a Square Deal." *New York Times,* March 20, 1912.

Allen, Francis A. *The Decline of the Rehabilitative Ideal.* New Haven, CT: Yale University Press, 1981.

American Bar Association. *Draft Report of the Judicial Disqualification Project* (September 2008), at http://www.aja.org/ethics/pdfs/ABAJudicialdisqualification projectreport.pdf.

American Bar Association. *Justice in Jeopardy: Report of the American Bar Association Commission on the 21st Century Judiciary.* Chicago: American Bar Association, 2003.

———. Standards of State Judicial Selection (2000), at http://www.abanet.org /judind/downloads/reformat.pdf.

———. Standing Committee on Judicial Independence. *Public Financing of Judicial Campaigns: Report of the Commission on Public Financing of Judicial Campaigns.* Chicago: American Bar Association, 2002.

American Judicature Society. "Judges Relieved of Political Stress." *Journal of the American Judicature Society* 23 (August 1939): 13–41.

———. "Judicial Selection in the States," at http://www.judicialselection.us/.

———. *Merit Selection: The Best Way to Choose Judges,* at http://www.judicial selection.us/uploads/documents/ms_descrip_1185462202120.pdf.

———. "Retention Evaluation Programs," at http://www.judicialselection.us/judicial _selection/methods/judicial_performance_evaluations.cfm?state=.

Annenberg Judicial Independence Survey (2006). At www.annenbergpublicpolicy center.org/NewsDetails.aspx?myld=218.

Ansolabehere, Stephen, John M. de Figueirdo, and James M. Snyder Jr. "Why Is There So Little Money in U.S. Politics?" *Journal of Economic Perspectives* (winter 2003): 105–30.

Aspin, Larry T., and William K. Hall. "Retention Elections and Judicial Behavior." *Judicature* 77 (May–June 1994): 306–15.

Atkinson, David N. *Leaving the Bench: Supreme Court Justices at the End.* Lawrence: University Press of Kansas, 1999.

Balkin, Jack M., and Sanford Levinson. "Understanding the Constitutional Revolution." *Virginia Law Review* 87 (October 2001): 1045–109.

Ballantine, Henry Winthrop. "Labor Legislation and the Judicial Veto." *Case and Comment* 19 (September 1912): 227.

Barber, Sotirios A., and James E. Fleming, *Constitutional Interpretation: The Basic Questions.* New York: Oxford University Press, 2007.

Baum, Lawrence. *Judges and Their Audiences: A Perspective on Judicial Behavior.* Princeton, NJ: Princeton University Press, 2006.

———. "Judicial Election and Appointment at the State Level: Voter's Information in Judicial Elections: The 1986 Contests for the Ohio Supreme Court." *Kentucky Law Review* 77 (1988–89): 645–70.

———. "Judicial Elections and Judicial Independence: The Voter's Perspective." *Ohio State Law Journal* 64 (2003): 21.

Baum, Lawrence, and Bradley C. Canon. "State Supreme Courts as Activists: New Doctrines in the Law of Torts." In Mary Cornelia Porter and G. Alan Tarr, eds., *State Supreme Courts: Policymakers in the Federal System.* Westport, CT: Greenwood Press, 1982.

Baum, Lawrence, and David Klein. "Voter Responses to High-Visibility Judicial Campaigns." In Matthew J. Streb, ed., *Running for Judge: The Rising Political, Financial, and Legal Stakes of Judicial Elections.* New York: New York University Press, 2007.

Bauries, Scott R. "State Constitutions and Individual Rights: Conceptual Convergence in School Finance Litigation." *George Mason Law Review* 18 (winter 2011): 301–66.

Bayne, William C. "Lynchard's Candidacy: Ads Putting Spice into Judicial Race: Hernando Attorney Challenging Cobb." *Commercial Appeal,* October 29, 2000.

Beard, Charles A., and Birl E. Shultz, eds. *Documents on the State-Wide Initiative, Referendum, and Recall.* New York: DaCapo Press, 1970.

Behn, Robert D. *Rethinking Democratic Accountability.* Washington, DC: Brookings, 2001.

Behrens, Mark A., and Cary Silverman. "The Case for Adopting appointive Judicial Selection Systems for State Court Judges." *Cornell Journal of Law and Public Policy* 11 (spring 2002): 273–313.

Bemar, Lamar T., ed. *Election vs. Appointment of Judges.* New York: H. W. Wilson, 1926.

Benjamin, Gerald. "Constitutional Amendment and Revision." In G. Alan Tarr and Robert F. Williams, eds., *Constitutional Politics in the States: The Agenda of State Constitutional Reform.* Albany: State University of New York Press, 2006.

Bergan, Francis. *The History of the New York Court of Appeals, 1847–1932.* New York: Columbia University Press, 1985.

Berger, Raoul. *Impeachment: The Constitutional Problems.* Cambridge, MA: Harvard University Press, 1973.

Berkson, Larry C., and Rachel Caufield. *Judicial Selection in the United States: A Special Report*, at www.ajs.org/selection/docs/Berkson.pdf .

Bierman, Luke. "Comment on Paper by Cheek and Champagne: The Judiciary as a 'Republican' Institution." *Willamette Law Review* 39 (fall 2003): 1387–91.

Black, Earl, and Merle Black. *The Rise of the Southern Republicans.* Cambridge, MA: Harvard University Press, 2002.

Blackmar, Charles B. "Missouri's Nonpartisan Court Plan from 1942 to 2005." *Missouri Law Review* 72 (winter 2007): 199–218.

Blackstone, William. *Commentaries* 1:259–60 (1765). In Philip B. Kurland and Ralph Lerner, eds., *The Founders' Constitution,* vol. 4. Chicago: University of Chicago Press, 1987.

Bloomfield, Maxwell H. *American Lawyers in a Changing Society, 1776–1876.* Cambridge, MA: Harvard University Press, 1976.

Bonneau, Chris W. "The Effects of Campaign Spending in State Supreme Court Elections." *Political Research Quarterly* 60 (September 2007): 489–99.

———. "Electoral Verdicts: Incumbent Defeats in State Supreme Court Elections." *American Politics Research* 33 (November 2005): 818–41.

———. "Patterns of Campaign Spending and Electoral Competition in State Supreme Court Elections." *Justice System Journal* 25 (2004): 21–38.

———. "Vacancies on the Bench: Open-Seat Elections for State Supreme Court." *Justice System Journal* 27 (2006): 143–59.

Bonneau, Chris W., and Melinda Gann Hall. *In Defense of Judicial Elections.* New York: Routledge, 2009.

———. "Predicting Challengers in State Supreme Court Elections: Context and the Politics of Institutional Design." *Political Research Quarterly* 56 (June 2003): 337–49.

Bopp, James, Jr., and Josiah Neeley. "How Not to Reform Judicial Elections: *Davis, White,* and the Future of Judicial Campaign Financing." *Denver University Law Review* 86 (2008): 208–18.

Botein, Stephen. "'What We Shall Meet Afterwards in Heaven': Judgeship as a Symbol for Modern American Lawyers." In Gerald L. Geison, ed., *Professions and Professional Ideologies in America*. Chapel Hill: University of North Carolina Press, 1983.

Brace, Paul, and Melinda Gann Hall. "Studying Courts Comparatively: The View from the American States." *Political Research Quarterly* 48 (March 1995): 5–24.

Brandenburg, Bert. "Citizens United: Silver Linings and Opportunities," at http://www.acslaw.org/node/15157.

Branning, Rosalind L. *Pennsylvania Constitutional Development*. Pittsburgh, PA: University of Pittsburgh Press, 1960.

Brennan Center for Justice. "Judicial Public Financing in Wisconsin—2011," at http://www.brennancenter.org/content/resource/judicial_public_financing_in_wisconsin_2011.

Brennan, Patrick M. "Locating Authority in Law." In Patrick M. Brennan, ed., *Criticizing Authority*. Lanham, MD: Lexington Books, 2007.

Brewer, Mark D. "The Rise of Partisanship and the Expansion of Partisan Conflict Within the American Electorate." *Political Science Quarterly* 58 (June 2005): 219–29.

Bridges, Amy. "Managing the Periphery in the Gilded Age: Writing Constitutions for the Western States." *Studies in American Political Development* 22 (spring 2008): 32–58.

Briffault, Richard. "Judicial Campaign Codes after *Republican Party v. White*." *University of Pennsylvania Law Review* 153 (November 2004): 181–238.

Bright, Stephen B. "Can Judicial Independence Be Attained in the South: Overcoming History, Elections, and Misperceptions about the Role of the Judiciary." *Georgia State Law Review* 14 (July 1998) 817–60.

———. "Political Attacks on the Judiciary: Can Justice Be Done Amid Efforts to Intimidate and Remove Judges from Office for Unpopular Decisions?" *New York University Law Review* 72 (May 1997): 308–30.

Bright, Stephen B., and Patrick J. Keenan. "Judges and the Politics of Death: Deciding Between the Bill of Rights and the Next Election in Capital Cases." *Boston University Law Review* 75 (May 1995): 759–835.

Brody, David C. "The Use of Judicial Performance Evaluation to Enhance Judicial Accountability, Judicial Independence, and Public Trust." *Denver University Law Review* 86 (2008): 115–56.

Brooks, Richard R. W., and Steven Raphael. "Life Terms or Death Sentences: The Uneasy Relationship between Judicial Elections and Capital Punishment." *Journal of Criminal Law and Criminology* 92 (spring/summer 2003): 609–38.

Brown, George D. "Political Judges and Popular Justice: A Conservative Victory or Conservative Dilemma?" *William and Mary Law Review* (April 2008): 1543–619.

Bryce, James. *The American Commonwealth*, 2 vols. Indianapolis, IN: Liberty Fund Classics, 1995.

———. *Modern Democracies*. New York: Macmillan, 1924.

Bugliosi, Vincent T. "None Dare Call It Treason." *The Nation*, February 5, 2001.

Burbank, Stephen B. "Is It Time for a National Commission on Judicial Independence and Accountability?" *Judicature* 73 (December–January 1990): 177–78.

———. "Judicial Accountability to the Past, Present, and Future: Precedent, Politics, and Power." *University of Arkansas Little Rock Law Review* 28 (fall 2005): 19–61.

———. "What Do We Mean by 'Judicial Independence'?" *Ohio State Law Journal* 64 (2003): 323–38.

Burbank, Stephen B., and Barry Friedman, eds. *Judicial Independence at the Crossroads: An Interdisciplinary Approach.* Thousand Oaks, CA: Sage Publications, 2002.

———. "Reconsidering Judicial Independence." In Steven R. Burbank and Barry Friedman, eds., *Judicial Independence at the Crossroads: An Interdisciplinary Approach.* Thousand Oaks, CA: Sage Publications, 2002.

Burke, Thomas F. *Lawyers, Lawsuits, and Legal Rights: The Battle over Litigation in American Society.* Berkeley: University of California Press, 2002.

Butler, Nicholas Murray. *Why Should We Change Our Form of Government?* New York: Charles Scribner's Sons, 1912.

Bybee, Keith J. *All Judges Are Political—Except When They Are Not: Acceptable Hypocrisies and the Rule of Law.* Stanford, CA: Stanford University Press, 2010.

———. *Bench Press: The Collision of Courts, Politics, and the Media.* Stanford, CA: Stanford University Press, 2007.

Cain, Bruce E., and Roger G. Noll, "Malleable Constitutions: Reflections on State Constitutional Reform." *Texas Law Review* 87 (2008–9): 1517–44.

Calabresi, Guido. *A Common Law for the Age of Statutes.* Cambridge, MA: Harvard University Press, 1982.

"Call to Action Statement of the National Summit on Improving Judicial Selection." *Loyola Los Angeles Law Review* 34 (June 2001): 1353–59.

Campbell, James E., and Steve J. Jurek, "The Decline of Competition and Change in Congressional Elections." In Sunil Ahuja and Robert Dewhirst, eds., *The United States Congress: A Century of Change.* Columbus: Ohio State University Press, 2003.

Campbell Public Affairs Institute, the Maxwell Poll on Civic Engagement and Inequality (October 2005). At http://www.maxwell.syr.edu/campbell/Poll/2005Poll/MaxwellPoll.pdf.

Cann, Damon M. "Justice for Sale? Campaign Contributions and Judicial Decisionmaking." *State Politics and Policy Quarterly* 7 (fall 2007): 281–99.

Cann, Damon M., and Jeff Yates. "Homegrown Institutional Legitimacy: Assessing Citizens' Diffuse Support for State Courts." *American Politics Research* 36 (March 2008): 297–329.

Carbon, Susan B. "Judicial Retention Elections: Are They Serving Their Intended Purpose?" *Judicature* 64 (November 1980): 210–33.

Carpenter, William S. *Judicial Tenure in the United States with Especial Reference to the Tenure of Federal Judges.* New Haven, CT: Yale University Press, 1918.

Carrington, Paul D. "Judicial Independence and Democratic Accountability in Highest State Courts." *Law & Contemporary Problems* 61 (summer 1998): 79–125.

———. *Stewards of Democracy: Law as a Public Profession.* Boulder, CO: Westview, 1999.

Carrington, Paul D., and Adam R. Long. "The Independence and Democratic Accountability of the Supreme Court of Ohio." *Capital University Law Review* 30 (2002): 455–87.

Carrington, Paul D., Daniel J. Meador, and Maurice Rosenberg. *Justice on Appeal.* St. Paul, MN: West, 1976.

Cass, Ronald A. *The Rule of Law.* Baltimore, MD: Johns Hopkins University Press, 2001.

Caufield, Rachel Paine. "The Foreboding National Trends in Judicial Elections," at http://www.ajs.org/selection/docs/caufield_ia_judges_conference.pdf.

———. "Reconciling the Judicial Ideal and the Democratic Impulse in Judicial Retention Elections." *Missouri Law Review* 74 (summer 2009): 573–604.

———. "In the Wake of *White*: How States Are Responding to *Republican Party of Minnesota v. White* and How Judicial Elections Are Changing." *Akron Law Review* 38 (2005): 625–47.

———. "What Makes Merit Selection Different?" *Roger Williams University Law Review* 15 (fall 2010): 765–92.

Center for Governmental Studies. "Public Campaign Financing: North Carolina Judiciary," at http://cgs.org/images/publications/cgs_nc_judg_061709.pdf.

Champagne, Anthony. "Parties, Interest Groups, and Systemic Change." *Missouri Law Review* 74 (summer 2009): 555–62.

———. "Interest Groups and Judicial Elections." *Loyola of Los Angeles Law Review* 34 (June 2001): 1391–409.

———. "The Politics of Criticizing Judges," at www.justiceatstake.org/files/ChampagneThePolitics ofCriticizingJudges.pdg.

———. "Television Ads in Judicial Campaigns." *Indiana Law Review* 35 (2002): 669–88.

Champagne, Anthony, and Kyle Cheek. "The Cycle of Judicial Elections: Texas as a Case Study." *Fordham Urban Law Review* 29 (February 2002): 907–40.

———. "Money in Texas Supreme Court Elections, 1980–1998." *Judicature* 84 (July–August 2000): 20–25.

Chemerinsky, Erwin. "Evaluating Judicial Candidates." *Southern California Law Review* 61 (September 1988): 1985–994.

Choi, Stephen J., G. Mitu Gulati, and Eric A. Posner. "Professionals or Politicians: The Uncertain Empirical Case for an Elected Rather than Appointed Judiciary." *Journal of Law, Economics, & Organization* 26 (August 2010): 290–336.

———. "Which States Have the Best (and Worst) High Courts?" University of Chicago Law School Working Paper No. 217, 2008.

Clinton, Joshua D., and John S. Lapinski. "'Targeted' Advertising and Voter Turnout: An Experimental Study of the 2000 Presidential Election." *Journal of Politics* 66 (February 2004): 69–96.

Clinton, Robert L. *Marbury v. Madison and Judicial Review.* Lawrence: University Press of Kansas, 1989.

Constitution Project. "The Cost of Justice: Budgetary Threats to America's Courts," at www.constitutionproject.org/court/.

Cook, Charles M. *The American Codification Movement: A Study of Antebellum Legal Reform.* Westport, CT: Greenwood, 1981.

Corwin, Edward S. "The Extension of Judicial Review in New York: 1783–1905." *Michigan Law Review* 15 (February 1917): 283–85.

Court Statistics Project of the National Center for State Courts. At http://www.ncsconline.org/D_Research/csp/CSP_Main_Page.html.

Cover, Robert M. "The Uses of Jurisdictional Redundancy: Interest, Ideology, and Innovation." *William & Mary Law Review* 22 (summer 1981): 639–81.

Cramton, Roger C., and Paul D. Carrington, eds. *Reforming the Court: Term Limits for Supreme Court Justices.* Durham: University of North Carolina Press, 2006.

Croley, Steven P. "The Majoritarian Difficulty: Elective Judiciaries and the Rule of Law." *University of Chicago Law Review* 62 (spring 1995): 689–790.

Crosson, Scott. "Impact of the 2004 North Carolina Judicial Voter Guide: Exit Poll Study Report." *North Carolina Center for Voter Education and Justice at Stake Campaign,* reported in *Public Campaign Funding,* pp. 28–29, at http://www.cgs.org/images/publications/cgs_nc_judg_061709.pdf.

Dear, Jake, and Edward W. Nessen. "'Followed Rates' and Leading State Court Cases, 1940–2005." *University of California Davis Law Review* 41 (December 2007): 683–711.

DeMary, Michele. "Legislative-Judicial Relations on Contested Issues: Taxes and Same-Sex Marriage." *Judicature* 89 (January–February 2006): 202–11.

Democracy North Carolina. "A Profile of the Judicial Public Financing Program, 2004–06," at http://www.ncvce.org/image_uploads/judicial%20program%20overview%20january%202007.pdf.

DeMuniz, Paul J. "Eroding the Public's Confidence in Judicial Impartiality: First Amendment Federal Jurisprudence and Special Interest Financing of Judicial Campaigns." *Albany Law Review* 67 (2004): 763–68.

———. "Politicizing State Judicial Elections: A Threat to Judicial Independence." *Willamette Law Review* 38 (summer 2002): 367–96.

Desan, Christine A. "The Constitutional Commitment to Legislative Adjudication in the Early American Tradition." *Harvard Law Review* 111 (April 1998): 1381–446.

———. "Contesting the Character of the Political Economy in the Early Republic: Rights and Remedies in *Chisholm v. Georgia.*" In Kenneth R. Bowling and Donald R. Kennon, eds., *The House and Senate in the Early 1790s: Petitioning, Lobbying, and Institutional Development.* Athens: Ohio University Press, 2002.

De Tocqueville, Alexis. *Democracy in America.* Trans. by Harvey Mansfield and Delba Winthrop. Chicago: University of Chicago Press, 2000.

"Developments in the Law—Voting and Democracy, Judicial Elections and Free Speech." *Harvard Law Review* 119 (February 2006): 1127–200.

Devins, Neal, and Nicole Mansker. "Public Opinion and State Supreme Courts." *University of Pennsylvania Journal of Constitutional Law* 13 (February 2011): 455–96.

Dimino, Michael R. "Accountability Before the Fact." *Notre Dame Journal of Law, Ethics & Public Policy* 22 (2008): 451–72.

———. "The Futile Quest for a System of Judicial 'Merit' Selection." *Albany Law Review* 67 (2004): 803–19.

———. "The Worst Way of Selecting Judges—Except for All the Others That Have Been Tried." *Northern Kentucky Law Review* 32 (2005): 267–304.

Dinan, John. "Foreword: Court-Constraining Amendments and the State Constitutional Tradition." *Rutgers Law Journal* 38 (summer 2007): 983–1039.

Dodd, Walter F. "The Recall and Political Responsibility." *Michigan Law Review* 10 (December 1911): 79–92.

Dodson, J. Michael, and Donald W. Jackson. "Judicial Independence and Instability in Central America." In Peter L. Russell and David M. O'Brien, eds., *Judicial Independence in the Age of Democracy.* Charlottesville: University Press of Virginia, 2001.

Douglas, James W., and Roger E. Hartley. "State Court Budgeting and Judicial Independence: Clues from Oklahoma and Virginia." *Administration & Society* 33 (2001): 54–78.

Dowdle, Michael W. "Public Accountability: Conceptual Historical, and Epistemic Mappings." In Michael W. Dowdle, ed., *Public Accountability: Designs, Dilemmas, and Experiences.* Cambridge: Cambridge University Press, 2006.

"Drawing the Line on Inappropriate Criticism." At www.justiceatstake.org/content Viewer.asp?breadcrumb=3,551,866.

Drew, Richard. "The Surge and Consolidation of American Judicial Power: Judicial Review in the States, 1840–1880." Unpublished paper presented at the 2004 Annual Meeting of the American Political Science Association.

Dubois, Philip L. "Accountability, Independence, and the Selection of State Judges: The Role of Popular Judicial Elections." *Southwestern Law Journal* 40 (May 1986): 31–52.

———. *From Ballot to Bench: Judicial Elections and the Quest for Accountability.* Austin: University of Texas Press, 1980.

Dunne, Gerald T. *The Missouri Supreme Court: From Dred Scott to Nancy Cruzan.* Columbia: University of Missouri Press, 1993.

Duxbury, Neil. *Patterns of American Jurisprudence.* Oxford: Clarendon Press, 1995.

Eisenstein, James. "Financing Pennsylvania's Supreme Court Candidates." *Judicature* 84 (July–August 2000): 10–19.

Eisgruber, Christopher L. "Judicial Supremacy and Constitutional Distortion." In Sotirios A. Barber and Robert P. George, eds., *Constitutional Politics: Essays on Constitution Making, Maintenance, and Change.* Princeton, NJ: Princeton University Press, 2001.

Elhauge, Einer. "Preference-Eliciting Statutory Default Rules." *Columbia Law Review* 102 (December 2002): 2162–290.

Ellis, Richard E. *The Jeffersonian Crisis: Courts and Politics in the Young Republic.* New York: Oxford University Press, 1971.

Epstein, Lee. "Shedding (Empirical) Light on Judicial Selection." *Missouri Law Review* 74 (summer 2009): 565–67.

Epstein, Lee, and Jack Knight. *The Choices Justices Make.* Washington, DC: CQ Press, 1998.

Epstein, Lee, and Jeffrey A. Segal. *Advice and Consent: The Politics of Judicial Appointments.* New York: Oxford University Press, 2005.

Equal Justice Initiative, "Criminal Justice Reform in Alabama," at http://eji.org/eji/files/judicialselectionreportsm.pdf.

Erickson, Robert S., Michael B. Mackuen, and James A. Stimson. *The Macro Polity.* New York: Cambridge University Press, 2002.

Eskridge, William, Jr. *Dynamics of Statutory Interpretation.* Cambridge, MA: Harvard University Press, 1994.

———. "Overriding Supreme Court Statutory Interpretation Decisions." *Yale Law Journal* 101 (November 1991): 331–417.

Farber, Daniel A., and Suzanna Sherry. *Judgment Calls: Principle and Politics in Constitutional Law.* New York: Oxford University Press, 2009.

Farganis, Dion. "Court Curbing in the Modern Era: Should Supreme Court Justices Really Worry About Attacks from Congress?" at http://personal.bgsu.edu/~fargard/Research_files/CURBING.pdf .

Feeley, Malcolm, and Edward L. Rubin. *Judicial Policy Making and the Modern State: How the Courts Reformed America's Prisons.* Cambridge: Cambridge University Press, 1998.

Fehrenbacher, Don E. *Constitutions and Constitutionalism in the Slaveholding South.* Athens: University of Georgia Press, 1989.

Feldman, Stephen M. *American Legal Thought from Premodernism to Postmodernism: An Intellectual Voyage.* New York: Oxford University Press, 2000.

Fellowes, Matthew C., and Patrick J. Wolf. "Funding Mechanisms and Policy Instruments: How Business Campaign Contributions Influence Congressional Votes." *Political Research Quarterly* 57 (June 2004): 315–24.

Ferejohn, John A., and Larry D. Kramer. "Independent Judges, Dependent Judiciary: Institutionalizing Judicial Restraint." *New York University Law Review* 77 (October 2002): 962–1039.

Finley, Tillman J. "Judicial Selection in Alaska: Justifications and Proposed Courses of Reform." *Alaska Law Review* 20 (June 2003): 49–77.

Fitzpatrick, Brian T. "The Politics of Merit Selection." *Missouri Law Review* 74 (summer 2009): 675–710.

Flango, Victor Eugene, and Nora F. Blair. "Creating an Intermediate Appellate Court: Does It Reduce the Caseload of a State's Highest Court?" *Judicature* 64 (August 1980): 74–84.

Flanigan, William H., and Nancy H. Zingale. *Political Behavior of the American Electorate.* 12th ed. Washington, DC: CQ Press, 2010.

Fogelsong, Todd. "The Dynamics of Judicial (In)dependence in Russia." In Peter H. Russell and David M. O'Brien, eds., *Judicial Independence in the Age of Democracy.* Charlottesville: University Press of Virginia, 2001.

Forbath, William E. *Law and the Shaping of the American Labor Movement*. Cambridge, MA: Harvard University Press, 1989.

Franklin, Charles H. "Behavioral Factors Affecting Judicial Independence." In Stephen B. Burbank and Barry Friedman, eds., *Judicial Independence at the Crossroads*. Thousand Oaks, CA: Sage, 2002.

Frederick, Karl T. "The Significance of the Recall of Judicial Decisions." *Atlantic Monthly*, July 1912.

Freedman, Monroe H. "The Threat to Judicial Independence by Criticism of Judges—A Proposed Solution to the Real Problem." *Hofstra Law Review* 25 (spring 1997): 729–43.

Freedman, Paul, Michael Franz, and Kenneth Goldstein. "Campaign Advertising and Democratic Citizenship." *American Journal of Political Science* 48 (October 2004): 723–41.

Freund, Paul A. "Appointment of Justices: Some Historical Perspectives." *Harvard Law Review* 101 (April 1988): 1146–63.

Frey, Andrew L., and Jeffrey A. Berger. "A Solution in Search of a Problem: The Disconnect between the Outcome in *Caperton* and the Circumstances of Justice Benjamin's Election." *Syracuse Law Review* 60 (2010): 279–92.

Friedman, Lawrence M. *The History of American Law*. 3d ed. New York: Simon & Schuster, 2005.

Fritz, Christian G. *American Sovereigns: The People and America's Constitutional Tradition Before the Civil War*. Cambridge: Cambridge University Press, 2008.

Frohnmayer, David B. "Election of State Appellate Judges: The Demise of Democratic Premises." *Willamette Law Review* 39 (fall 2003): 1251–64.

Frost, Amanda, and Stefanie A. Lindquist. "Countering the Majoritarian Difficulty." *Virginia Law Review* 96 (June 2010): 719–96.

Galie, Peter J. *Ordered Liberty: A Constitutional History of New York*. New York: Fordham University Press, 1996.

Gallagher, Michael. "Disarming the Confirmation Process." *Cleveland State Law Review* 50 (2002): 516–17.

Gardner, James A. "New York's Inbred Judiciary: Pathologies of Nomination and Appointment of Court of Appeals Judges." *Buffalo Law Review* 58 (June 2010): 15–28.

Garnett, Richard W. "The Virtue of Humility," at www.pennumbra.com/debates/debate.php?did=3.

Garwood, W. St. John. "Democracy and the Popular Election of Judges: An Argument." *Southwestern Law Journal* 16 (April 1962): 216–43.

Gavison, Ruth. "The Implications of Jurisprudential Theories for Judicial Election, Selection, and Accountability." *University of Southern California Law Review* 61 (September 1988): 1617–61.

Gawalt, Gerard W. *The Promise of Power: The Emergence of the Legal Profession in Massachusetts, 1760–1840*. Westport, CT: Greenwood Press, 1979.

Geison, Gerald L., ed. *Professions and Professional Ideologies in America*. Chapel Hill: University of North Carolina Press, 1983.

Gerber, Elisabeth R., and Arthur Lupia. "Voter Competence in Direct Legislation Elections." In Stephen L. Elkin and Karol Edward Soltan, eds., *Citizen Competence and Democratic Institutions*. University Park: Pennsylvania State University, 1999.

Gerber, Scott. *A Distinct Judicial Power: The Origins of an Independent Judiciary, 1606–1787*. New York: Oxford University Press, 2011.

Gerhardt, Michael J. *Constitutional Theory: Arguments and Perspectives*. Charlottesville, VA: Michie, 1993.

Geyh, Charles Gardner. "Can the Rule of Law Survive Judicial Politics?" *Cornell Law Review* 97 (January 2012): 191–254.

———. "Informal Methods of Judicial Discipline." *University of Pennsylvania Law Review* 142 (November 1993): 243–312.

———. "Preserving the Delicate Balance between Judicial Independence and Judicial Accountability: Merit Selection in the Post-*White* World." *Cornell Journal of Law and Public Policy* 17 (spring 2008): 343–81.

———. "Preserving Public Confidence in the Courts in an Age of Individual Rights and Public Skepticism." In Keith J. Bybee, ed, *Bench Press: The Collision of Courts, Politics, and the Media*. Stanford, CA: Stanford University Press, 2007.

———. "Publicly Financed Judicial Elections: An Overview." *Loyola of Los Angeles Law Review* 34 (June 2001): 1467–86.

———. "Rescuing Judicial Accountability from the Realm of Political Rhetoric." *Case Western Law Review* 56 (summer 2006): 911–35.

———. *When Courts and Congress Collide: The Struggle for Control of America's Judicial System*. Ann Arbor: University of Michigan Press, 2006.

———. "Why Judicial Elections Stink." *Ohio State University Law Review* 64 (2003): 43–80.

Geyh, Charles, and Emily Field Van Tassel. "The Independence of the Judicial Branch in the New Republic." *Chicago-Kent Law Review* 74 (1998): 31–87.

Geyh, Charles, and Kathleen Lee, "Taking Disqualification Seriously." *Judicature* 92 (July–August 2008): 12–17.

Gibson, James L. "Challenges to the Impartiality of State Supreme Courts: Legitimacy Theory and 'New Style' Judicial Campaigns." *American Political Science Review* 102 (February 2008): 59–75.

———. "The Effects of Electoral Campaigns on the Legitimacy of Courts." *Syracuse Law Review* 59 (2009): 397–415.

———. "Judging the Politics of Judging: Are Politicians in Robes Inevitably Illegitimate?" In Charles Gardner Geyh, ed., *What's Law Got to Do with It? What Judges Do and Why It Matters*. Stanford, CA: Stanford University Press, 2011.

Gibson, James L., and Gregory A. Caldeira. *Citizens, Courts, and Confirmations: Positivity Theory and the Judgments of the American People*. Princeton, NJ: Princeton University Press, 2009.

Gillman, Howard. *The Constitution Besieged: The Rise and Demise of Lochner Era Police Powers*. Durham, NC: Duke University Press, 1993.

Ginsburg, Tom. *Judicial Review in New Democracies: Constitutional Courts in Asian Cases*. Cambridge: Cambridge University Press, 2003.

Glick, Henry R. "The Promise and Performance of the Missouri Plan: Judicial Selection in the Fifty States." *University of Miami Law Review* 32 (June 1978): 509–42.

Gluck, Abbe R. "The States as Laboratories of Statutory Interpretation: Methodological Consensus and the New Modified Textualism." *Yale Law Journal* 119 (June 2010): 1750–862.

Goldberg, Deborah. *The New Politics of Judicial Elections 2000*, at http://faircourts.org/files/JASMoneyReport.pdf.

Goldberg, Deborah, James Sample, and David E. Pozen. "The Best Defense: Why Elected Courts Should Lead Recusal Reform." *Washburn Law Journal* 46 (spring 2007): 503–34.

Goldberg, Deborah, et al. *The New Politics of Judicial Elections 2006*, at www.justiceatstake.org.

Goldstein, Ken, and Paul Freedman. "Campaign Advertising and Voter Turnout: New Evidence for a Stimulation Effect." *Journal of Politics* 64 (August 2002): 721– 40.

Goldstein, Leslie Friedman. *Constituting Federal Sovereignty: The European Union in Comparative Perspective.* Baltimore, MD: Johns Hopkins University Press, 2001.

Goodwyn, Lawrence. *Democratic Promise: The Populist Movement in America.* New York: Oxford University Press, 1976.

Graber, Mark A. "The Problematic Establishment of Judicial Review." In Howard Gillman and Cornell W. Clayton, eds., *The Supreme Court in American Politics: New Institutional Interpretations.* Chicago: University of Chicago Press, 1999.

Grant, Ruth W., and Robert O. Keohane. "Accountability and Abuses in World Politics." *American Political Science Review* 99 (February 2005): 29.

Greenberg Quinlan Rosner Research, Inc., Justice at Stake Campaign, Justice at Stake National Survey Results (2001). At http://www.faircourts.org/files/JASNational SurveyResults.pdf.

Griffin, Kenyon N., and Michael J. Horan. "Patterns of Voter Behavior in Judicial Retention Elections for Supreme Court Justices in Wyoming." *Judicature* 67 (August 1983): 68–77.

Griffin, Steven M. *American Constitutionalism: From Theory to Politics.* Princeton, NJ: Princeton University Press, 1996.

Grodin, Joseph R. *In Pursuit of Justice: Reflections of a State Supreme Court Justice.* Berkeley: University of California Press, 1989.

Groot, Roger D. "The Effects of an Intermediate Appellate Court on the Supreme Court Work Product: The North Carolina Experience." *Wake Forest Law Review* 7 (October 1971): 548–72.

Grow, Doug. "Tuesday's Wisconsin Supreme Court Election Morphs into Referendum on Scott Walker." *Minnesota Post*, April 4, 2011, at http://www.minnpost.com /stories/2011/04/04/27149/tuesdays_wisconsin_supreme_court_election_ morphs_into_referendum_on_scott_walker .

Gryski, Gerard S., Eleanor C. Main, and William J. Dixon. "Models of State High Court Decision Making in Sex Discrimination Cases." *Journal of Politics* 48 (February 1986): 143–55.

Guarnieri, Carlo, and Patrizia Pederzoli. *The Power of Judges: A Comparative Study of Courts and Democracy*. Cambridge: Oxford University Press, 2002.

Haber, Samuel. *The Quest for Authority and Honor in the American Professions, 1750–1900*. Chicago: University of Chicago Press, 1991.

Haines, Charles Grove. *The American Doctrine of Judicial Supremacy*. New York: DaCapo Press, 1973.

Hall, Kermit L. "Constitutional Machinery and Judicial Professionalism: The Careers of Midwestern State Appellate Court Judges, 1861–1899." In Gerard W. Gawalt, ed. *The New High Priests: Lawyers in Post-Civil-War America*. Westport, CT: Greenwood Press, 1984.

———. "The Irony of the Federal Constitution's Genius: State Constitutional Development." In Peter Nardulli, ed., *The Constitution and American Political Development: An Institutionalist Perspective*. Urbana: University of Illinois Press, 1992.

———. "The Judiciary on Trial: State Constitutional Reform and the Rise of an Elected Judiciary, 1846–1860." *Historian* 45 (1983): 337–54.

———. *The Magic Mirror: Law in American History*. New York: Oxford University Press, 1989.

———. "Progressive Reform and the Decline of Democratic Accountability: The Popular Election of State Supreme Court Judges, 1850–1920." *American Bar Foundation Research Journal* (1984): 345–69.

Hall, Melinda Gann. "Competition as Accountability in State Supreme Court Elections." In Matthew J. Streb, ed., *Running for Judge: The Rising Political, Financial, and Legal Stakes of Judicial Elections*. New York: New York University Press, 2007.

———. "Constituent Influence in State Supreme Courts: Conceptual Notes and a Case Study." *Journal of Politics* 49 (November 1987): 1117–24.

———. "Electoral Politics and Strategic Voting in State Supreme Courts." *Journal of Politics* 54 (May 1992): 427–46.

———. "Justices as Representatives: Elections and Judicial Politics in the American States." *American Politics Quarterly* 29 (October 1995): 485–503.

———. "State Supreme Courts in American Democracy: Probing the Myths of Judicial Reform." *American Political Science Review* 95 (June 2001): 315–30.

———. "Voting in State Supreme Court Elections: Competition and Context as Democratic Incentives." *Journal of Politics* 60 (November 2007): 1147–59.

Hall, William K., and Larry T. Aspin. "What Twenty Years of Judicial Retention Elections Have Told Us." *Judicature* 70 (April–May 1987): 340–47.

Hamburger, Philip. *Law and Judicial Duty*. Cambridge, MA: Harvard University Press, 2008.

Handlin, Oscar, and Mary Flug Handlin. *Commonwealth: A Study of the Role of Government in the American Economy: Massachusetts, 1774–1861*. Cambridge, MA: Belknap Press, 1969.

———. "Return of the Town of Sutton on the Massachusetts Constitution of 1778." In Oscar and Mary Handlin, eds., *The Popular Sources of Political Authority: Documents on the Massachusetts Constitution of 1780*. Cambridge, MA: Belknap Press, 1966.

Hanssen, Andrew. "Learning About Judicial Independence: Institutional Change in the State Courts." *Journal of Legal Studies* 33 (June 2004): 431–73.

Hardin, Peter. "More News on Wisconsin Public Financing." In *Gavel Grab*, November 6, 2009, available at http://www.gavelgrab.org/?p=4983.

Harrington, Matthew P. "The Law-Finding Function of the American Jury." *Wisconsin Law Review* (1999): 377–440.

Hartley, Roger E., and James W. Douglas. "The Politics of Court Budgeting in the States: Is Judicial Independence Threatened?" *Public Administration Review* 63 (July/August 2003): 441–54.

Hartz, Louis. *Economic Policy and Democratic Thought: Pennsylvania, 1776–1860*. Cambridge, MA: Harvard University Press, 1938.

Haussameh, Heath. "Judicial Candidate Appeals Public Finance Ruling." *New Mexico Independent*, March 1, 2010, at http://newmexicoindependent.com/50606/judicial-candidate-appeals-public-financing-ruling.

Haynes, Evan. *The Selection and Tenure of Judges*. Littleton, CO: Fred W. Rothman & Co., 1981.

Henschen, Beth M., Robert Moog, and Stephen Davis, "Judicial Nominating Commissioners: A National Profile." *Judicature* 73 (April–May 1990): 328–34.

Herschkoff, Helen. "State Courts and the 'Passive Virtues': Rethinking the Judicial Function." *Harvard Law Review* 114 (May 2001): 1833–940.

Hill, Melvin B., Jr. *The Georgia State Constitution: A Reference Guide*. Westport, CT: Greenwood Press, 1994.

Hobson, Charles F. *The Great Chief Justice: John Marshall and the Rule of Law*. Lawrence: University Press of Kansas, 1966.

Hoffer, Peter Charles, and N. E. H. Hull. *Impeachment in America, 1635–1805*. New Haven, CT: Yale University Press, 1984.

Hofstadter, Richard. *The Progressive Movement, 1900–1915*. Englewood Cliffs, NJ: Prentice-Hall, 1963.

Holmes, Lisa M., and Jolly A. Emrey. "Court Diversification: Staffing the State Courts of Last Resort through Interim Appointments." *Justice System Journal* 27 (2006): 1–13.

Horwitz, Morton J. *The Transformation of American Law, 1780–1860*. Cambridge, MA: Harvard University Press, 1975.

Hovenkamp, Herbert. *Enterprise and American Law, 1836–1937*. Cambridge, MA: Harvard University Press, 1991.

Huber, Gregory A., and Sanford C. Gordon. "Accountability and Coercion: Is Justice Blind When It Runs for Office?" *American Journal of Political Science* 48 (April 2004): 247–63.

Hurst, James Willard. *The Growth of American Law: The Law Makers*. Boston: Little, Brown, 1950.

Hutson, James L. "The American Revolutionaries, the Political Economy of Aristocracy, and the American Concept of the Distribution of Wealth, 1765–1900." *American Historical Review* 98 (October 1993): 1079–105.

Jacobson, Gary. "Party Polarization in National Politics: The Electoral Connection." In Jon R. Bond and Richard Fleisher, eds., *Polarized Politics: Congress and the President in a Partisan Era*. Washington, DC: CQ Press, 2000.

Jamieson, Kathleen Hall. *Dirty Politics: Deception, Distraction, and Democracy*. New York: Oxford University Press, 1992.

Jefferson, Thomas. *Notes on the State of Virginia*, at http://etext.virginia.edu/toc/modeng/public/JefVirg.html.

Johnson, John W. *American Legal Culture, 1908–1940*. Westport, CT: Greenwood Press, 1981.

Jordan, Winthrop E. *Courting Votes in Alabama: When Lawyers Take Over a State's Politics*. Lafayette, LA: Prescott Press, 1999.

Judicial Roulette: Report of the Twentieth Century Fund Task Force on Judicial Selection. New York: Priority Press, 1988.

Justice at Stake. "2001 Poll of State Judges," at www.gavelgrab.org/wp-content/resources/polls/JASJudgesSurveyResults.pdf.

———. "2004 National Opinion Poll," at http://www.justiceatstake.org/media/cms/ZogbyPollFactSheet_54663DAB970C6. pdf.

———. *Justice at Stake & Judicial Issues*, at http://www.justiceatstake.org/issues/state_court_issues/justice_at_stake__judicial_elections.cfm.

———. "Nasty Campaign Deepens 'Crisis' for Wisconsin High Court," at http://www.justiceatstake.org/newsroom/press_releases.cfm/nasty_campaign_deepens_crisis_for_wisconsin_high_court?show=news&newsID=10401.

———. "The New Politics of Judicial Elections in the Great Lake States," at http://www.justiceatstake.org/media/cms/NPJEGreatLakes20002008_DE945C4A0839D.pdf.

Kagan, Robert A., Bliss Cartwright, Lawrence M. Friedman, and Stanton Wheeler. "The Business of State Supreme Courts, 1870–1970." *Stanford Law Review* 30 (November 1977): 121–56.

———. "The Evolution of State Supreme Courts." *Michigan Law Review* 76 (May 1978): 961–1005.

Kales, Albert M. "Methods of Selecting Judges." *Central Law Journal* 85 (December 1917): 425–29.

———. *Unpopular Government in the United States*. Chicago: University of Chicago Press, 1914.

Kaufmann, Karen M., John R. Petrocik, and Daron R. Shaw. *Unconventional Wisdom: Facts and Myths About American Voters*. New York: Oxford University Press, 2008.

Kaye, Judith S. "Safeguarding a Crown Jewel: Judicial Independence and Lawyer Criticism of the Courts." *Hofstra Law Review* 25 (spring 1997): 703–27.

———. "State Courts at the Dawn of a New Century: Common Law Courts Reading Statutes and Constitutions." *New York University Law Review* 70 (April 1995): 1–35.

Keeton, Robert E. *Venturing to Do Justice: Reforming Private Law*. Cambridge, MA: Harvard University Press, 1969.

Kelleher, Christine A., and Jennifer Wolak. "Explaining Public Confidence in the Branches of State Government." *Political Research* 60 (December 2007): 707–21.

Keller, Morton. *Affairs of the State: Public Life in Late Nineteenth Century America.* Cambridge, MA: Belknap Press, 1977.

Kens, Paul. *Judicial Power and Reform Politics: The Anatomy of* Lochner v. New York. Lawrence: University Press of Kansas, 1990.

Kenzevich, Alison. "Public Finance Campaign Supporters Worried about Pilot Program." *Charleston Gazette,* March 15, 2011, at http://sundaygazettemail.com/News/201103150658.

Keyssar, Alexander. *The Right to Vote: The Contested History of Democracy in the United States.* New York: Basic Books, 2000.

"Kilbridge and Madigan." *Chicago Tribune,* October 26, 2010, at www.chicagotribune.com/news/opinion/editorials/ct-edit-kilbride-20101026,4009319.story.

Kimball, Bruce A. *The "True Professional Model" in America: A History.* Lanham, MD: Rowman & Littlefield, 1995.

King, Linda. *Indecent Disclosure.* National Institute on Money in State Politics Report (2007), at www.followthemoney.org/press/Reports/200708011.pdf .

Klein, David, and Lawrence Baum. "Ballot Information and Voting Decisions in Judicial Elections." *Political Research Quarterly* 54 (December 2001): 709–28.

Klots, Alan T. "The Selection of Judges and the Short Ballot." In Glenn R. Winters, ed., *Judicial Selection and Tenure.* Chicago: American Judicature Society, 1973.

Kmiec, Keenan D. "The Origin and Current Meanings of 'Judicial Activism.'" *California Law Review* 92 (October 2004): 1441–77.

Korbitz, Adam. "Legislature Sends State Budget Bill to Gov. Walker," at http://www.wisbar.org/AM/Template.cfm?Section=News&Template=/CM/ContentDisplay.cfm&ContentID=103301.

Kourles, Rebecca Love, and Jordan M. Singer. "Using Judicial Performance Evaluations to Promote Judicial Accountability." *Judicature* 90 (March–April 2007): 200–207.

Kozinski, Alex. "The Real Issues of Judicial Ethics." *Hofstra Law Review* 32 (summer 2004): 1095–106.

Kramer, Larry D. "The Supreme Court, 2000 Term—Foreword: We the Court." *Harvard Law Review* 115 (November 2001): 4–167.

———. *The People Themselves: Popular Constitutionalism and Judicial Review.* New York: Oxford University Press, 2004.

Kramer, Matthew H. *Objectivity and the Rule of Law.* Cambridge: Cambridge University Press, 2007.

Kritzer, Herbert J. "Competitiveness in State Supreme Court Elections, 1946–2009." *Journal of Empirical Legal Studies* 8 (June 2011): 237–59.

Kurland, Philip B., and Ralph Lerner, eds. *The Founders' Constitution.* 4 vols. Chicago: University of Chicago Press, 1987.

Landsman, Stephen. "The Civil Jury in America: Notes from an Unappreciated History." *Hastings Law Journal* 44 (March 1993): 579–619.

Larson, John Lauritz. *Internal Improvement.* Chapel Hill: University of North Carolina Press, 2001.

Larson, Magali Sarfatti. *The Rise of Professionalism: A Sociological Analysis.* Berkeley: University of California Press, 1977.

Lasser, William. *The Limits of Judicial Power: The Supreme Court in American Politics.* Chapel Hill: University of North Carolina Press, 1988.

Latzer, Barry. "California's Constitutional Revolution." In G. Alan Tarr, ed., *Constitutional Politics in the States.* Westport, CT: Greenwood Press, 1996.

Lau, Richard, Lee Sigelman, Caroline Heldman, and Paul Babbit. "The Effects of Negative Political Advertisements: A Meta-Analytic Assessment." *American Political Science Review* 93 (December 1999): 851–75.

Lau, Richard R., and Gerald M. Pomper, "The Effectiveness of Negative Campaigning in U.S. Senate Elections." *American Journal of Political Science* 46 (January 2002): 47–66.

Leahy, James E. *The North Dakota State Constitution.* New York: Oxford University Press, 2011.

Lerner, Renée Lettow. "The Transformation of the American Civil Trial: The Silent Judge." *William & Mary Law Review* 42 (October 2000): 195–264.

Leshy, John D. *The Arizona State Constitution.* New York: Oxford University Press, 2011.

Levin, Mark R. *Men in Black: How the Supreme Court is Destroying America.* Washington, DC: Regnery, 2005.

Lewis, William Draper. "A New Method of Constitutional Amendment." *The Annals of the American Academy of Political and Social Science* 43 (September 1912): 319–25.

Linde, Hans A. "Elective Judges: Some Comparative Comments." *Southern California Law Review* 61 (September 1998): 1995–2005.

———. "The Judge as Political Candidate." *Cleveland State Law Review* 40 (1992): 1–17.

Lindquist, Stefanie A., and Frank B. Cross. *Measuring Judicial Activism.* New York: Oxford University Press, 2009.

Lochner, Todd. "Judicial Recusal and the Search for the Bright Line." *Justice System Journal* 26 (2005): 231–37.

Locke, John. *Second Treatise on Government.* Ed. C. B. McPherson. Indianapolis: Hackett, 1980.

Lubet, Steven. "It Takes a Court." *Syracuse Law Review* 60 (2010): 221–28.

———. "Judicial Discipline and Judicial Independence." *Law & Contemporary Problems* 61 (summer 1998): 59–74.

Lublin, David. *The Republican South: Democratization and Partisan Change.* Princeton, NJ: Princeton University Press, 2004.

Lupia, Arthur, and Matthew D. McCubbins. *The Democratic Dilemma: Can Voters Learn What They Need to Know?* New York: Cambridge University Press, 1998.

Lutz, Donald S. *Popular Consent and Popular Control: Whig Political Theory in the Early State Constitutions.* Baton Rouge: Louisiana State University Press, 1980.

———. "Toward a Theory of Constitutional Amendment." *American Political Science Review* 88 (June 1994): 355–70.

Malbin, Michael J., and Thomas L. Gais. *The Day After Reform: Sobering Campaign Finance Lessons from the American States.* Albany, NY: Rockefeller Institute Press, 1998.

Malleson, Kate, and Peter H. Russell, eds. *Appointing Judges in an Age of Judicial Power.* Toronto: University of Toronto Press, 2006.

Manweller, Matthew. *The People Versus the Courts: Initiative Elites, Judicial Review, and Direct Democracy in the American Legal System.* Bethesda, MD: Academica Press 2005.

Marshall, Margaret. "The Promise of Neutrality: Reflections on Judicial Independence." *Human Rights* 36 (winter 2009): 3–4.

Marshall, William P. "Constitutional Law as Political Spoils." *Cardozo Law Review* 46 (January 2005): 925–41.

———. "Judicial Accountability in a Time of Legal Realism." *Case Western Reserve Law Review* 56 (summer 2006): 937–45.

Mate, Manoj, and Matthew Wright. "The 2000 Presidential Election Controversy." In Nathaniel Persily, Jack Citrin, and Patrick J. Egan, eds., *Public Opinion and Constitutional Controversy.* New York: Oxford University Press, 2008.

McCall, Madhavi. "Buying Justice in Texas: The Influence of Campaign Contributions on the Voting Behavior of Texas Supreme Court Justices." *American Review of Politics* 22 (fall 2001): 349–73.

———. "Campaign Contributions and Judicial Decisions: Can Justice Be Bought?" *America Review of Politics* 22 (fall 2001): 349–73.

———. "The Politics of Judicial Elections: The Influence of Campaign Contributions on the Voting Patterns of Texas Supreme Court Justices, 1994–1997." *Politics and Policy* 31 (June 2003): 314–43.

McCarty, Nolan, Keith T. Poole, and Howard Rosenthal. "The Hunt for Party Discipline in Congress." *American Political Science Review* 95 (September 2001): 673–87.

McKeown, M. Margaret. "Don't Shoot the Cannons: Maintaining the Appearance of Propriety Standard." *Journal of Appellate Practice and Process* 45 (spring 2005): 45 58.

McLauchlan, William P. *The Indiana State Constitution: A Reference Guide.* New York: Oxford University Press, 2011.

McLeod, Aman. "Bidding for Justice: A Case Study about the Effect of Campaign Contributions on Judicial Decision-Making." *University of Detroit Mercy Law Review* 85 (spring 2008): 385–405.

———. "An Excess of Participation: A Critical Examination of Judicial Elections and Their Consequences for American Democracy." Unpublished PhD dissertation, University of Michigan, 2004.

———. "If at First You Don't Succeed: A Critical Analysis of Judicial Selection Reform Efforts." *West Virginia Law Review* 107 (winter 2005): 499–522.

———. "The Party on the Bench: Party Politics and State High Court Appointments." *Justice System Journal* (forthcoming 2012).

McMillan, Malcolm C. *Constitutional Development in Alabama, 1798–1901: A Study in Politics, the Negro, and Sectionalism.* Chapel Hill: University of North Carolina Press, 1955.

Melhorn, Donald F., Jr. *Lest We Be Marshall'd: Judicial Powers and Politics in Ohio, 1806–1812.* Akron, OH: University of Akron Press, 2003.

Meyers, Marvin. *The Jacksonian Persuasion: Politics and Belief.* Madison: University of Wisconsin Press, 1956.

Michael Moncur's (Cynical) Quotations, at http://www.quotationspage.com/quote/181 .html.

Miewald, Peter D., and Peter J. Longo. *The Nebraska State Constitution.* New York: Oxford University Press, 2011.

Miles, Edwin Arthur. *Jacksonian Democracy in Mississippi.* Chapel Hill: University of North Carolina Press, 1960.

Miller, Ben Robertson. *The Louisiana Judiciary.* Baton Rouge: Louisiana State University Press, 1932.

Miller, F. Thornton. *Juries and Judges Versus the Law: Virginia's Provincial Legal Perspective, 1783–1828.* Charlottesville: University Press of Virginia, 1994.

Mowry, George E. *Theodore Roosevelt and the Progressive Movement.* Madison: University of Wisconsin Press, 1946.

Nagle, John Copeland. "The Recusal Alternative to Campaign Finance Legislation." *Harvard Journal of Legislation* 37 (winter 2000): 69–103.

Nancarrow, William J. "Vox Populi: Democracy and the Progressive Era Judiciary, 1890–1916." Unpublished PhD dissertation, Boston College, 2004.

Nardulli, Peter F. *Popular Efficacy in the Democratic Era: A Reexamination of Electoral Accountability in the United States, 1828–2000.* Princeton, NJ: Princeton University Press, 2007.

Nash, Jonathan Remy. "Prejudging Judges." *Columbia Law Review* 106 (December 2006): 2168–206.

National Center for State Courts. "Examining the Work of State Courts: An Analysis of 2007 State Court Caseloads," at http://www.ncsonline.org/d_research /csp/2007B_files/EWSC-2007–v21.online.pdf.

National Institute on Money in State Politics. "High Court Candidates," at http://www.followthemoney.org/database/StateGlance/state_candidates .phtml?s=NM&y=2008&f=J.

Neely, Richard. *How Courts Govern America.* New Haven, CT: Yale University Press, 1981.

Nelson, Caleb. "A Re-Evaluation of Scholarly Explanations for the Rise of the Elective Judiciary in Antebellum America." *American Journal of Legal History* 37 (July 1993): 190–224.

Nelson, Margaret V. *A Study of Judicial Review in Virginia, 1789–1928.* New York: Columbia University Press, 1947.

Nelson, Michael J. "Uncontested and Unaccountable? Rates of Contestation in Trial Court Elections." *Judicature* 94 (March–April 2011): 208–17.

Nelson, William E. *Americanization of the Common Law: The Impact of Legal Change on Massachusetts Society, 1760–1840.* Athens: University of Georgia Press, 1994.

———. "Changing Conceptions of Judicial Review: The Evolution of Constitutional

Theory in the States, 1790–1860." *University of Pennsylvania Law Review* 120 (1972): 1166–85.

———. Marbury v. Madison: *The Origins and Legacy of Judicial Review.* Lawrence: University Press of Kansas, 2000.

Norton, Clark F. "Michigan's First Supreme Court Elections, 1850–51." *Papers of the Michigan Academy of Science, Arts, and Letters* 29 (1943): 507–24.

Note. "The State Advisory Opinion in Perspective." *Fordham Law Review* 44 (1975): 81–113.

O'Brien, David M. *Storm Center: The Supreme Court in American Politics.* 8th ed. New York: W. W. Norton, 2008.

O'Callaghan, Jerome. "Another Test for the Merit Plan." *Justice System Journal* 14 (1991): 477–85.

O'Connor, Sandra Day. Project on the State of the Judiciary, at http://www.law .georgetown.edu/judiciary/.

Paul, Arnold M. *Conservative Crisis and the Rule of Law: Attitudes of Bar and Bench, 1887–1895.* New York: Harper & Row, 1969.

Peck, Robert S. "In Defense of Fundamental Principles: The Unconstitutionality of Tort Reform." *Seton Hall Law Review* 31 (2001): 939–51.

Peretti, Terri Jennings. "Does Judicial Independence Exist? The Lessons of Social Science Research." In Stephen B. Burbank and Barry Friedman, eds., *Judicial Independence at the Crossroads.* Thousand Oaks, CA: Sage, 2002.

Perry, Michael J. *The Constitution in the Courts: Law or Politics?* New York: Oxford University Press, 1994.

Peters, C. Scott. "Campaigning for State Supreme Court, 2006." *Justice System Journal* 29 (2008): 166–86.

Phillips, Thomas R. "Comment." *Law & Contemporary Problems* 61 (summer 1998): 127–39.

———. "Electoral Accountability and Judicial Independence." *Ohio State Law Journal* 64 (2003): 137–47.

Pinello, Daniel R. *The Impact of Judicial-Selection Method on State-Supreme-Court Policy: Innovation, Reaction, and Atrophy.* Westport, CT: Greenwood Press, 1995.

———. "Linking Party to Ideology in American Courts: A Meta-Analysis." *Justice System Journal* 54 (1992): 427–46.

Popkin, Samuel L. *The Reasoning Voter: Communication and Persuasion in Presidential Elections.* Chicago: University of Chicago Press, 1991.

Popkin, Samuel L., and Michael A. Dimock. "Political Knowledge and Civic Competence." In Stephen L. Elkin and Karol Soltan, eds., *Citizen Competence and Democratic Institutions.* University Park: Pennsylvania State University, 1999.

Posner, Richard A. *How Judges Think.* Cambridge, MA: Harvard University Press, 2008.

———. "Judicial Autonomy in a Political Environment." *Arizona State Law Journal* 38 (spring 2006): 1–14.

Pound, Roscoe. "The Causes of Popular Dissatisfaction with the Administration of Justice." *Journal of the American Judicature Society* 20 (February 1937): 178–86.

Pozen, David E. "The Irony of Judicial Elections." *Columbia Law Review* 108 (March 2008): 265–330.

Preston, Bryan. "Iowa Holds a Major Judicial Election You've Heard Next to Nothing About," at http://pajamasmedia.com/blog/iowa-holds-a-major-judicial-election-youve-heard-next-to-nothing-about/2/.

Provine, Doris Marie, and Antoine Garapon. "The Selection of Judges in France: Searching for a New Legitimacy." In Kate Malleson and Peter H. Russell, eds., *Appointing Judges in an Age of Judicial Power.* Toronto: University of Toronto Press, 2006.

Rakove, Jack N. "The Origins of Judicial Review: A Plea for New Contexts." *Stanford Law Review* 49 (May 1997): 1031–64.

Reddick, Malia. *Judging the Quality of Judicial Selection Methods: Merit Selection, Elections, and Judicial Discipline,* at http://www.ajs.org/elections/docs/JudgingQuality JudSelectMethods.pdf.

———. "Merit Selection: A Review of the Social Scientific Literature." *Dickinson Law Review* 106 (spring 2002): 729–45.

Reed, Douglas. *On Equal Terms: The Constitutional Politics of Educational Opportunity.* Princeton, NJ: Princeton University Press, 2001.

Reid, John Phillip. *Controlling the Law: Legal Politics in Early National New Hampshire.* DeKalb: Northern Illinois University Press, 2004.

———. *Legislating the Courts: Judicial Dependence in Early National New Hampshire.* DeKalb: Northern Illinois University Press, 2009.

Reid, Traciel V. "The Politicization of Judicial Retention Elections: The Defeat of Justices Lanphier and White." In *Research on Judicial Selection, 1999.* Chicago: American Judicature Society, 1999.

Resnick, Judith. "Judicial Selection and Democratic Theory: Demand, Supply, and Life Tenure." *Cardozo Law Review* 26 (January 2005): 579–647.

Richardson, Glenn W., Jr. *Pulp Politics: How Political Advertising Tells the Stories of American Politics.* Lanham, MD: Rowman & Littlefield, 2008.

Roe, Gilbert E. *Our Judicial Oligarchy.* New York: B. W. Huebsch, 1912.

Roeber, A. G. *Faithful Magistrates and Republican Lawyers: Creators of Virginia Legal Culture, 1680–1810.* Chapel Hill: University of North Carolina Press, 1981.

Romero, Francine Sanders, David W. Romero, and Victoria Ford. "The Influence of Selection Method on Racial Discrimination Cases: A Longitudinal State Supreme Court Analysis." In *Research on Judicial Selection* 2. Chicago: American Judicature Society, 2002.

Rosenberg, Morris. "The Qualities of Justice—Are They Strainable?" *Texas Law Review* 44 (June 1966): 1063–80.

Rosenman, Samuel E. "A Better Way to Select Judges." *American Judicature Society Journal* 48 (October 1964): 88–92.

Ross, William G. *A Muted Fury: Populists, Progressives, and Labor Unions Confront the Courts, 1890–1937.* Princeton, NJ: Princeton University Press, 1994.

———. "Attacks on the Warren Court by State Officials: A Case Study of Why Court- Curbing Movements Fail." *Buffalo Law Review* 50 (spring/summer 2002): 483– 612.

Rowe, G. S. *Embattled Bench: The Pennsylvania Supreme Court and the Forging of a Democratic Society, 1684–1809.* Newark: University of Delaware Press, 1994.

Ruger, Theodore W. "'A Question Which Convulses a Nation': The Early Republic's Greatest Debate About the Judicial Review Power." *Harvard Law Review* 117 (January 2004): 826–97.

Rumble, Wilfrid E. *American Legal Realism: Skepticism, Reform, and the Judicial Process.* Ithaca, NY: Cornell University Press, 1968.

Rusk, Jerrold G. "The Effect of the Australian Ballot Reform on Split Ticket Voting: 1876–1908." *American Political Science Review* 64 (December 1970): 1220–38.

Russell, Peter H., and David M. O'Brien, eds. *Judicial Independence in the Age of Democracy: Critical Perspectives from Around the World.* Charlottesville: University Press of Virginia, 2001.

Rutledge, Jesse. *The New Politics of Judicial Elections in the Great Lake States,* at http://www.justiceatstake.org/media/cms/NPJEGreatLakes20002008_DE945C4A0839D.pdf.

Salokar, Rebecca Mae, D. Jason Berggren, and Kathryn A. DePalo, "Merit Selection Redefined: The New Politics of Judicial Selection in Florida." *Justice System Journal* 27 (2006): 123–42.

Salokar, Rebecca Mae, and Kimberly A. Shaw. "The Impact of National Politics on State Courts: Florida after Election 2000." *Justice System Journal* 23 (2002): 57–74.

Sample, James. "*Caperton*: Correct Today, Compelling Tomorrow." *Syracuse Law Review* 60 (2010): 293–304.

Sample, James, David Pozen, and Michael Young. *Fair Courts: Setting Recusal Standards.* New York: Brennan Center for Justice, 2008.

Sample, James, Adam Skaggs, Jonathan Blitzer, and Linda Casey. *The New Politics of Judicial Elections 2000–2009,* at http://www.justiceatstake.org/resources/new_politics_of_judicial_elections_20002009/

Sample, James, and Michael Young. "Invigorating Judicial Disqualification: Ten Potential Reforms." *Judicature* 92 (July–August 2008): 26–33.

Samples, John. *The Fallacy of Campaign Finance Reform.* Chicago: University of Chicago Press, 2006.

Samuels, Dorothy. "Hanging a 'For Sale' Sign over the Judiciary." *New York Times,* February 15, 2010, at www.nytimes.com/2010/01/30/opinion/30sat4.html?sq=SupremeCourt&st=nyt&scp.

Saye, Albert. *A Constitutional History of Georgia, 1732–1945.* Athens: University of Georgia Press, 1948.

Scalia, Antonin. *A Matter of Interpretation: Federal Courts and the Law: An Essay.* Princeton, NJ: Princeton University Press, 1997.

———. "The Rule of Law as a Law of Rules." *University of Chicago Law Review* 56 (fall 1989): 1175–88.

Scalia, Laura J. *America's Jeffersonian Experiment: Remaking State Constitutions, 1820–1850.* DeKalb: Northern Illinois University Press, 1999.

Schaffner, Brian F., and Jennifer Segal Diascro. "Judicial Elections in the News." In Matthew J. Streb, ed., *Running for Judge: The Rising Political, Financial, and Legal Stakes of Judicial Elections.* New York: New York University Press, 2007.

Schaffner, Brian F., Matthew Streb, and Gerald Wright. "Teams Without Uniforms: The Nonpartisan Ballot in State and Local Elections." *Political Research Quarterly* 54 (March 2001): 7–30.

Schick, Marvin. *Learned Hand's Court.* Baltimore, MD: Johns Hopkins University Press, 1970.

Schotland, Roy A. "A Plea for Reality." *Missouri Law Review* 74 (summer 2009): 507–29.

———. "Comment." *Law and Contemporary Problems* 61 (summer 1998): 147–53.

———. "Financing Judicial Elections." In David B. Magleby, ed., *Financing the 2000 Election.* Washington, DC: Brookings Institution Press, 2002.

———. "New Challenges to States' Judicial Selection." *Georgetown Law Journal* 95 (April 2007): 1077–105.

———. "To the Endangered Species List, Add: Nonpartisan Judicial Elections." *Willamette Law Review* 39 (fall 2003): 1397–423.

Schultz, David, ed. *Money, Politics, and Campaign Finance Reform Law in the States.* Durham, NC: Carolina Academic Press, 2002.

Schwartz, Victor E., and Leah Lorber. "Judicial Nullification of Civil Justice Reform Violates the Fundamental Federal Constitutional Principle of Separation of Powers: How to Restore the Right Balance." *Rutgers Law Journal* 32 (summer 2001): 907–76.

See, Harold. "An Essay on Judicial Selection: A Brief History." In Keith J. Bybee, ed, *Bench Press: The Collision of Courts, Politics, and the Media.* Stanford, CA: Stanford University Press, 2007.

Segal, Jeffrey A., and Harold J. Spaeth. *The Supreme Court and the Attitudinal Model Revisited.* New York: Cambridge University Press, 2002.

Semonche, John E. *Charting the Future: The Supreme Court Responds to a Changing Society, 1890–1920.* Westport, CT: Greenwood Press, 1978.

Sensenbrenner, James. "Zola Lecture in Public Policy" at Stanford University (2005), at http://judiciary.house.gov/media/pdfs/stanfordjudgesspeechpressversion505.pdf.

Shaman, Jeffrey M., and Jona Goldschmidt. *Judicial Disqualification: An Empirical Study of Judicial Practices and Attitudes.* Chicago: American Judicature Society, 1995.

Shaman, Jeffrey M., Steven Lubet, James J. Alfini, and Charles Gardner Geyh. *Judicial Conduct and Ethics.* 4th ed. Charlottesville, VA: LexisNexis, 2007.

Shane, Peter M. "Interbranch Accountability in State Government and the Constitutional Requirement of Judicial Independence." *Law and Contemporary Problems* 61 (summer 1998): 21–54.

Shane-DuBow, Sandra, Alice P. Brown, and Erik Olsen. *Sentencing Reform in the*

United States: History, Content, and Effect. Washington, DC: U.S. Government Printing Office, 1985.

Shankman, Andrew. "Malcontents and Tertium Quids: The Battle to Define Democracy in Jeffersonian Philadelphia." *Journal of the Early Republic* 19 (spring 1999): 43–72.

Shapiro, Martin. *Courts: A Comparative and Political Analysis.* Chicago: University of Chicago Press, 1981.

———. "Toward a Theory of *Stare Decisis*." *Journal of Legal Studies* 1 (January 1972): 125–34.

Sheldon, Charles H., and Nicholas P. Lovrich. "Voter Knowledge, Behavior, and Attitudes in Primary and General Judicial Elections." *Judicature* 82 (March–April 1999): 216–23.

Sheldon, Charles H., and Linda S. Maule. *Choosing Justice: The Recruitment of State and Federal Judges.* Pullman: Washington State University Press, 1998.

Shepard, Randall T. "Judicial Independence: Telephone Justice, Pandering, and Judges Who Speak Out of School." *Fordham Urban Law Journal* 29 (February 2002): 811–25.

Shepherd, Joanna M. "The Influence of Retention Politics on Judges' Voting." *Journal of Legal Studies* 38 (January 2009): 169–203.

———. "Money, Politics, and Impartial Justice." *Duke Law Journal* 58 (January 2009): 623–85.

Sherry, Suzanna. "The Founders' Unwritten Constitution." *University of Chicago Law Review* 54 (fall 1987): 1127–77.

———. "The Intellectual Background of *Marbury v. Madison*." In Mark Tushnet, ed., *Arguing* Marbury v. Madison. Stanford, CA: Stanford University Press, 2005.

Shugerman, Jed Handelsman. "Economic Crisis and the Rise of Judicial Elections and Judicial Review." *Harvard Law Review* 123 (March 2010): 1061–150.

———. *The People's Courts: The Rise of Judicial Elections and Judicial Power in America.* Cambridge, MA: Harvard University Press, 2012.

Skaggs, Adam. "Buying Justice: The Impact of *Citizens United* on Judicial Elections," at http://www.brennancenter.org/page/-/publications/BCReportBuyingJustice .pdf?nocdn+1.

Skowronek, Stephen. *Building a New American State: The Expansion of National Administrative Capacities, 1877–1920.* Cambridge: Cambridge University Press, 1982.

Smith, Eric R. A. N. *The Unchanging American Voter.* Berkeley: University of California Press, 1989.

Sniderman, Paul M., Richard A. Brody, and Philip E. Tetlock. *Reasoning and Choice: Explorations in Political Psychology.* Cambridge: Cambridge University Press, 1991.

Snowiss, Sylvia. *Judicial Review and the Law of the Constitution.* New Haven, CT: Yale University Press, 1990.

Snyder, James M., Jr., and Tim Groseclose. "Estimating Party Influence in Congressional Roll Call Voting." *American Journal of Political Science* 44 (April 2000): 193–211.

Solum, Lawrence B. "Indeterminacy and Equity." In Steven M. Griffin and Robert C.

L. Moffat, eds., *Radical Critiques of the Law.* Lawrence: University Press of Kansas, 1997.

Spellicsy, Ciara Torres. *Transparent Elections After Citizens United.* New York: Brennan Center for Justice, 2011, at http://www.brennancenter.org/content/resource /transparent_elections_after_citizens_united/.

Stagner, Stephen. "The Recall of Judicial Decisions and the Due Process Debate." *Journal of Legal History* 24 (July 1980): 257–72.

"The Statistics." *Harvard Law Review* 123 (November 2009): 382–96.

Steinglass, Steven H., and Gino J. Scarselli. *The Ohio State Constitution.* New York: Oxford University Press, 2011.

Stephenson, D. Grier, Jr. *Campaigns and the Court: The U.S. Supreme Court in Presidential Elections.* New York: Columbia University Press, 1999.

Stimson, Shannon C. *The American Revolution in the Law: Anglo-American Jurisprudence Before John Marshall.* Princeton, NJ: Princeton University Press, 1990.

Stone, Alec Sweet. *Governing with Judges: Constitutional Politics in Europe.* New York: Oxford University Press, 2000.

Stoner, James. "Constitutionalism and Judging in *The Federalist.*" In Charles R. Kesler, ed., *Saving the Revolution: The Federalist Papers and the American Founding.* New York: Free Press, 1987.

Stratmann, Thomas. "Can Special Interests Buy Congressional Votes? Evidence from Financial Services Legislation." *Journal of Law and Economics* 45 (October 2002): 345–73.

———. "Some Talk: Money in Politics: A (Partial) Review of the Literature." *Public Choice* 124 (July 2005): 135–46.

Streb, Matthew J. "Judicial Elections: A Different Standard for the Rulemakers?" In Matthew J. Streb, ed., *Laws and Election Politics: The Rules of the Game.* Boulder, CO: Lynne Riener, 2005.

Streb, Matthew J., and Brian Frederick. "Judicial Reform and the Future of Judicial Elections." In Matthew J. Streb, ed., *Running for Judge: The Rising Political, Financial, and Legal Stakes of Judicial Elections.* New York: New York University Press, 2007.

"Summary of Initial Selection Methods" complied by the American Judicature Society, at www.judicialselection.us.

"Taft Shows Peril in Roosevelt Policy." *New York Times*, March 9, 1912.

Taft, William Howard. "The Selection and Tenure of Judges." *American Bar Association Report* 38 (1913): 418.

Tarr, G. Alan. "Designing an Appointive System: The Key Issues." *Fordham Urban Law Journal* 34 (summer 2006): 291–92.

———. "Do Retention Elections Work?" *Missouri Law Review* 74 (summer 2009): 605–33.

———. "Interpreting the Separation of Powers in State Constitutions." *New York University Annual Survey of American Law* 59 (2003): 329–40.

———. "The Judicial Branch." In G. Alan Tarr and Robert F. Williams, eds., *State*

Constitutions for the Twenty-first Century: The Agenda of Constitutional Reform. Albany: State University of New York Press, 2006.

———. *Judicial Process and Judicial Policymaking.* 5th ed. Boston: Wadsworth Cengage, 2010.

———. "Politicizing the Process: The New Politics of State Judicial Selections." In Keith J. Bybee, ed., *Bench Press: The Collision of Courts, Politics, and the Media.* Stanford, CA: Stanford University Press, 2007.

———. *Understanding State Constitutions.* Princeton, NJ: Princeton University Press, 1998.

Tarr, G. Alan, and Mary Cornelia Aldis Porter. *State Supreme Courts in State and Nation.* New Haven, CT: Yale University Press, 1988.

Task Forces of Citizens for Independent Courts. *Uncertain Justice: Politics and America's Courts.* New York: Century Press, 2000.

Thach, Charles C. *The Creation of the Presidency, 1775–1789: A Study in Constitutional History.* Baltimore, MD: Johns Hopkins University Press, 1922.

Thomas, Clive S., Michael L. Boyer, and Ronald J. Hrebenar. "Interest Groups and State Court Elections: A New Era and Its Challenges." *Judicature* 87 (November–December 2003): 135–49.

Toma, Eugene F. "Congressional Influence and the Supreme Court: The Budget as a Signaling Device." *Journal of Legal Studies* 20 (1991): 131–46.

Topf, Mel A. *A Doubtful and Perilous Experiment: Advisory Opinions, State Constitutions, and Judicial Supremacy.* New York: Oxford University Press, 2011.

Traut, Carol Ann, and Craig F. Emmert. "Expanding the Integrated Model of Judicial Decision Making: The California Justices and Capital Punishment." *Journal of Politics* 60 (November 1998): 1166–80.

Treanor, William Michael. "Judicial Review Before *Marbury.*" *Stanford Law Review* 58 (November 2005): 455–561.

Uclman, Gerald F. "Crocodiles in the Bathtub: Maintaining the Independence of State Supreme Courts in an Era of Judicial Politicization." *Notre Dame Law Review* 72 (May 1997): 1133–53.

Urofsky, Melvin I. "State Courts and Protective Legislation during the Progressive Era: A Reevaluation." *Journal of American History* 72 (June 1985): 63–92.

Van Alstyne, William W. "A Critical Guide to *Marbury v. Madison.*" *Duke Law Journal* (1969): 1–48.

Vile, M. J. C. *Constitutionalism and the Separation of Powers.* Oxford: Clarendon Press, 1967.

Volcansek, Marly L., and Jacqueline Lucienne Lafon. *Judicial Selection: The Cross-Evolution of French and American Practices.* Westport, CT: Greenwood Press, 1988.

Walker, James L. "The Ohio Constitution: Normatively and Empirically Distinctive." In George E. Connor and Christopher W. Hammons, eds., *The Constitutionalism of American States.* Columbia: University of Missouri Press, 2008.

Wallis, John. "Constitutions, Corporations, and Corruption: American States and Constitutional Change, 1842 to 1852." *Journal of Economic History* 65 (March 2005): 211–56.

Wallison, Peter J., and Joel M. Gora. *Better Parties, Better Government: A Realistic Program for Campaign Finance Reform*. Washington, DC: AEI Press, 2009.

Waltenberg, Eric N., and Charles S. Lopeman. "Tort Decisions and Campaign Dollars." *Southeastern Political Review* 28 (2000): 241–63.

Ware, Stephen J. "The Missouri Plan in National Perspective." *Missouri Law Review* 74 (summer 2009): 751–76.

———. "Money, Politics, and Judicial Decisions: A Case Study of Arbitration Law in Alabama." *Journal of Law & Politics* 15 (fall 1999): 645–86.

Watson, Richard A., and Rondal G. Downing. *The Politics of the Bench and the Bar: Judicial Selection under the Missouri Nonpartisan Court Plan*. New York: John Wiley & Sons, 1969.

Wefing, John B. "State Supreme Court Justices—Who Are They?" *New England Law Review* 32 (fall 1997): 89–95.

Weisz, Rachel. "Alabama's Supreme Court Primary Campaigns Highlight Radical Transformation of State Judicial Elections," at www.justiceatstake.org.

"What Do Judges Think About the Feeney Amendment?" *Judicature* 88 (July–August 2004): 8–11.

White, G. Edward. *History and the Constitution: Collected Essays*. Durham, NC: Carolina Academic Press, 2007.

White, Penny J. "Relinquished Responsibilities." *Harvard Law Review* 123 (November 2009): 120–51.

———. "Using Judicial Performance Evaluations to Supplement Inappropriate Voter Cues and Enhance Judicial Legitimacy." *Missouri Law Review* 74 (summer 2009): 635–66.

White, Penny J., and Malia Reddick. "A Response to Professor Fitzpatrick: The Rest of the Story." *Tennessee Law Review* 75 (spring 2008): 501–43.

Whittington, Keith E. *Constitutional Construction: Divided Powers and Constitutional Meaning*. Cambridge, MA: Harvard University Press, 1999.

Wilcox, Delos F. *Government by All the People*. New York: Macmillan, 1912.

Wilentz, Sean. *The Rise of American Democracy: Jefferson to Lincoln*. New York: W. W. Norton, 2005.

Williams, Margaret S., and Corey A. Ditslear. "Bidding for Justice: The Influence of Attorneys' Contributions on State Supreme Courts." *Justice System Journal* 28 (2007): 135–56.

Williams, Robert F. *The Law of American State Constitutions*. New York: Oxford University Press, 2009.

———. *State Constitutional Law Cases and Materials*. 4th ed. Charlottesville, VA: LexisNexis, 2006.

Winters, Glenn R., ed. *Judicial Selection and Tenure: Selected Readings*. Rev. ed. Chicago: American Judicature Society, 1973.

Winters, Glenn R., and Robert E. Allard, "Judicial Selection and Tenure in the United States." In Harry W. Jones, ed., *The Courts, the Public, and the Law Explosion*. Englewood Cliffs, NJ: Prentice-Hall, 1965.

Wiseman, Rebecca. "So You Want to Stay a Judge: Name and Politics of the Moment May Decide Your Future." *Journal of Law and Politics* 18 (summer 2002): 643–90.

Wold, John T., and John H. Culver. "The Defeat of the California Justices: The Campaign, the Electorate, and the Issue of Judicial Accountability." *Judicature* 70 (April–May 1987): 348–55.

———. "Rose Bird and the Politics of Judicial Accountability in California." *Judicature* 70 (August–September 1986): 81–89.

Wood, Gordon S. *The Creation of the American Republic, 1776–1787.* New York: W. W. Norton, 1969.

———. "The Origins of Judicial Review." *Suffolk University Law Review* 22 (winter 1988): 1293–307.

Zainaldin, Jamil. *Law in Antebellum Society: Legal Change and Economic Expansion.* New York: Alfred A. Knopf, 1983.

Zemans, Frances Kahn. "The Accountable Judge: Guardian of Judicial Independence." *Southern California Law Review* 72 (January/March 1999): 625–55.

Zimmerman, Joseph F. *The Recall: Tribunal of the People.* Westport, CT: Praeger, 1997.

Zimring, Franklin E. *Punishment and Democracy: Three Strikes and You're Out in California.* New York: Oxford University Press, 2001.

Zuckert, Michael. "Founder of the Natural Rights Republic." In Thomas S. Engeman, ed., *Thomas Jefferson and the Politics of Nature.* Notre Dame, IN: University of Notre Dame Press, 2000.

Cases

Arizona Free Enterprise Club's Freedom Club PAC v. Bennett, 131 S.Ct. 2806 (2011).

Ass'n of Am. Physicians and Surgeons v. Brewer, 494 F.3d 1145, 1146 (9th Cir. 2007).

Avery v. State Farm Mutual Insurance Company, 835 N.E.2d 801 (Ill. 2005).

Baehr v. Lewin, 852 P.2d 44 (1993).

Bayard v. Singleton (1786).

Blakely v. Washington, 542 U.S. 296 (2004).

Boykin v. State, 818 S.W.2d 782, 786 (Tex. Crim. App. 1991).

Bridges v. California, 314 U.S. 252, 273 (1940).

Brown v. Allen, 344 U.S. 443, 539 (1953).

Bush v. Gore, 531 U.S. 98 (2000).

Caperton v. A. T. Massey Coal Co., 129 S.Ct. 2252 (2009).

Carey v. Wolnitzek, No. 3:06–36–KKc (E.D. Ky. Oct. 10, 2006).

Chambers v. Florida, 309 U.S. 227 (1940).

Chisholm v. Georgia, 2 U.S. 419 (1793).

Citizens United v. Federal Election Commission, 558 U.S. 50 (2009).

Claremont School District v. Governor, 703 A.2d 1353 (N.H. 1997).

Daggett v. Comm'n on Governmental Ethics and Election Practices, 205 F.3d 445 (1st Circ. 2000).

Day v. Holhan, 34 F.3d 1356 (8th Cir. 1994).

District Attorney v. Watson, 411 N.E.2d 1274 (Mass. 1980).

Eakin v. Raub, 12 Sergeant & Rawl 330 (Pa. 1825).

Fletcher v. Peck, 10 U.S. 87 (1810).

Herb v. Pitcairn, 324 U.S. 117, 126 (1945).

Holden v. James, 11 Mass. 396 (1814).

In re Marriage Cases, 183 P.3d 384 (2008).

Kansas Judicial Watch v. Stout, 440 F.Supp. 2d 1209 (D. Kan. 2006).

Lochner v. New York, 198 U.S. 45 (1905).

Michigan v. Long, 463 U.S. 1032 (1983).

Minnesota Citizens Concerned for Life v. Swanson, application 10A422 (2010).

N. C. Right to Life Comm. Fund for Indep. Political Expenditures v. Leake, 524 F.3d 427 (4th Cir. 2008), *cert. denied*, 129 S.Ct. 490 (2008).

New York State Bd. of Elections v. Lopez Torres, 552 U.S. 196 (2008).

New York Times v. Sullivan, 376 U.S. 254, 270 (1964).

Norris v. Clymer, 2 Pa. 277 (1845).

North Dakota Family Alliance v. Bader, 361 F.Supp.2d 1021 (D.N.D. 2005).

People v. Anderson, 439 P.2d 880 (Calif. 1972).

People v. Max, 198 P .2d 150 (1921).

People v. Western Union, 198 P.2d 146 (1921).

Planned Parenthood of Southeastern Pennsylvania v. Casey, 505 U.S. 833 (1992).

Portland General Electric Co. v. Bureau of Labor and Industries, 850 P.2d 1143 (Or. 1993).

Prentis v. Atlantic Coast Line Co., 211 U.S. 210 (1908).

Republican Party of Minnesota v. White, 536 U.S. 765 (2002).

Republican Party of Minnesota v. White (White II), 416 F.3d 738 (8th Cir. 2005) (*en banc*).

Spargo v. New York State Commission on Judicial Conduct, 244 F. Supp. 2d 72 (N.D.N.Y. 2003).

Standard Oil Co. of New Jersey v. United States, 221 U.S. 1 (1911).

State v. Courchesne, 816 A.2d 562 (Conn. 2003).

State v. Gerald, 549 A.2d 792 (1988).

State ex rel. Warren v. Nusbaum, 198 N.W.2d 630 (Wisc. 1972).

Strauss v. Horton, 46 Cal. 4th 364 (2009).

Texas v. Johnson, 491 U.S. 397 (1989).

United States v. Butler, 297 U.S. 62 (1936).

Weaver v. Bonner, 309 F.3d 1312 (11th Cir. 2002).

Worcester v. Georgia, 31 U.S. 515 (1832).

Constitutional Convention Debates

Constitutional Debates of 1847, ed., Arthur Charles Cole. Springfield: Illinois State Historical Society Library, 1919.

Debates and Proceedings of the Constitutional Convention of the State of Illinois. 2 vols. Springfield, IL: E. L. Merritt & Brother, 1870.

Debates and Proceedings of the Maryland Reform Convention, to Revise the State Constitution, Commenced at Annapolis, November 4, 1850. 2 vols. Annapolis, MD: W. M'Neir, 1851.

Debates and Proceedings of the Minnesota Constitutional Convention. St. Paul, MN: Earle S. Goodrich of the Pioneer and Democrat Office, 1857.

Debates in the Convention for the Revision and Amendment of the Constitution of the State of Louisiana. New Orleans, LA: W. R. Fish, 1864.

Debates of the Convention to Amend the Constitution of Pennsylvania. 9 vols. Harrisburg, PA: Benjamin Singerley, 1873.

Goff, John S., ed. *The Records of the Arizona Constitutional Convention of 1910.* Phoenix, AZ: Supreme Court of Arizona, 1991.

Official Report of the Proceedings and Debates in the Convention Assembled at Frankfort, on the Eighth Day of September, 1890, to Adopt, Amend, or Change the Constitution of the State of Kentucky. 2 vols. Frankfort, KY: E. Polk Johnson, 1890.

Official Report of the Debates and Proceedings in the State Convention, Assembled May 4th, 1853, to Revise and Amend the Constitution of the Commonwealth of Massachusetts. 3 vols. Boston, MA: White & Potter, 1853.

Official Report of the Proceedings and Debates of the Third Constitutional Convention of Ohio. 2 vols. Cleveland, OH: W. S. Robison, 1873–74.

Proceedings and Debates of the Convention of Louisiana. New Orleans, LA: Besancon, Ferguson, 1845.

Proceedings of the Maryland State Convention, to Frame a New Constitution, Commenced at Annapolis, November 4, 1850. 3 vols. Annapolis, MD: 1850.

Report of the Debates and Proceedings of the Convention for the Revision of the Constitution of the State of Indiana. 2 vols. Indianapolis, IN: A. H. Brown, 1850.

Report of the Debates and Proceedings of the Convention for the Revision of the Constitution of the State of Ohio, 1850–51. 2 vols. Columbus, OH: 1851.

Report of the Debates and Proceedings of the Convention for the Revision of the Constitution of the State of New York. Albany, NY: Office of the Evening Atlas, 1846.

Index

Hunstein, Carol, 82

Idaho, 59, 144, 198n114, 206n8
Illinois, 59; judicial selection in, 45,
    48, 49, 50, 68, 71, 83, 124, 144, 192n31;
    retention elections in, 124; Supreme
    Court, 83, 140, 152, 220n5
Illinois Civil Justice League, 83
impeachment of judges. *See* removal of
    judges, by impeachment
Indiana: Constitution of 1816, 42–43;
    Constitution of 1851, 194n65; judicial
    review in, 28, 195n69; judicial
    selection in, 42, 43, 45, 49, 200n10;
    Supreme Court, 28
In re Marriage Cases, 178, 179, 206n20
interpretation of law, 6, 21, 29, 52, 88, 92,
    95, 144, 165; and accountability to
    the law, 102–4; and appellate review,
    98, 104–7; Bashers on, 5, 58, 60, 61,
    112–15, 120, 135–36, 171; common law
    vs. statutory law, 22–23; Defenders
    on, 5, 112, 116, 120–21, 126–27, 136, 172;
    as judicial responsibility, 25, 34–35,
    58, 120–21, 127; legal indeterminacies,
    5, 31, 103, 104, 112–13, 117–21, 135–36,
    207n36; in Oregon, 174, 224n98,
    225n102; originalism/textualism,
    113–15, 117, 118–19, 174–75; and state
    legislatures, 174–75, 176, 178, 224n100,
    225nn101,102; in Texas, 225n102. *See
    also* judicial review
Iowa: judicial selection in, 42, 45, 81, 84;
    same-sex marriage in, 178, 214n42;
    Supreme Court, 45, 81, 84, 178, 179,
    214n42
Iowa for Freedom, 81, 82
Italy: Constitutional Court, 165; judicial
    selection in, 164–65

Jackson, Andrew, 42, 196n91
Jacobson, Gary, 79
JAIL4Judges, 110

James, Dorothy, 87
Jefferson, Thomas, 14, 19, 99; on judicial
    independence, 15; on juries, 22
judgmental heuristics, 116, 128
judicial accountability, 25, 65, 66–67,
    176, 177–79, 205n6; abolition of
    courts and judgeships, 4, 12, 30, 38,
    40, 41; accountability to the law,
    95, 96, 102–4, 114–15, 116, 207n39;
    appellate review as, 95, 96, 98, 99,
    100, 101, 104–7, 112, 115, 134–35, 208n47;
    Bashers on, 3, 4–5, 57, 58, 59, 60–61,
    110–16, 118, 120, 142, 171; behavioral
    accountability, 5, 93, 94, 96, 97, 99,
    100, 101–2; decisional accountability,
    5, 92–93, 96, 98, 99, 100–101;
    Defenders on, 4–5, 59–60, 98, 101–10,
    114, 115–16, 118, 119–20; institutional
    accountability, 5, 93, 94, 96, 101–2,
    206n10; and judicial elections, 1, 5–6,
    35, 36, 38, 44, 55, 56, 58–59, 64, 74,
    100–101, 107–8, 122, 123–25, 136, 142,
    150, 151, 200n15, 207n36, 211n7; judicial
    performance evaluations, 95, 96,
    97, 133, 134, 215nn71,76; relationship
    to judicial independence, 1–2, 3, 8,
    38, 70, 89, 90, 97, 120, 121, 151, 152, 154,
    172; relationship to public financing
    of judicial elections, 161–64; self-
    enforced accountability, 95, 96–97,
    101; and unpopular rulings, 1, 2, 3, 5,
    6, 12, 14, 15–16, 17, 20, 30, 37, 38, 40–41,
    42, 43, 44, 56, 59, 60–61, 66, 75, 76, 81,
    82–84, 94, 98, 99, 100, 107, 125, 126, 129,
    130, 136, 144, 208n56. *See also* judicial
    elections; judicial performance
    evaluations; judicial selection;
    judicial tenure; recall of judicial
    decisions; removal of judges
judicial activism: Bashers on, 2, 66, 112–
    13, 115, 166–67, 171; criticism of, 1, 2, 3,
    66, 81, 88, 112–13, 118, 144–45, 166–67,
    171, 172–73, 205n114, 208n56, 210n97